THE ARK OF SPEECH

The Ark of Speech investigates the interplay of speech and silence in the dialogue between God and human beings, one human being and another, and human beings and the world. Ranging from the Old Testament and its depiction of God's creative word and responsiveness to human beings, via the New Testament and its focus on the life and words of Jesus as the Word of the Father, the book shows how important it is for the believer to listen, both to God and to others, in silence and devoutness.

Jean-Louis Chrétien lectures at the Sorbonne, University of Paris, and is one of France's leading philosophers. He is author of *The Unforgettable and the Unhoped For* (2002) and a contributor to *Phenomenology and the 'Theological Turn': The French Debate* (2001).

THE ARK OF SPEECH

Jean-Louis Chrétien,
translated by Andrew Brown

Routledge
Taylor & Francis Group
LONDON AND NEW YORK

First published by Presses Universitaires de France as *L'arche de la parole*

First published in English 2004 by Routledge

2 Park Square, Milton Park, Abingdon, Oxon OX14 4RN
Simultaneously published in the USA and Canada
by Routledge
711 Third Avenue, New York, NY 10017

Routledge is an imprint of the Taylor & Francis Group

© 1998, Presses Universitaires de France

Translation © 2004 Routledge

Typeset in Galliard by Prepress Projects Ltd, Perth, Scotland

First issued in paperback 2013

British Library Cataloguing in Publication Data
A catalogue record for this book is available from the British Library

Library of Congress Cataloging in Publication Data
A catalog record has been requested for this title

ISBN13: 978-0-415-86302-5 (pbk)

CONTENTS

v

INTRODUCTION

How far does our hospitality go? How far *can* it go? What can we welcome and gather in, and how? Hospitality is, first and foremost, the hospitality that we give each other, exchanging words and silences, glances and voices. And yet, this conversation cannot take place in a vacuum: it is in the world, this world that we never cease to share – among ourselves but also with other forms of presence, the presence of animals, of vegetables, of things. In our speech, we are equally responsible for them, just as we respond to them. Even though the light of speech dawned only because of man, it cannot dawn for him alone. What we have here is another hospitality, indissociable from the first, but with its own proper modes of vigilance, attention, and responsibility. The two hospitalities are brought into play by what I here call the ark of speech, an expression that may seem disconcerting. What does it mean? It takes inspiration from the biblical tradition of the origins of human language and from the polyphonic meditation based on it that theologians and philosophers have never ceased to develop, from Philo to Hegel and beyond. The French word *parole* (word, speech) derives from *parabola* (the Greek word for parable); it will not constitute a betrayal of this word if we use a parable to commence our questioning of human speech and its powers.

According to the Genesis story, the first human act of speech is not that of saying something but of naming. This is the act through which man confers a name on the animals that God has brought before him. As they appear before man they come into the light of speech, and they do not leave unchanged but bearing a name that calls them. God 'brought them to the man to see what he would call them; each one was to bear the name the man would give it. The man gave names to all the cattle, all the birds of heaven and all the wild animals.'[1] This first human act of speech cannot however constitute the origin of speech or language. When he speaks for the first time, man does not enter language: he must already inhabit it. Indeed, as the very letter of the story puts it, God has already addressed man, has already spoken to him before man starts to speak, so that he will start to speak in his turn. Man has already

1

listened, and so he has already replied, even if his reply was a silent one. As for the living things that man considers and names, they too have already had to obey the divine speech, if the miracle of their summoning and their gathering before man is to be possible. Speech is thus prior in two ways, preceding as it does, in its very dissymmetry, the first human speech.

This first speech, far from coinciding with itself in the perfect transparency and plenitude of a language seen as original, is, in itself and in the way it is used, nothing but the discovery of its own inadequacy and failure, as the whole passage shows. Indeed, when man names the animals, what he learns from gazing on them is the knowledge of his own solitude, of the absence of an interlocutor. 'But no helper suitable for the man was found for him.'[2] Although it is an act of inauguration, the naming of the animals by Adam does not, for all that, allow human speech to deploy the highest of its powers. He names, but he has nobody to say anything to. So it is pointless to use this story as a pretext for feeling nostalgia for a primitive and perfect language, as so many different authors have done through the ages. Thus Calvin writes, 'As to the names which Adam imposed, I do not doubt that each of them was founded on the best reason; but their use, with many other good things, has become obsolete.'[3] And Bossuet, in turn: 'He would never have been able to name the animals without knowing their nature and their differences, so that he could give them suitable names, in accordance with the primitive roots of the language that God had taught him.'[4] A language like this, established by God, is not mentioned by the story.

Much more essential, and worthy of consideration, is the fact that this story makes human speech into the *first ark*. The animals have been gathered for human speech and brought together in this speech, which names them long before they are brought together, according to this same story, in Noah's ark to be saved from the flood and the destruction it brings.[5] Noah must take the animals with him when he makes them board the ark, whereas the animals themselves had spontaneously come before Adam so as to be named. Their first guardian, their first safeguard, is that of speech, which shelters their being and their diversity. This is true for more than just the animals. No protective gesture could take responsibility for the least being if the latter had not been taken up into speech. However, to this understanding of the first human speech as hospitality, as first and last ark, two distinct but related objections can be raised. The first objection involves the very meaning of this act, and the second the extent and significance of this naming.

The summoning of the animals before man is indeed frequently interpreted as the demonstration of his domination and his mastery over them. The power of giving a name to that which as yet has none is said to constitute an act of sovereignty, laying the basis of all expropriation and all mastery.[6] By naming, man – on this reading – exercises for the first time, on his own account, that superiority and that power which God has conferred on him, and truly avails himself of them; so what is at issue is an act of seizure and not of safeguard. To speak, in this relation, of hospitality in the ark would be quite out of place. However, St Thomas Aquinas sees in this scene what Francis Ponge later called 'the gaze as it is spoken'. He observes, in fact, that, in the state of innocence, men, in the biblical account, needed animals not for clothes, nor for food, nor for transport. But, he continues, what humans needed animals for 'was to acquire an experiential knowledge of their natures. This is suggested by God leading the animals to Adam for him to give them their names, which designate their natures.'[7] The animals had to be seen and considered so as to be named, their nature had to be apprised so that they could be apprehended in speech. So Adam could not invent nature: it was his duty to respect it. So names come from a gaze that obeys the very nature of things.

The fact remains – and this is an important element in the story – that God himself waits: waits for man to invent his own language. This face-to-face encounter between man, who is still solitary, and animality, an encounter in which he becomes a man of speech, has the character of a *test* or ordeal. The first act of speech is *testing*. Philo of Alexandria emphasized this point. The way man 'calls' to what is not himself, to what he receives and welcomes, 'became the name not only of the thing called but of him who called it'.[8] In what I allow to come to myself in and through language, I also reveal what I am myself. How could the confrontation between man and the different forms of animal life be anything other than a test in which he himself is at stake and on trial? His humanity, for the biblical story, is defined simultaneously through his relation to God, in whose image he was created, and through his relation to the other things that live on the earth, with whom he is constantly interacting. Man alone can fall into bestiality, when he tries desperately to efface or to forget, in himself or in the other, the image of God. A whole host of authors have seen in animals the figures or symbols of the different possibilities of human existence.[9] We have our own bestiary, which the grotesque illustrations of Granville for La Fontaine's *Fables* depict as comical or terrifying. This is also one of the dimensions of the test that Adam undergoes.

Certain Christian authors daringly transposed this scene of naming, comparing it to the scrutiny of human souls by the second Adam. This was the case, in the seventeenth century, with Louis Bail in his *Théologie affective*, with its admirable style:

> These things regard us and matter to us most entirely. For this sacrosanct soul full of knowledge and truth knew all men who had ever been since Adam, and which would be until the fulfilling of the

Resurrection, all their meritorious or impious works, all their words, thoughts, affections and intentions being represented as in a theatre before his inner eyes: and Jesus then knew all men much better than Adam knew the animals in the fields of the Earthly Paradise, and then he imposed on them names that fitted the works and merits of their whole life.[10]

Louis Bail proceeds to evoke, following an ancient author, the eagles, the oxen, the doves, the foxes or the vipers that we can be, his meditation ending with a prayer to receive from Jesus a name that will be propitious. From this perspective, the testing of Adam announces ours; the origin is also a promise. The scene derives a supplementary meaning from this interpretation.

Returning to this scene, Franz von Baader, in an interpretation the esoteric ramifications of which are untenable, nonetheless correctly brought out the character of this test. 'If man was to accomplish his vocation and attain the full mastery of the whole of (animal) nature, he could not let himself be given this power in a simply passive way, nor could he take possession of it without making his own contribution.'[11] What has been created for a higher position 'must first and foremost fix itself in this situation, or realize its higher nature' through an act and the undergoing of a trial. And Baader adds, 'What I name, what bears my name, belongs to me (obeys me or follows my call)'. For Adam to come and stand before animality constitutes, for Baader, his first temptation. Instead of seeing in the act of naming a mere demonstration of man's power, as if this were already established, he locates in it the moment at which this power, caught between the opportunities it can seize on and the perils that threaten it, really risks itself and forges its own identity. 'The mind can produce only by thinking and speaking (naming), but in naming the product, it introduces its name into it, and by this means – as from what comes from it without however being separated from it – the effective relation between it and the product has its consistency.'[12] This domination is not simply a juridical act, nor is it indifferent to the being of what it dominates. It presupposes seeing and hearing and thus hospitality.

But – and this is a second objection to the idea of an ark of speech – modern philosophies of language, while taking this inaugural scene as the point of departure for their own meditation, have seen in it the revelation of a completely different power of human speech from the power to welcome, namely negation. This is true of Hegel in his writings of the Jena period. Adam's words provide an opportunity for Hegel to describe the real potential of naming. The evanescent sensible intuition gives way to the interiorizing memory, which gathers within itself the meaning of things while gathering itself together also. By grasping the meaning of the things that he fixes in names, man denies them in their simple exteriority.

In the *name* its empirical being as a concrete internally manifold living entity is cancelled, it is made into a strictly ideal, internally simple [factor]. The first act, by which Adam established his lordship over the animals, is this, that he gave them a name, i.e., he nullified them as beings on their own account (*sie als Seiende vernichtete*), and made them into ideal [entities].[13]

Later analyses point out that this move from a 'kingdom of images' to a 'kingdom of names' constitutes an 'awakening', in which the dream element is left behind. The name is one of the first acts in which the spirit starts to come into possession of itself.

Language, says Hegel:

speaks only with this self, with the meaning of the thing; it gives it a name and expresses this as the being of the object . . . What *is* this? We answer, It *is* a lion, a donkey, etc. – [namely] it *is*. Thus it is not merely something yellow, having feet, etc., something on its own, [existing] independently. Rather, it is a *name*, a sound made by my voice, something entirely different from what it is in being looked at – and this [as named] is its true *being*. . . . By means of the name, however, the object has been born out of the I [and has emerged] as *being* [*seyend*]. This is the primal creativity exercised by Spirit. Adam gave a name to all things. This is the sovereign right [of spirit], its primal taking-possession of all nature – or the creation of nature out of Spirit [itself]. . . . Man speaks to the thing as *his*.[14]

To be sure, Hegel is describing the negative dimension of language, in which is affirmed a higher act of the spirit than that of mere receptivity. From henceforth, to paraphrase Claudel, we have flowers that cannot fade, flowers of language; but for this to be possible it was necessary for the flower that fades to fade completely and for the troubling thoughts that this aroused in us to be overcome.

However, it is not right, as certain people have done, to give an overimaginative reading to these thoughts, which after all foreground the transcending of mere imagination, or to orchestrate in an overemotional way the sober words of philosophy. Hegel's intention is to describe the different potentialities and different acts of the spirit: to deny the thing as an existent being means denying it as accessible to me in mere sensible intuition, and thus gathering up its meaning, thinking its truth beyond all images. This determinate negation is productive and positive, it means that I appropriate things, without which the spirit would be nothing but stupor and night. What is needed is a way of understanding – in an idealist sense – the ark of speech, and not a way of transforming that ark into its opposite. Nature is reborn from spirit so as to come into its truth.

The use Maurice Blanchot makes of these pages of Hegel's – or the fate he reserves for them – in his study 'Literature and the Right to Death' is quite different. It depends heavily on the analysis of Alexandre Kojève, in which the latter stated, 'The *word* "dog" does not run, drink, and eat; in it the Meaning (Essence) *ceases* to live – that is, it *dies*. And that is why the *conceptual* understanding of empirical reality is equivalent to a *murder*.'[15] This is to forget that, since the empirical dog is not its own essence, this essence cannot 'die' at the same time that it is 'born', in other words comes to thought, through the negation of the empirical dog. Murder in effigy is precisely *not* murder, unless in some magical sense. And it is not really the empirical dog that is denied but the mute and imprecise sensible intuition that *we* had of it and that we imagined gave us full access to its being. Maurice Blanchot is not content with such a paltry murder as that of a dog. He transposes, strangely enough, what Kojève said about the dog to 'this woman', thus explicitly making speech into a 'deferred assassination'.[16] 'For me to be able to say "This woman," I must somehow take her flesh-and-blood reality away from her, cause her to be absent, annihilate her.'[17] This slippage from one episode of the biblical story to another, quite different one, from the naming of the animals to the sudden arrival of the first woman as speech partner, is laden with meaning. Adam exclaims, 'This one at last is bone of my bones and flesh of my flesh! She is to be called Woman':[18] henceforth, he can pass from naming to saying, from the imposing of names on mute beings to a dialogue that takes place within a liberty that is at once intimate and open. Blanchot reduces all this to the same thing, so that coming into being coincides with disappearance.

His basic thesis makes of Adam's speech, not the first ark, but the first flood: 'The meaning of speech, then, requires that before any word is spoken, there must be a sort of immense hecatomb, a preliminary flood plunging all of creation into a total sea. God has created living things, but man had to annihilate them.'[19] And little by little, speech, far from being the song of the world, becomes, with nihilistic jubilation, the song of death: 'Therefore it is accurate to say that when I speak, death speaks in me. . . . When I speak, I deny the existence of what I am saying, but I also deny the existence of the person who is saying it.'[20] While claiming to develop Hegel's thought, all these hyperboles blunt his point and obscure his clarity. If to speak is already to kill, if to think is already to assassinate, are we not in hell?

But if the 'death' that is supposed to speak in language is linked to its ideality, it is, by the same token, a death in idea only. It is the charm, and also the limit, of certain poems by Supervielle that they transform this death-in-idea into a death-in-reality. Speech is described as a material relation, acting at a distance but still perfectly adequately, with what it names. Thus, in 'The

Bird', the poet's speech reached the bird, in the very depths of the distant forest, and the bird laments, saying:

> Leave me on my branch and keep your words,
> I fear your thought like a gunshot

before it does indeed die.[21] The famous poem that gives its title to the collection *The Unknown Friends* finishes with a request for forgiveness for the harm we do to the animals dreamt up by our words, a forgiveness

> For the phrases that come from unknown lips
> Which touch you from afar like stray bullets.[22]

The negativity of language as it is conceptualized by modern philosophy comes to it from the way it tears itself from the transience of that which appears to the senses. Speech is the sole ark, for it is the sole memorial and the sole promise. It is in speech alone that what is absent still, or already, presents itself and that the distant confines of space and time come to attest to their existence and to resonate here and now. This here and now, which cannot be separated from the very act of speaking, in no way resembles a simple point: here and now are in excess of themselves, responses to the world, an appeal to the world, bringing within themselves ever-receding new horizons. Does describing speech as one of man's powers, whose many different aspects we can then survey, mean that we have taken the measure of the word? ' "Man behaves," says Heidegger, "as if he were the shaper and master of language, whereas it is, on the contrary, language which remains the sovereign of man." '[23] We can make everything enter the ark of speech only because it first safeguards us.

To what extent can speech be this ark? This is the question to which the following pages, developing and focusing more sharply an investigation into the voice, the body and the world that I have undertaken in various previous works, try to be remain fully attentive. Much space is given to what other voices – those of philosophers, those of poets, those of mystics – can teach us when it comes to seeing more clearly the phenomena described here. The first chapter, 'The unheard-of', asks what is involved in listening, and in giving hospitality within us to the speech of the other. The second chapter, 'Wounded speech', attempts a phenomenology of *vocal* prayer: why is prayer not a purely inner act, an invisible movement towards the invisible? How and why can prayer, in accordance with various different configurations, be incarnated in the voice that resonates and gain a hearing for itself in the world? What role does the body play in this? The third chapter, 'The hospitality of silence', describes that without which we could neither receive speech nor utter it on

7

our own behalf. However, silence is too often hypostatized and transformed into an autonomous entity; it is thus absolutely essential to discern and to order the various acts through which we impose or keep silence and, in parallel to this, the silences to which we can open ourselves. The fourth chapter, 'Does beauty say adieu?' studies beauty in so far as beauty constitutes, par excellence, a provocation to speak and to sing. How can we reply to it? And to what extent? The fifth and final chapter, 'The offering of the world', treats of the ark of speech properly speaking. How and why can our speech, in admiration and praise, be the place of a welcoming of the world and of nature – a place in which these are illuminated by the very offering of our song?

To the friends, the students, the readers, who have, through their attention, their speech, their encouragements, their questions and their objections too, supported and fortified me throughout the years when this book was being written: a heartfelt thank you!

1

THE UNHEARD-OF

The first hospitality is nothing other than listening. It is the hospitality that we can grant to others, with our body and our soul, even out on the streets and on the roadside, when we would not be able to offer a roof, or warmth or food. And it is at any instant that this hospitality can be granted. Of all other forms of hospitality it is the precondition, for bitter is the bread that is eaten without speech having been exchanged, heavy and burdensome is the insomnia of the beds in which we sleep without our weariness having been welcomed and respected. And is not the ultimate hospitality, that of the Lord, the hospitality that falls, dizzyingly, into the luminous listening of the Word, listening to it so as to speak, speaking so as to listen to it? Listening is big with eternity.

The freshness and openness of this hospitality comes to it from its humility. It is the first hospitality, to be sure, but nobody has ever inaugurated it. No man has ever been the first to listen. We can offer it only because we have always already been received in it. It is consubstantial with the very transmission of speech. In order to speak, I have to be able to hear myself, but in order to hear myself, someone must already have heard me and spoken to me, in a way that forestalls me – that is, comes before me, in both spatial and temporal terms. We have been listened to even before we speak. Between our ears and our voice, other voices and other kinds of listening are already active. The hospitality of listening thus has a common quality, in the sense in which people used to talk of a common bakehouse. It is in a common space, or, more precisely, it is in what founds any possible community, that we welcome the other. When I really listen, I occupy the place of any other man, and it is equally true that, as everyone knows, there is no attention without a sort of effacement.

But how is it possible to think that, on the one hand, by listening I tend to be nothing but the place holder or surrogate of humanity, allowing the other to raise his voice into the light of the universal, and that, on the other hand, this place holding does not constitute an anonymity or interchangeability, since hospitality can only be truly given if it is given as our own – in our own words ('from our own hands', as we also say), in the form of a phrase such as, 'Here I am, I'm listening'? These two dimensions do not form an alternative, and to think as much would mean missing out on an essential aspect of the phenomenon of listening. For to listen *with* my particularities, in other words with my habits and my prejudices, with my predilections and my resentments, with my memories and my dreams, means forcing the words of the other into the Procrustean bed of everything that is most contingent and most accidental about me, it means listening in a way that the Greeks would have called *idiotic*. And so it is not really listening, but rather *reacting*, as in those 'reactions' to this or that event that journalists require from curious bystanders – in other words those reactions that professionally curious bystanders require from merely occasional curious bystanders. Nothing of the other is received and taken in, for there is then no place in which he can be received, but merely a stand-offish reserve, and thus something that is as interchangeable as one can imagine – as in everything that depends on opinion.

On the other hand, when a man burns in the fire of attention the dead wood of his particularities, when he allows the words of the other to unfold in a silence that is rustling with meaning, what happens is that, by effacing himself, he becomes properly himself, and offers a kind of listening that nothing can replace by very virtue of the fact that it is universal. How are we to understand this paradox? The act of speech cannot be thought on the basis of the simple duality of you and me. As soon as you speak to me, we are already all there, even the dead, and those who will one day come also. The interlocutors do not address one another in the vacuum of a telepathic communication, they speak to each other in the world within which they exist along with everyone and in the language of a community. They are thus never only two people: even a face-to-face conversation is heavy with a distant rumour, and even intimacy has its own wide-open spaces.

Listening to the other does not simply mean listening to what he says, but to what it is, in the world or, in other words, to which his words are replying – what is calling his words, requesting them, menacing them or overwhelming them. To begin listening means having to break through the frightening closure of duality: indeed, it is not a question of the two interlocutors forming two halves that finally reunite and come together in a single sphere, as in the ancient myth. When I really listen *with* the other to what he himself, as he speaks, is listening to or has listened to, then it is really *he* to whom I am listening. And it is when I listen in this way that *I* really listen, for listening with the other is not the same as fusing with him, or coinciding with him: we hear twice over, from two distinct places, what has called our exchange into being. This alone gives to listening its solidity and its gravity.

These remarks are enough to dismiss the utopian idea of a perfect act of listening, of an adequate act of listening – in the sense in which philosophers speak of an adequate knowledge. To be sure, we speak in order to be heard, and who would not wish to be listened to as well as possible, with the most perfect attention? If we put to one side – as requiring to be thought through in different terms – the situations in which we speak so as *not* to be heard, two questions arise. Does being listened to constitute – and *can* it constitute – the ultimate and essential aim of my acts of speech? And, on the other hand, in what might the perfection of listening consist? A word that aims merely to be listened to is a word that inveigles: it enjoins, it orders, it seduces, it charms, it acts in many other fashions too, or at least it seeks to do so, but it excepts itself and withdraws from the dialogue of truth or in truth. I aim to be listened to only as a moment of the reply, as the precondition of another act of speech. To speak means first and foremost to *say*, to articulate a meaning on the basis of which we can exist together in the world, and even a word of revelation, with all its critical, decisive and imperious implications, can have this weightiness only because it *says* something about God and the world and the relation between them, and thus, in order to say this, it calls on a response *from us*, without which it would not be itself. A *cry* forces itself on to listening, it seizes us, as it were, in spite of ourselves, but it does not form the first moment of a dialogue. It shows something, it discloses the joy, suffering, horror, surprise to which, if I hear it, I must reply, but it says, properly speaking, nothing. Speech lives off the stifling of these cries, it forbids them so that it can speak itself – which does not mean, far from it, that it denies or fails to recognize their intensity as an essential possibility of the human voice. By making itself into the luminous monstrance of their meaning, by saying, tremulously, what in them is always unheard-of, it only makes them all the more piercing. For the voice brings into itself their piercing quality, which is the only way of not forgetting it. Only speech, by saying, and not by starting to howl in turn, really listens to the cries, for it alone can grant their desire, by bearing – and this is its very own responsibility – what is unbearable about them, and by bearing it as such, that is, without denying it. So listening cannot be separated from replying to and taking up what we listen to.

Where can we find the perfection of listening, supposing there is one? If perfect listening were a listening so full of insight and understanding that it to some degree enveloped my words with its lucid anticipation, understood my merest hint, without fail, in all I say and all I do not say – that it always knew in advance the movement of my phrases without ever being taken by surprise – then it would tend to suppress my speech and suppress itself as listening. And this, far from constituting a desirable aim, would merely lead to ruin and violence. There are senses in which perfect listening changes over into its opposite: complete violence and expropriation. We do not want to talk to those who know everything all too well, long in advance; we do not want to speak if others are going to finish our sentences for us; we do not start speaking to relinquish the ground of our being. Interpretation has its violence, too, and perhaps it is always a certain violence that founds and gives rise to interpretation. If listening understands too much (and we doubtless always understand *too much*), it tends to become vision, autopsy, a perspicacity that sees through me, instead of greeting me around the hearth of language. The gift that is attributed, in various traditions, to philosophers or visionaries of the spirit, enabling them to know at a glance with whom they are dealing and to see their innermost secrets without even needing to speak – is it really a gift? It takes away more than it gives, if it tears from the other his burden of language, that is, the unique and irreplaceable weight of his humanity.

As opposed to such a dire utopia, however dazzling it might make itself out to be, we have to imagine that the perfection of listening lies in its imperfection, to borrow a Taoist formula. Listening begins in a void, in dispossession – and not in bringing into action and setting to work a 'know-how' of listening that has already been acquired and possessed. The 'know-how' of listening has something obscene and pornographic about it, if the essence of pornography is the sterile and empty interchangeability of intimacy, its invasion by anonymous techniques and a gaze that wants to see everything. The only know-how or knowledge of which it can be a question in this domain is that there should be a question, that I should allow myself to be dispossessed of what I thought I knew by the words of the other, which are thus the occasion of a reciprocal openness. In other terms, what is at stake is what the Socratic tradition calls *learned ignorance* – the act of knowing what I do not know. Knowing that you do not know means knowing how to learn, knowing each time how to learn. And knowing each time how to learn means encountering the other and allowing the other to encounter you and speak to you. *Each time* – these words are important.

For, with this learned ignorance, we are not talking about a posture, a position, an attitude. It is learned only because it has been burned by the epiphany of the other. It is learned only by being born anew and starting over again. Its knowledge is not a kind of baggage, it means you lose whatever baggage you had. The hospitality of listening, like that of the Epiphany, is hospitality in a stable, that is, in a place normally unsuitable for receiving kings, a hospitality caught short, because it has nothing else to offer than a vacant and unadorned place. Its deficiency is its nakedness and thus its perfection.

What is there to hear and understand in this epiphany, and how is it to be understood? Every authentic word runs risks, ventures out, and listening can be faithful to it only if it measures up to this venture. Which venture? To start to speak, to *take* up the conversation, if we pay attention to the force of this expression, which has been concealed by habit, does not mean receiving it where it is held out to me, as when you ask questions round the table or at a conference, but to take it up from silence. No human speech comes before all other, as if it were indistinguishable from the origin and brought meaning into being, but every speech worthy of the name is a new dawn, and rises tremulously in the uncertain light of daybreak. It moves forward, to adopt the fine title of Henri Michaux's work, 'face à ce qui se dérobe' – 'in the face of what slips away'. What I say, I cannot say. The full measure of speech is that it speaks to the impossible.

This paradox reveals itself to be a self-evident truth. For if, in speaking, I need only draw on a stock of already available sentences, ready-made turns of phrase, pre-existing commonplaces, whether they are indeed commonplace or, on the contrary, precious, then my task is reduced to that of putting new wine in old wineskins and thus corrupting and wasting its newness. A man with the gift of the gab is a man who is always repeating things, even if the variety of his utterances conceals the fact. But if I have something new to say, even if it is merely this joy or this trial I am going through, it cannot be a question merely of actualizing a meaning that was already potentially there within me, and I have to say something I do not understand and cannot manage, something that has broken into me by coming upon me unawares. No rhetoric will do the job.

Speech takes risks because it is always the *unheard-of* that it wants to say, when it really wants to say something. The silence within events is what we want to bring into speech. In this way, the voice blazes for itself a trail that was not marked out in advance, a trail that it can in no way follow. It can be strong only in its weakness. Its sole authority lies in being venturesome, and so its trembling must always bear the hallmark of the silence from which it emerges: sometimes it is a toneless voice that alone can express the unheard-of. The distress inherent to airport novels and hit songs lies precisely in the fact that, by providing simple-hearted people with formulae of pure convention and worn-out, devalued expressions with which to express their joys and their pains, they deprive them of access to speech, they forbid its stammerings, and they thus deprive men of their own existence. There is something really vampiric about this. An arrogant vulgarity flourishes at the expense of all who listen to it. Then there is nothing left between the nakedness of the unsayable and the off-the-peg formulae that are all ready to wear, in which nobody speaks and nothing is said.

If speech is born from the unheard-of, listening, too, can live from it alone. And if we indeed speak only to the impossible, we also indeed listen only to and towards the impossible. How? It is towards what I myself do not understand and cannot master, towards what escapes me, that I must lend an ear. This is the only way to listen, for it is only in this way that I can let myself be shaken and transformed, rather than just instructed, by what occurs (even if this is only a new thought, which also constitutes an event). I listen where I do not know any more than the other about what he is saying to me, where I can share with him the surprise at what happens. To listen, we have, as a striking expression of Péguy puts it, 'to be prepared to be caught off our guard': only thus can we be reached by, and, as it were, united with, everything that is lofty, for the man who is on his guard, and sticks to the commands set out in his programme of possibilities, will never see anything happening but what he has already seen and will never hear anything but what has already been said.

Being with the other, attuned to the unheard-of, does not at all mean that I am, like a psychologist or an interpreter, lying in wait for the unsaid in the other's speech, nor that I thereby adopt a position of superiority and mastery. Something quite different is at stake. Listening to the unheard-of in what the other is saying means following a patient, laborious path, sometimes getting lost and needing to start all over again, with all that is improvisational and, as it were, caressing in the act of attention, towards the singularity of the event that calls for his speech. It is only on this basis, on the basis of this perpetually inchoative fraternity in which what is *to be said* sets the tone, that the words of the other become audible, that is, respected. Their stammerings, their clumsiness, their inadequacy, their contradictions are no longer an obstacle, they are no longer privations or deficiencies from the point of view of some masterful speech: they mean something. But this meaningfulness has nothing in common with that of a symptom, which I decipher by myself in a supposedly expert fashion. It bears witness to the agonistic dimension of speech, it demonstrates that every act of speech is a hand-to-hand combat with silence, with what cannot be said and yet will be said.

All the same, this listening to the unheard-of has nothing in common with a mute contemplation. We are all ears only if we are all lips, just as we are all lips only if we are all ears. Heidegger has shown, with great profundity, that speaking means listening and that listening means speaking. To bear with the other the burden and responsibility of his words can only happen if we ourselves bring our offering, the fresh air of our whispered meanings. To allow myself to be questioned by what he has to say means also having, myself, to question and interrogate him. It is not certain that listening can always reply *to* what is said to it, for it does not have at its disposal a magical power that enables it to untie or to cut all the Gordian knots of existence, but it is certain that it must always be answerable *to and for* what is said to it. Its hospitality is active, and forms the perpetual noviciate of speech. Everyone has experienced how the attention with which we are listened to has a heuristic force and bears our speech beyond itself, fertilizes our thoughts and reinforces them quite unexpectedly. This is because this attention is not directed towards us but towards the unheard-of, from which our speech arises; thus it is on this unheard-of, and not on us, that it casts its light, which is our godsend. What we have here is an itinerant attention, which accompanies us, whereas in the quite different case of attention scrutinizing us with the aim of judging us, as in an examination or an audition, it includes much more of a dimension of constraint and inhibition. In one case, the silence of listening speaks, and, in the other, it is silent.

To these considerations, however, an objection can nonetheless be raised. If we listen towards the unheard-of, if we listen with what we do not know, and if listening with what we do not know constitutes the beginnings of deafness, do we not arrive at the idea of an attention that is, as it were, ecstatic? What distinguishes this surprise from a sort of stupor in the face of the unforeseeable? Is this not an entirely negative conception, which disables all understanding in its structures and its potentialities?

This would be to misunderstand and, quite literally, to remain deaf to this novitiate of speech. It is in following the movement of the other's words, it is in following too the movement of my own questionings, that I am attentive to the unheard-of, as to the origin of our exchange. Learned ignorance does not consist of making ourselves amnesic and stupid so that we can listen better but of silencing within us the noise of what has already been said so that we can, in Heidegger's apt words, let ourselves be said. This ignorance suspends my knowledge, it does not destroy it. It frees me from my blind adhesion to the belief that my knowledge is sufficient to hear and understand everything that will ever be said to me. It is a question of mobilizing my knowledge and my experience, and making them fluid and lively, so that they will serve the attention instead of replacing it.

The radical difference between the act of speech and the deciphering of a message or the reception of a piece of information is thereby made manifest. Listening is not the same as decoding, for words do not constitute a code. A machine can decode by bringing its programmes into play. But it will never be able to listen. Listening is a truly palpitating activity, it can happen only with this heart that beats, this air breathed in and breathed out, this patient activity of the entire body. It is with all one's body that one listens, as the act of speech is never separable from an act of the body. The always unfinished truth of listening is a heartfelt truth.

2

WOUNDED SPEECH

A phenomenology of prayer

Prayer is the religious phenomenon par excellence, as it is the human act that alone opens up the religious dimension and never ceases to sustain, to bear, to suffer that opening. There are, of course, other specifically religious phenomena, but prayer constantly belongs among their conditions of possibility. If we could not address our words to God or the gods, no other act would be capable of aiming at the divine. Thus, sacrifice forms an act that is, at least at first sight, distinct from prayer, but it is impossible to imagine any sacrifice that prayer does not in one way or another accompany and constitute as such. With prayer, the religious phenomenon begins and ends.

This appearance can indeed, in certain cases, open only on to a virtual dimension, as when Supervielle, in his 'Prayer to the Unknown', speaks to a God whose existence he does not presuppose and whom he does not know whether he is listening to him:

And see, I surprise myself addressing my words to you,
My God, even though I do not yet know whether you exist.[1]

And yet this prayer to a virtual God, however one judges it from a religious and poetic point of view, is not itself a virtual prayer but an effective and authentic prayer, and this poem belongs quite properly to the religious order, the virtual character of the God whom it addresses familiarly as 'thou' constituting a moment of the meaning of its religiosity. What we have here is the weakest and least strenuous form of a possibility of which the Gospel presents particularly acute and vibrant examples, such as 'Lord, teach us to pray', which is a prayer, or the 'I have faith. Help my lack of faith!'[2]

The most diverse thinkers emphasize how the religious dimension is thus founded on prayer. Thus, Novalis writes in a fragment of his *Encyclopedia*: '*Praying* is, in religion, what thinking is in *philosophy*. Praying is *producing religion* (*Religion-machen*) . . . . The religious sense *prays* – just as the mental organ thinks',[3] and Ludwig Feuerbach, taking up from a heuristic point of view what Novalis affirms in a genetic way, states in *The Essence of Christianity*: 'The ultimate essence of religion is revealed by the simplest act of religion – prayer'.[4]

Simple? That is the question. And even supposing that it *is* simple, its simplicity is no easier to grasp here than it is elsewhere. This fundamental phenomenon, irreducible to any other, is difficult to describe, so varied are the forms that it can assume and the definitions that have been given of it. The most commonly accepted and most traditional typologies and classifications can be phenomenologically impure and conceal the phenomenon instead of patterning themselves on it. The same is true of the distinction between vocal prayer and mental prayer. It appears clear when we separate silent acts from acts in which prayer is uttered or pronounced. But it becomes much less clear as soon as we note, as did St Teresa of Avila, that for prayer to be mental, it is not a question of keeping your mouth shut (*tener cerrada la boca*). If prayer is uttered merely by the lips (*solo con la boca*), it is not a Christian prayer, even though certain practices involving the recitation of a formula or the repetition of a word, to the point of intoxication, occur in various religions; but, if authentic vocal prayer is always accompanied by mental prayer, as St Teresa claims, this distinction can no longer be claimed to describe rigorously the phenomenon of prayer.[5]

On the other hand, and here we encounter another and no less challenging difficulty for our description, in the constitution of the meaning of prayer its addressee is absolutely essential. But even if, as a phenomenologist, one does not posit the existence or non-existence of the latter, the fact remains that the way we address him, name him, speak to him, the nature of what we ask from him and feel able to ask from him, the fear or the trust with which the person praying turns to him, all depend on the being of this addressee as he appears to the believer. Prayer cannot be described unless the power to which it is addressed is also described. But in that case, does not the attempt to describe prayer relapse into a presentation of the various real and possible theologies, without regard for their existence or non-existence? Does not a phenomenology of prayer then dissolve into the cataloguing of the various possible modes in which the divine can appear, as for every prayer there is a face of the divine, and vice versa? Furthermore, every established religion has its *lex orandi*; its prayer has a norm that the phenomenologist cannot ignore, since it is a part of the phenomenon, any more than he can simply adopt it and make it his own.

In order to find a way through these difficulties, the best thing is to limit our study, which could, taken in itself, be indefinitely prolonged. We will examine only prayer as an *act of speech*, even if the history of religion naturally describes all sorts of prayers that are not in the slightest, at least at first sight,

18

acts of speech, and our guiding question will be that of the role played, in this act, by the *voice*. How and why, in prayer, do we come out with our voice, do we give voice, our voice? What is the meaning, within it, of the diverse means of utterance? This is not a matter of an arbitrary or purely opportunistic limitation, as these questions include one on the essence of prayer: is vocal prayer merely one form of prayer among others, or is it the form of prayer par excellence, in relation to which alone all others can be defined and constituted, by derivation or antithetically? Is it true that, as Feuerbach puts it, 'audible prayer is only prayer revealing its nature'?[6]

While still being incomplete, a first description of prayer can show how it inhabits an act of presence to the invisible. Prayer is the act by which the person praying stands in the presence of a being in whom he believes, but whom he cannot see, and makes himself manifest to that being. If prayer is the response to a theophany, it is first and foremost an anthropophany, a manifestation of man. The invisible to which man shows himself may at one extreme be the radical invisibility of Spirit and at the other the inner sacredness or power of a being that is in itself visible, such as a mountain, a star or a statue. This act of presence brings the whole of man into play, in all the dimensions of his being; it exposes him in every sense of the term, and unreservedly. It concerns our body, its bearing, its posture, its range of gestures, and it can include certain requirements for preliminary bodily purification, such as ablutions, requirements as to clothing, such as covering or uncovering certain parts of our body, certain positions, such as holding up the hands or kneeling, and certain directions in which one must face. All these practices, whether they are obligatory or left to the choice of the person praying, come together in an appearance (as in the juridical sense) that incarnates the act of presence. Even the person who turns towards the incorporeal does so with his body, with his whole body. This is a *sine qua non*, for to say, as does St Augustine, that one can pray in any 'bodily position' at all does not mean that the body is, in prayer, bracketed, or that it has no role and no importance, but that in his view everyone must take up the position most appropriate and most likely to favour his prayer.[7] With its dances and its capers, the Hasidic movement has demonstrated, in this domain, a vital and indeed uncanny freedom.[8] Written into the body, this presence to the invisible and this appearance before it comprise, essentially, acts by which the person praying declares to God or the gods his desires, his thoughts, his needs, his love, his repentance, in accordance with the various possibilities of speech, from crying out to soundlessly moving his lips, via speaking aloud and murmuring. The person praying before God is in his very being an active manifestation of himself to God. All modes of prayer are forms of this self-manifestation, whether individual or collective.

19

This description raises a question. What do we see when we see a man praying, independently of the existence or non-existence of the one he is addressing? A man who is talking all by himself, who is the only one talking. But does talking by yourself mean talking with yourself, talking to yourself, or addressing another who cannot be perceived by the senses? The two phenomena are essentially distinct. To reduce prayer to a pure soliloquy, to a dialogue with oneself, is not to describe but to interpret and to construct, in a way that does violence to the phenomenon. I can indeed address myself, and speak to myself in a familiar way (as 'thou'), to screw up my courage or impel myself to take a particular action; but this is in no way a prayer and this act is quite different from that in which I turn to another and address another familiarly (as 'thou'). When Kant writes that when one prays one speaks 'within oneself and in fact *with oneself* (*in und eigentlich mit sich selbst*), though allegedly all the more comprehensibly with God', when he compares the person praying to someone who is 'talking to himself (*mit sich selbst laut redend*)', so as to give rise to the suspicion that he is having 'a slight fit of madness (*Wahnsinn*)',[9] when Feuerbach states that prayer is 'the self-division of man into two beings, – a dialogue of man with himself, with his heart',[10] the essence of this act of speech is misunderstood and deformed, all the more maliciously in the first case than in the second, for the second presents itself as an interpretative construction. It is not 'altogether unjustly,' says Kant furthermore, that we consider the person we come across all by himself 'occupied in practices or gestures that we expect only of one who sees somebody else before him'. Kant distinguishes the pure 'spirit of prayer' of allocution or address (*Anrede*): the latter presupposes the belief in a personal presence of the other, and in so far as it does so it can be considered as a 'superstitious delusion (*ein abergläubischer Wahn*)', a 'fetish-making (*Fetischmachen*)'.[11] This was before Schopenhauer went as far as to view all prayer addressed to a personal being as 'idolatry'.[12] To judge that a phenomenon is absurd is too facile a way of relieving oneself of the obligation to think about the meaning it might have and, first and foremost, of describing it as it appears and gives itself. The metaphysical prejudice following which the spirit is necessarily voiceless, and all the purer in so far as it does not manifest itself, has never – fortunately! – sufficed to silence the human voice.

What are the functions of speech in prayer? What is the importance in prayer of address, indeed of familiar address (as 'thou')? Why give voice to it? These are the questions that we will successively need to tackle if we are to describe prayer more adequately, although they are necessarily interdependent and interwoven with one another.

That a God for whom everything is clear has no need of anyone telling him anything whatsoever, that an omniscient God has nothing to learn from us, not even our most secret desires: this was the objection repeatedly raised against monotheistic prayer. This objection aims, if not to suppress prayer, at least to suppress it as an act of speech. But this objection is in its own way judicious, in that it includes its own solution within itself, namely the fact that the function of speech is not in this case to communicate a piece of information or to transmit something we know to our invisible interlocutor. At the beginning of his dialogue *De magistro*, St Augustine supposes that speech has two functions, *docere* and *discere*, teaching and learning, to which his son Adeodatus comes up with the counter-example of song, which we can sing all by ourselves. St Augustine then distinguishes properly musical pleasure from the very words of the song which, addressed to ourselves, are a *commemoratio*, in which we remind ourselves of something. Then Adeodatus raises a new objection: 'When we pray, we certainly do speak; and – there is the rub – it is not right to think that God should be taught by us or that we should remind Him of anything.' St Augustine's reply is complex, but it essentially comes down to making a distinction within prayer between an act, the 'sacrifice of justice', which is not in itself directly an act of speech, and a linguistic dimension, whether internal and silent or external and audible; the latter is assimilated to the commemorative function of speech, to the act of recalling something to oneself or others, to the meditative ingathering of our thought. [13]

How should this be understood? We speak when we address another, and turn towards him, but it is we ourselves who are taught by this speech, and it is on us that it acts. The words of our speech affect and modify the addresser, and not the addressee. We affect ourselves as we stand before the other, in a movement towards him. This is the first wound of speech in prayer: the gap introduced by the addressee has broken the closed circle of speech, opened within it a fault that alters its nature. Another has silently introduced himself into my dialogue with myself, and has radically transformed and broken it. My speech rebounds on to myself and affects me, as indeed would any speech of mine of the kind I always hear, but it affects me much more in so far as it is not aimed at me, and has a completely different addressee from me. It is precisely because I am not talking to myself, because I am not talking for myself, that my own speech, altered at its very origin, and perhaps even before that, turns back on me with such singular force.

St Thomas Aquinas puts it very well: 'We must pray, not in order to inform God of our needs and desires, but in order to remind ourselves that in these matters we need divine assistance.'[14] To ask God, to accomplish in speech an act of question and request, means that, as we speak to him, we at one and the same time say something about him and something about ourselves, inseparably. We make ourselves manifest to ourselves, we are through speech made manifest to ourselves as we manifest ourselves to him. To ask is actively to acknowledge that we are not the origin of every good and every gift, and it is actively to acknowledge that the one whom we address is what he is. All prayer confesses God as giver, by dispossessing us of our self-centredness, in a speech that at every instance the addressee alone, in our eyes, makes possible. By returning to me, prayer does not speak to me of myself alone.

Prayer, says St Bonaventure, needs the fervour of attention, the concentration of thought, the firmness of patience. This is why God wished us 'not only to pray mentally but also to pray verbally to recollect our thoughts through words (*ad recollectionem cogitationum*)'.[15] We are far from the mute spiritualism that sees in vocal expression a mere movement of effusion and dispersal into outwardness, one that is, furthermore, vain and superfluous in the sight of God. The movement of speech is like that of air breathed out and in again. It brings me together before the other, it gives me a being for him, since it paradoxically gives me what it presupposes if it is to take place. One has to be recollected in order to pray, but that is the point: prayer itself, in so far as it is speech, is alone capable of really gathering me and recollecting me. Does this mean that we are turning speech into a mere means, the instrument, so to speak, of a technique of concentration? This may, of course, in some cases be true. But St Bonaventure does not separate the gift of our voice from the meaning of what we say. It is around what it says that the voice gathers and gathers us, just as what it says gathers around the person it addresses. The first function of speech in prayer is thus a self-manifestation to the invisible other, a manifestation that becomes a manifestation of oneself to oneself through the other, in which the presence of self to other and that of other to self cannot be separated, as in the invisible poem of breathing evoked by Rilke. This manifestation does not merely bring to light what was there before it, it has its own light, that of an event, the event in which what is invisible to me illuminates me, in a way that is phenomenologically different from a conversation with oneself or an examination of conscience.

The speech of prayer has its tenor of meaning, and the question arises as to its relationship with truth. Aristotle, in the famous words of his *De interpretatione*, states that 'a prayer is a sentence but is neither true nor false', it is not a *logos apophantikos*.[16] A question or request, a supplication, a complaint are not, after all, capable of being true in the same way that a predicative proposition is. But prayer still has its norms of correctness, which also involve the truth, including that of the *logos apophantikos*. It cannot avoid including a theology, explicit or implicit, which can be true or false – so that one might describe the way that the divine is thought of in a particular religion simply by examining the way people of that religion pray. The mere linguistic form of petitionary prayer is not enough to bracket the question of truth. Thus, Proclus makes a knowledge of the gods the first stage of prayer,[17] and in all religions the correctness of the divine names is something that is always being questioned: is God (or a god) being named as he should be named and as he wants to be named? To be sure, this desire for correctness may become merely pragmatic, and may simply bear on the minute attention to correctness in the way that a rite is carried out, as for the Ancient Romans, for whom the fact that a priest got his words mixed up, or that he stumbled over a ritual prayer, was enough to invalidate the whole ceremony.[18] But this concerns the problem of the rite rather than that of prayer. Prayer always involves a profession of faith, which may be expressed in ways other than in its optative or imperative form.

In the first words of the Christian prayer par excellence, 'Our Father', John Cassian says that 'we confess with our own voice that the God and Lord of the universe is our Father, we profess that we have in fact been admitted from our servile condition into an adopted sonship'.[19] We are after all affirming something about God and something about ourselves. The history of salvation, and Trinitarian theology, as well as ecclesiology (for, even when alone, one prays with the words 'Our Father' and not 'My Father')[20] are, in these two single vocative words, already implied.

Of course, the potential truth of prayer as an act of speech cannot be reduced solely to that of the predicative theological propositions that it expresses or presupposes. It involves the correctness of the prayer itself. The adverb *recte*, 'correctly' or 'rightly', occurs several times over when St Thomas Aquinas is studying desire and request in prayer. This correctness concerns the object of the request as much as the form in which it is couched.[21] How should we think of this correctness? As a preliminary to prayer, or as the stake of prayer itself? Is not the truth of prayer as an act of speech agonistic – the truth of a combat and a struggle for truth, or indeed a struggle *with* truth?

A moral objection frequently raised against prayer involves this very question. If we are corrupt, will our prayer not bear within it the imprint of our unjust nature, and thereby become a cause of scandal? And if we are virtuous, through our own acts and by their light, what is the use of praying? The prayer of the just man would be superfluous, and that of the unjust would be yet one more injustice, putting off the reformation of himself that he himself must perform. Montaigne was shocked by the prayers of hardened sinners, and this brought down on him, at the time of his trip to Rome, the troublesome attentions of the Holy Office.[22] And Proclus, whose thinking in this domain is nuanced and complex, nonetheless claims, on the authority of Plato's notion in the *Phaedo,* that the impure must not have any contact with the pure, that 'only the man who is supremely good can even deserve to be able to pray'.[23] As for Louis-Claude de Saint-Martin, he goes so far as to write, 'Will you pray to God, and will you ask him for his gifts and favours before you have purified yourselves, and established in yourselves all the virtues? This would be the same as asking him to prostitute himself.'[24] Transposing this type of investigation into contemporary, existential terms and distinguishing an authentic from an inauthentic way of praying, would not fundamentally transform this moralistic attitude. It rests on a failure to attend to the phenomenon of prayer as a manifestation of self to the other. This manifestation in speech is, on every occasion and every day it happens, epoch-making, for it is the event of an encounter. Hugo von Hofmannsthal says that each new encounter breaks us and recomposes us, and this is particularly true of the encounter we know as prayer.

Restricting ourselves just to prayer to the one God, whoever addresses God always does so *de profundis*, from the depths of his distress whether manifest or hidden, from the depths of his sin. He confesses in his prayer the divine holiness, before which he stands and which he addresses. If he really stands before it, he is thereby dispossessed of all the beliefs that he may previously have held about his own holiness. It is in the light of prayer, at once discrete and inescapable, that he now sees himself, and in this light he discovers that no man is worthy to pray, if 'worthy' means that we can rely on any pre-existing merit in order to pray. He also discovers how he has fallen short of rectitude, and realizes that this lack of justice must certainly pervade his very requests, to a degree that he cannot discern. In the Bible, Moses replies to God that he does not know how to speak, and this is often the first response of prophets to their vocation – and as such, the very moment they really understand that vocation.

But it is part and parcel of prayer itself that in it alone the person praying learns that he does not know how to pray. 'We do not know how to pray properly', says St Paul.[25] The painful and joyful adventures of the encounter take place only in the encounter itself. The gaps in speech open up only when we speak. Such is the circularity of prayer: the person praying prays so as to learn how to pray, and first and foremost to learn that he does not know, and he gives thanks for his prayer as for a gift from God. One can be turned to God only by praying, and one can pray only by being turned to God. Only a leap can enable us to enter this circle. There are no prolegomena or preliminaries to prayer. Proclus puts it very well:

> To wish to pray is to desire to turn towards the gods; and this desire leads and links the desiring soul to the divine, and it is here that we find what seemed to us to be the altogether principal work of prayer. The act of wanting and the act of praying should thus not constitute two successive stages, but it is at one and the same time that we want to pray and possesses the prayer, in proportion as one wants it.[26]

He thus resolves the aporia of an infinite regress in prayer, which would require us to pray before praying and in order to pray. As he puts it: 'Whatever business one prays about, the one who prays must first of all give thanks to the gods for the very fact that he has received from the gods the ability to turn towards them.'[27]

Prayer appears, in its own eyes, as always forestalled and always preceded by the person it addresses. It does not begin, it responds, and this is the only thing which, in the very uncertainty it harbours about its rightness, gives it confidence. The circle is not absurdly circular: it leads us to the event of an encounter. This act of speech takes its assurance not from itself, but it is assured of standing in the only place where it can in truth struggle for truth and become upright. For the stumblings of speech are overcome in speech alone, just as lovers' quarrels are resolved in love alone, and thus by keeping on going, together – not by separating and waiting for those difficulties to disappear spontaneously. This completes our first description of prayer: this manifestation of self to other through speech is agonistic and transformative, as it is a dialogue and conversation with the other in an encounter in which our truth is at stake. The person before God is drawn into involvement only in and through prayer.

The Christian tradition has particularly insisted on this agonistic dimension. A very fine discourse by Kierkegaard is called 'One Who Prays Aright Struggles in Prayer and Is Victorious – in that God Is Victorious'.[28] Many centuries earlier, we find St Macarius's powerful commentary on the phrase in the gospel, which says that the violent are taking the kingdom of heaven by force. He invites man, still a prisoner to his hardness of heart, to 'force himself to charity when he has no charity – force himself to meekness, when he has no meekness'. And he continues that a man must 'force himself to prayer, when he has not spiritual prayer; and thus God, beholding him thus striving, and compelling himself by force, in spite of an unwilling heart, gives him the true prayer of the Spirit'.[29] And what would gentleness be without the fire of this inner violence of which it becomes the clarity, what would prayer be without this intimate combat against the muteness within us? This violent prayer, at first uttered only with reluctance – who will say whether it is authentic or inauthentic? Does not the mere possibility that it raises exclude such a distinction, which aims at ensuring a clear boundary between the proper and the improper, the clean and the unclean?

Before describing in greater detail these welcome wounds in speech, we have to ponder what it is that makes them possible: address, allocution, familiar speech (saying 'thou'). Feuerbach notes, indeed, 'In prayer, man addresses God with the word of intimate affection – Thou', before interpreting this familiar form of address tendentiously by claiming, 'He thus declares articulately that God is his *alter ego*'.[30] For a philosopher who, like Karl Jaspers, makes of disenchantment a virtue, this second person singular already constitutes a slide towards a misunderstanding of God:

When man addresses the divinity *in prayer*, this divinity becomes for him a Thou with whom, lost as he is in his own solitude, he would like to enter into communication. It is thus for him a *personal figure* . . . . However, an authentic awareness of transcendence refrains from thinking of the absolute God as a person. I resist the impulse to make a Thou of the divinity the minute I sense that I am thereby infringing transcendence.[31]

To be on terms of easy familiarity with the absolute would mean improperly bringing its distance closer, so that this proximity is no longer its own and it is replaced by a mythic image that I have forged for myself.

Thus, dialogue with God, far from being the very place where I find him in finding myself, in other words by being first and foremost detached from myself, would on the contrary be the place where I lose him by covering over and concealing 'the abyss of transcendence' that lies beyond all address. To this, a historical objection can be made first of all: the freedom, the trust, the heartfelt intimacy in the speech addressed to God, what Christians call *parrhesia*, instead of diminishing and weakening with the acknowledgement of its absolute transcendence, on the contrary always accompany it. This is clear if we compare Jewish and Christian prayer with the Greek and Roman prayer of antiquity. Kerenyi points out that the word 'god', *theos*, in the vocative, is introduced only by the Jews and Christians. And a formula of appropriation such as *my God* does not mean that God is degraded into a thing or into a property of man, but, on the contrary, puts its seal on the fact that in speech the one who speaks belongs, without reserve, to the one who is addressed. In any case, it must be a very strange and narrow conception of the other, of speech, and of the familiar form of address (saying 'thou') that decrees that address can only be an excessive familiarity. For it is only in familiar address that objectification comes up against an uncrossable limit, it is only in the hymn in which we sing for the one we sing that 'the abyss of transcendence' can be really recognized and confessed. Indeed, even silence as a mark of respect and adoration, the *favete linguis* of the Romans or the *euphemia* of the Greeks, is a silence with an addressee, a silence before, and for, the other. It is silence before You, and it forms a possibility proper to speech, which alone can *fall silent*, transforming, by the act of standing in silence, silence into an act of presence and not into a privation. Silence is still an allocution.

A fine hymn by Synesios of Cyrene may cast light on this phenomenon. The first four lines start with a 'you' (*se*, the Greek accusative: it is you – singular – whom I sing) and announce that the hymn is sung at every hour of day and night, before the poet invites the various creatures of nature to fall silent – the wind, the birds, the waters – and finally cries, 'I sing you, blessed one, with my voice, and I sing you also, blessed one, with my silence; for all that the intelligence says with its voice, you hear and understand also from its silence.'[32] The almost irresistible widening of horizons in the hymn is also the spreading fire of silence. Nature must fall silent so that silence can become a voice, and so that in silence, as in its jewel casket of attention, the human voice may echo – but the human voice is still a voice in the silence in which it finds its consummation. Silence that aims at divine transcendence, which is here strongly emphasized, does not constitute the interruption or suspension of the initial *You* but its consummation. Silence says *You*, beyond all names, like the opening of a gaze, but this gaze is opened only through speech and remains the silence of speech. The silence of prayer is here a silence that God *listens to*, it is still a dialogue, and can be so only because a first silence, different and purely privative, has been broken.

Prayer knows that it does not know how to pray, but it learns this only by praying, it knows it only for as long as it is praying, and is real – like everything about an encounter – only in the impossible. This agonistic dimension is nothing other than the ordeal of transcendence. For transcendence gives itself as such only when its distance approaches without ceasing to be distant, and it is encountered only in the ordeal of speech. The second person singular alone can open up the space of such an ordeal. It is only in saying *You* that the I can be completely exposed, in other words laid open to all that it cannot master.

A new characteristic can be added to the description of prayer: the manifestation of self to other through speech, an agonistic speech struggling for its truth, is an ordeal, an undergoing of God, a suffering of God, a theopathy. Prayer is a prey to its addressee. By measuring itself with God, prayer is a speech that has always already lost all measure, the power of measuring itself and knowing itself completely; it bears, even as it collapses under it – like all speech dictated by love – the weight of giving itself, that is, of losing itself, it suffers the other in its own self-detachment. In what way? How is the speech of prayer wounded by its addressee? The person praying addresses his speech to the divine capacity to listen. Unlike the capacity to listen of any particular human being, this listening is already vigilant, it does not need any call to attention in order to be aroused. The wavering speech of our voice echoes in, and in accordance with, a silent listening that has always preceded it and been expecting it. Being thus expected makes this speech unexpected to itself. To have God listening to you is an ordeal, a testing of speech incomparable with any other, for our speech is incomparably stripped bare by it, in all it seeks to hide, to excuse, to justify, to obtain in real terms. Speech appears in the attentive light of silence, the voice is really naked.

To listen, to grant – it is the same word: *audire, exaudire; hören, erhören*. The theological paradox which says that all true prayer is, in one way or another, granted is based in the phenomenon itself. The praying person speaks for a listening that always already forestalls his speech.

27

Knowing that the divine precedes human speech means that this speech appears to itself as a response to this listening, which awaits and summons. In all religions, it is stated – however this may be interpreted – that the divine wishes to be prayed to and addressed. Thus the act of speech appears to itself as rendered possible by the silence of the divine listening, it is silence which, properly speaking, gives speech to it; speech receives itself from the silence which brings it into being. This is why every prayer gives thanks for itself, for even the most supplicatory of petitionary prayers has already received – received the gift of being able to ask God, of being able to address him. Only in this way does it appear to itself, and on this alone do many of its properties as an act depend. The request always lags behind its granting, the appearing of self to self is merely lunar, and takes its light from elsewhere.

In his treatise *De dono perseverentiae*, St Augustine, against the errors of the Pelagians, puts it wonderfully well: 'What does this mean: *the Spirit himself pleads*, unless "to make one plead" (*interpellare facit*)?' And later on: 'And what does this word *crying* mean except making one cry (*clamare facientem*)? . . . Now you have not received a spirit of bondage so as to be again in fear, but you have received a spirit of adoption as sons, by virtue of which we cry, "Abba! Father!"'[33] What we have here, of course, is a thesis on grace, which really needs a theological commentary, but it is also a strict description of prayer as an act of speech, made possible by its addressee, in a possibility that is already a favour. Guillaume de Saint-Thierry puts it in terms as simple as they are clear: 'When it is I who speak to you, I am intent on you, and this alone is already good for me; and whatever direction the prayer takes, I never pray to you or adore you fruitlessly; the mere fact of praying to you is already for me a great reward.'[34] To speak to God is to belong to him and to be with him, and nothing can ever be asked from God that is not already written into the space opened up by this encounter and this ordeal. This is not without its consequences.

G. Van der Leeuw, in his considerable work *Religion in Essence and Manifestation*, curiously enough devotes only a few short pages to prayer. He distinguishes it from adoration, which he deals with later, and which evidently appears to him to be a higher and purer possibility, for, he says, 'prayer originates from care', and 'whoever adores has therefore forgotten his prayer and now knows only God's glory'.[35] Apart from the fact that it is not easy to see, at least in monotheism, how a prayer – whatever its object – could not be first and foremost an act of adoration, and apart from the fact that deliverance from all cares is not necessarily (far from it) the aim of religious existence, this would amount to forgetting that the very prayer that expresses our cares can give thanks of itself to the one whom it adores. The adoration of the Spirit making us cry aloud takes place in the cry itself. Thus it is superficial to contrast simplistically a prayer of request with a prayer that bears no request, considering exclusively the very object of the prayer, without paying any heed to the act of speech through which we make our request and the ways in which it turns towards its addressee. The link between desire and prayer is essential, and it can serve to unify the various definitions that have been given of the latter.

In the history of the Christian tradition, two definitions have often been put forward and discussed. The one makes of prayer an elevation of the mind towards God; the other, a request for God to grant what is suitable for us.[36] The first dissociates prayer from an act of speech, while the second is generally understood as vocal prayer.[37] But both presuppose desire. St Augustine says in a sermon, 'Desire is praying always, even if the tongue is silent. If you desire always, you are praying always. When does prayer nod off to sleep? When desire grows cold.'[38] Franz von Baader, who often described and meditated on the act of praying, went so far as to identify will and prayer, stating that man, by his very nature, that is, as will, is a religious being, a being that prays. Every form taken by the will is thus a prayer, whether aware or unaware of itself, turned towards God or towards an idol. [39]

When this desire for God appears to the person praying as a gift of God, when the very act by which he addresses a request to God occurs, it seems to him, in a space in which God is already responding to and responsible for him, prayer can accurately be described as a conversation or a dialogue with God, completely independently of extraordinary or supernatural events in which we would hear voices or receive signs. The great mystic Persian poet Rumi described it powerfully. He evokes a man praying insistently, to whom Satan objects, 'You blabberer, to all these "Allahs" where is the reply, "Here I am"? No reply comes from the throne of God.' This fills him with doubt and discouragement, before there comes to him, from the lips of a wise man, this divine reply:

> This 'Allah' that you are saying is my 'Here I am'. Your supplication, your pain, your fervour are My messenger towards you. Your advances to me and your efforts to find a way of reaching Me were in reality Myself drawing you to Me and freeing your feet . . . . In reply to each of your prayers to 'My Lord', I have often replied saying 'Here I am'.[40]

The reply lies in the act of calling on God, and echoes within it. The vocative of invocation is already not just the place of the presence to God of the person praying but that of the presence of God to the person praying. What we have here is the same structure of divine precedence as in the idea that 'You would not be seeking me if you had not already found me' as we encounter in St Bernard and Pascal.

In monotheism, the description of this envelopment, this interlacing of the human and divine calls, may extend to saying that it is God who is praying in us. Paul Claudel says with his usual profundity that God is not only with our plenitude but also with our need. 'It is together with Him that this need within us becomes an opening, a pronouncement and a summons. It is He, through our hearts and our mouths, who is invoking Himself.'[41] Franz von Baader likewise writes, 'The same God who prays within me will also grant his prayer within me.'[42] And in another place, describing prayer as being at one and the same time a gift and a task (*Gabe, Aufgabe*), he compares it to the movement of the breath; we receive it from God, we 'inspire' it from him, in order to give it back to him, to 'expire' it into him.[43] This circulation of the breath taken and given, received and returned, this 'conspiration' of the human and the divine is of such a kind, for Baader, that prayer appears to him as a function that is no less vital for the spirit than is breathing for the life of the body.[44]

If the ordeal of this circulation, in which the breath we draw in so as to make our request already a breath we have received, belongs to the essence of prayer, it is evidently experienced in very different ways, depending on the religion under consideration. In Christianity, the idea of the Mystical Body, in which Christians form the limbs of Christ, gives it a particular colouring: it is accompanied by an authentic exchange of voices. If God has taken a human voice, the relationship between our voice and his is thereby transformed. In a commentary on a psalm, St Augustine writes, with reference to Christ:

> We form with him one single man, head and body. So we pray towards him, by him, in him: and we speak with him, and he speaks with us. We say in him, and he says in us the prayer of this psalm which is called: *A Prayer of David*.[45]

Such quotations may seem to lead us towards strictly theological considerations, which would be somewhat tangential to a description of prayer. However, they raise two questions, which are decisive for any phenomenology. The first, already raised, is that of the breath and the voice in prayer. Why and how is prayer vocal? The second concerns the singularity of speech in prayer. One can pray freely, with one's own words invented for the occasion, but one can also 'recite' traditional prayers, such as the psalms for Jews and Christians. What exactly does it mean, to 'recite' a prayer? Is this the right word? How does the person praying appropriate the words composed by another so that they act as the highest expression of himself in this place of radical truth, irreplaceable and intimate: his presence to God? How does this appropriation of speech take place?

In his journey to Grande Garabagne, Henri Michaux refers to the god

Mna, 'the deafest and greatest of all the gods'. 'As soon as he knows what is required, he is a god who wishes only to satisfy men . . . (he cannot refuse them anything).' But there's the rub! For he cannot hear very well, and indeed his hearing is getting worse and worse. So he has been given an enormous artificial ear.

> And there are always grand official bawlers, priests and the children of priests, with the most high-pitched and piercing voices, to shout out to him the words of supplication, after they have been preceded, of course, by people they have sent ahead to alert him – cracker-throwers and trumpeters chosen from the most powerful sets of lungs to be found among the Gaurs.[46]

But when we are not in Grande Garabagne, this cannot, of course, be the function of the voice in prayer.

The study of prayer necessitates historical considerations, for the way that praying aloud is apprehended can vary remarkably from one period to another, and it is sometimes difficult to separate the description of the phenomenon from the way it is evaluated as either suitable or unsuitable. What an abyss there is, for example, between this admirable line in Aeschylus, 'How can our lips frame some force that will show for Orestes?',[47] in which prayer is literally the strength of people's mouths, and this couplet by Angelus Silesius: 'So do you think, poor man, that the cries of your mouth/ Are the song of praise that befits the silent Deity?'[48] As for Montaigne, he seems to make the utterance of prayers an inseparable aspect of their inauthenticity, writing, 'We say our prayers out of habit and custom, or to put it better, we merely read and utter the words of our prayers. It amounts, in the end, to show'.[49] And Ludwig Feuerbach sees in thus utterance an essential property of prayer: 'It is essential to the effectiveness of prayer that it be audibly, intelligibly, energetically expressed. Involuntarily prayer wells forth in sound; the struggling heart bursts the barrier of the closed lips.'[50]

The contrast between vocal prayer and silent prayer is, however, more complex than it appears. In those periods when praying aloud is the rule, a prayer that is said in a low voice or simply murmured can be called silent (*tacitus*).[51] And how are we to characterize the prayer of Hannah, described in the Bible? 'Eli was watching her mouth, for Hannah was speaking under her breath; her lips were moving but her voice could not be heard, and Eli thought that she was drunk'.[52] The Talmud deduced from this that 'one may not raise his voice and pray', but that 'one must mouth the Prayer with one's lips'.[53] The Latin poet Persius saw in this the characteristic of certain Jewish prayers: *Labra moves tacitus*, you silently twitch your lips,[54] rather like those who cannot read very well do nowadays. It is not an audible prayer,[55] and

31

in this sense it can be called silent, but it is still vocal and involves the same movements as if it were being pronounced. It is, on the edge of silence, the last stage of a murmur. Where does vocal prayer begin and where does it end? For us, to read, even a religious book, is an essentially different activity from praying. But when reading is always reading aloud, when, even when you are alone, you give voice to what you are reading, when you read body and soul, the distinction is less clear-cut and may even vanish. In the Christian Middle Ages, *lectio* tends to *meditatio*: reading the Holy Scriptures, you draw nourishment from them, you ruminate over them, you taste their savour and, as J. Leclercq puts it in his description of this practice, 'all this activity, necessarily, is a prayer, and *lectio divina* is a reading that is prayed'. [56]

In antiquity, pagan as well as Jewish, and then Christian, praying aloud, clearly and intelligibly, is the most normal and most common kind of prayer.[57] There are exceptions, but these are described precisely as exceptions, linked to particular circumstances or practices, and they are murmured prayers rather than altogether silent prayers. We even find the idea that the intensity and force of a prayer can be gauged from the clarity and liveliness with which it is said, sung or shouted. Not that the gods, or God, are deaf, like Mna for Michaux, and cannot hear our murmurs, but because a manifestation of self before God cannot be purely spiritual and acosmic. To manifest oneself is to manifest oneself for God in the world and to manifest oneself entire.

Where can one manifest oneself entire, if not through the voice, which is indissolubly spiritual and fleshly? Distress, joy, need and gratitude all crave articulate expression. To pray vocally is to make the body an essential element of prayer. St Thomas Aquinas says of vocal prayer that it is necessary since 'man ought to serve God with all that he has received from him, not only with the mind, but also with the body'.[58] The offering and the service of the voice, a gift of speech and a delivery of the breath, are the event in which everything, without division or restriction, can be sacrificed together. For if certain religions prescribe bodily purifications as a preliminary to prayer and if one praying may, before speaking, clear his voice (as we say 'clear his throat'), that voice will be or become purified and clear only in speaking; it is raised and transformed only in giving itself, at the cost sometimes of thereby being broken, made tremulous or stammering. Instead of being, in prayer, the simple external manifestation of an inner state, an expression, it thus becomes an effusion, which gathers, and an offering, which concentrates within itself. One receives oneself only by giving oneself, one exists as oneself only by throwing one's voice into the world, outside oneself. Paul Claudel says that vocal prayer 'is a sanctification, in short, of our breathing', which is not at all the same thing as a technique for mastering the breath; it is thereby, he continues, 'on the one hand a means of repressing vain thoughts, on the other a purification by rhythm of the chaotic ferment of our imagination and finally a way of alluring our sensibility and our attention'.[59] The discipline introduced by the voice means that speech itself listens, becomes a listening in its essence. Vocal prayer puts an end to the disorder of the murmurous noise within and is thus an act of attention to the person we are addressing. The voice is not instrumental for prayer.

A second aspect of vocal prayer, whether singular or collective, is its public aspect. We pray to God, but we pray in the world. We may go somewhere private to pray, but prayer cannot itself be secret, unless it be with a luminous secret that desires to be exposed, since it is an act of presence and manifestation. In antiquity, murmured or inaudible prayer was often associated with magical practices or requests of which one was ashamed. The magician wished to keep the secret of his formulae and his incantations: they must not be proclaimed. And there are certain wishes that we would be ashamed to utter aloud, even if only for ourselves. Ancient literature provides us with a certain number of examples.[60] This is why Seneca ends one of his letters to Lucilius by quoting a philosopher who stated, 'Know that thou art freed from all desires when thou hast reached such a point that thou prayest to God for nothing except what thou canst pray for openly,' which he himself transposes into a fine chiasmus: 'Live among men as if God beheld you; speak with God as if men were listening.'[61] Montaigne referred to the Pythagoreans, who believed that prayer should be 'public and heard by all, so that God should not be begged for things unseemly or unjust'.[62] This may seem naive or archaic to us, but it clearly brings out a property of vocal prayer: as manifestation in the world, it has, at least potentially, a public aspect, and in fact it is always heard by at least one man, the one who utters it. Even if I am the only witness, this act of speech preserves the responsibility proper to it. Is it necessarily a mark of naivety to take it seriously? Is it vain to emphasize that all human speech, even when solitary and addressed to God, always involves as its horizon the community of speech between men?

This raises the question of the respective importance of collective prayer and individual prayer. Even the opponents of vocal prayer agree that it is necessary to collective prayer, which, if it may include moments of silence, cannot be conceived of without the voice. And the superiority of collective prayer is emphasized by numerous religious traditions. The Talmud goes so far as to assert that 'only the prayers said in a synagogue are heard', and Maimonides writes that 'one must be associated with a community and not pray alone when there is a possibility of praying with others.'[63] Christianity also insists on this, as we clearly see from the words of the Gospel: 'For where two or three meet in my name, I am there among them.'[64] The community of men who have gathered together to pray to the invisible constitutes a visible manifestation of it. The community is all the more open to the invisible the more visible it is, and all the more spiritual the more corporeal it is. In certain beliefs, this community extends beyond its visibly present members. The voice shows the invisible which calls, summons and brings together.

Is the voice thereby just a means, a mere condition *sine qua non*? The mutual presence of men and their common presence to God in the sharing of speech go much further. Nobody prays for himself alone, and the collectivity also prays and speaks for those who can no longer speak or cannot yet speak, it speaks for the absent and the departed, it speaks for others, on their behalf but also in their stead. And it may be that each person, even in solitude, is merely the representative of community. This is why the phenomenological difference between communal prayer and solitary prayer, the difference which is one of essence, is not at all identical with the empirical difference between collective prayer and individual prayer. For Plotinus, for instance, who hardly ever refers to prayer, the truth of prayer is to tend towards God himself with our souls, and not with words, and to pray to him 'alone to him alone'.[65] Even if numerous philosophers were gathered together in the same place to pray in this way, this prayer would remain in its essence solitary. As for Proclus, he clearly differentiates between 'philosophical prayer' and 'legal prayer, that which conforms to the traditional usage of the *polis*' – a prayer that is necessarily collective; and this difference tallies with a difference between words, 'the words that one considers from within in a scientific spirit' and 'the words whose fate it is to be separated twice over from the intellect, those which are uttered outwardly with the aim of teaching, and in view of social relations'.[66] A polarization of this kind, in which the uttering of speech is a form of degradation and in which the most solitary prayer is necessarily the highest, is radically excluded elsewhere.

In Christianity, for example, all prayer is in essence communal, since every individual prays and can pray, even if it be in the greatest isolation, only as a member of the Mystic Body of Christ, and thus always within the Church. Individual prayer is of course distinguished from collective prayer, but only as variants of the same church-based prayer – something the 'Our Father' clearly shows in its very form. Each of these two variants relates to the other as to that without which it could not be fully complete: solitary prayer is only ever, as it were, a provisional detachment from collective prayer, since it is always based in the church, and collective prayer is in no way an imaginary entity floating above the individuals who utter it, but is rooted in the act proper to each of them. Everyone must after all say and repeat the *Credo,* in the first person singular, but the Christian *Credo* does not say that Christ died for me, but for us, *pro nobis*. Prayer thus establishes a *sui generis* mode of community through speech and in speech.

This is brought out by another characteristic: the insistence on the fact that one must pray for oneself, since prayer for oneself is a precondition of praying for others.[67] These two types of prayer are not in competition with each other, and there is nothing egotistic in the one forming the basis for the other, for it is the means whereby I stand before God and, far from deifying myself, am recalled to my own condition. This interlacing of voices and destinies gave rise to some eloquent considerations in St Augustine on the perpetuity of prayer. This theme has always aroused debate, for people have wondered how it was possible for an individual to be always praying. The most common solution is to state that any action can become a prayer when it is offered to God, which obviously dissociates prayer from an act of speech. But there is at least one perpetual vocal prayer, namely that of the community, in which, when one member falls silent, another one takes over and starts to speak. St Augustine describes the prayer of the Church as the incessant prayer of one single man across space and time.[68] Independently of this theological perspective, the singularity of prayer, which knows that it is one voice in the choir, one moment in a historical community of speech, is clearly emphasized.

Speech can be all the more proper to each person in that it does not belong to him exclusively, but passes and circulates and is transmitted from one voice to another and from one life to another, consuming and consummating them on the wing. The highest intimacy with God is expressed in words that we do not invent but that, rather, invent us, in that they find us and discover us where we were without knowing it. And formulary prayer, prayer that uses the traditional or scriptural formulae, is not a constrained prayer but the most free of all. All of these are essential characteristics of vocal prayer. To pray is not to summon up the words of another but to be summoned to appear by and before one's words, and in them. Of course, in other domains of life I can use, in order to communicate something altogether personal, the words of another and thus, for instance, make a declaration of love by quoting the words of a poet, or express my opinion by means of a proverb. I appropriate these words to myself, but it belongs to their particular stylistic effect that they should be identified as a quotation. In prayer, the situation is different. To say a prayer is to appropriate it to oneself, or to appropriate oneself to it in a quite different fashion.

This very common phenomenon has been little reflected on and treated thematically. John Cassian does so with great precision, in reference to the use of psalms in prayer:

> Thriving on the pasturage that they always offer and taking into himself all the dispositions of the psalms, he (the monk) will begin to repeat them and to treat them in his profound compunction of heart not as if they were composed by the prophet but as if they were his own utterances and his own prayer (*velut a se editos quasi orationem propriam*). Certainly he will consider that they are directed to his own

person (*vel certe ad suam personam aestimet eos fuisse directos*), and he will recognize that their words were not only achieved by and in the prophet in times past but that they are daily borne out and fulfilled in him.[69]

The actualization of the psalm in prayer could not be better described. To be sure, superficially, it might be felt to be over-bold to turn oneself into the author, so to speak, of words that one considers to be divinely inspired. But it is not pride, for belief in inspiration involves precisely this dimension of a perpetual newness and contemporaneity. To pray the psalms is not to add one theoretical interpretation to another, it is to allow oneself to be interpreted by them, to offer one's own life, to which they give a much deeper expression in the words of God, as a space in which they can echo and their promise be heard. Hence the temporal dimensions on which John Cassian goes on to insist: we pray the psalms by anticipating their meaning, as if we were inventing them, and also by remembering – remembering our own trials and tribulations, which are the best explanation of them.

This is why there is a life of prayer, 'a life,' says Claudel, 'which transports into the domain of the spirit the astonishingly complex, varied, ingenious and sometimes paradoxical activities of physiology', for 'the Word must be made flesh in us'.[70] This life is sustained by the voice that brings us together and gathers us in a place other than ourselves, before God. In the religions in which God is himself Word and speech, it seems that prayer springs forth on every side, as in the beautiful and surprising conclusion of Tertullian's treatise on prayer, in which he says that 'every creature' prays, even the animals: indeed (something that would have delighted Olivier Messiaen), the birds, having no hands, hold out to the sky the cross-shaped sign of their wings and 'utter something that seems a prayer'.[71] Is this merely an exaggeratedly rapturous statement, or the very rigorous perception that the human voice, in its unique and irreplaceable aspects, is always hymn-like, and cannot speak without giving voice to everything that has no voice and bringing to spoken expression everything that remains mute or can merely stammer? Thus, with the voice and in the voice, the entire world wounded by words is offered to God. Philo made man a 'eucharistic' creature, a creature whose most characteristic act, the one most wholly his, is to give thanks, since all that could be offered to God belongs to him already, except for the very act by which we thank him through 'whichever of its appointed functions the voice may exercise, be it eloquent speech or song'.[72] The human voice becomes a place in which the world can return to God. The voice gives what it does not have – which does not mean that it gives nothing, and in any case it can give itself only because it does not possess itself, since voice is that which, in all speech, does not belong to itself.

The exclusive insistence on vocal prayer in the preceding remarks does not involve an underestimation of the varied and profound forms of silent prayer. But the latter can be defined and constituted only with reference to the former. Only the voice can fall silent, and only speech can stop talking. The withdrawal or suspension of the voice cannot come first, and vocal prayer is always presupposed, even if there are states of religious life in which it can become impossible or inopportune. It is the foundation of all the other forms of prayer, which suspend or interiorize the voice. And this foundational character does not mean that it is merely an initial, crude, simple form of prayer, on which more subtle, pure and lofty forms can gradually be constructed. It appears simple only because it is the most common, but it has all the complexity of the voice, from the cry to the murmur, and that of an act of speech that can ask, thank, question, narrate, renounce, promise . . . . The other forms of prayer are, rather, simplifications of vocal speech, they preserve only this or that aspect of it, which are already contained actually or potentially in it. St Teresa of Avila shows that the highest states of contemplation can be produced in vocal prayer. This is why vocal prayer, in the diversity of its forms, is, so to speak, the index of religious existence, including, as it does, all of the phenomena that constitute religion. It is not a retreat into an imaginary world, not a flight from finitude, because it makes the entire world visible to the invisible, and by manifesting us to it body and soul it discloses to us our own condition and our own finitude in a light from which we cannot hide, in the incandescent clarity of the supplicant voice.

Why call it 'wounded speech'? It always has its origin in the wound of a joy or a distress; it always opens its lips in response to some tearing asunder. And if it does, it is still wounded, even more so. Wounded by this listening and this summons that have always already preceded it, that disclose it to itself, in its truth that is always in abeyance, always agonistic, wrestling like Jacob all night long in the dust to wrest God's blessing from him, and thereafter bearing the sign of a dislocated hip and a limp, which mean that speech is all the more confident the less sure it can be of its own capabilities. For the person praying learns in prayer that he does not know how to pray, he is called by a call that completely exceeds him, and he tries to find a way into the perfect prayer (this is not the place to examine whether such a prayer is possible), the prayer that from God goes to God, in a voice and thus in a human body: the prayer by which God calls upon himself. Wounded, too, is this speech because it attempts to give voice to all the voices that are silent, excluded as they are from prayer by the hollow echoing effect created when they address their individual or collective idols, or by the atrocious plight of the destiny they endure, whose despair does not even become a cry in which they could voice their complaint to God, which itself may be a way of praying.

This act of a speech wounded by the radical otherness of the person to whom it speaks is pure address. It does not speak in order to teach anyone anything, even if it always says something about ourselves and the world; it entrusts to the other what the other knows and asks the other for what he knows we need. Not for a single instant is speech dissociated from the idea of a test to be undergone, it is put to the test in every sense, by itself, and by what it says, and by what it does not manage to say, and by the person to whom it speaks. It learns, itself, by having to undergo this test, and this is why this wound makes it stronger – all the stronger in that it has not tried to heal it.

3

THE HOSPITALITY OF SILENCE

Introduction

Right from the start, and for all time, silence and speech belong to one another. There is not, and cannot be, any silence except for a creature of speech, for only the latter listens and can listen, just as he alone can fall silent and stop talking, suspending by an act the utterance of his words into the very depths of his inner murmur, so as to listen to silence as such. Silence cannot manifest itself, in all its multiple possibilities, except to someone who is able to speak. And speech itself comes from silence and tends towards it, just as it never ceases to accompany it. It comes from the silence that always precedes it, and which it interrupts or breaks, as we say, unless on a deeper level it makes it echo; it accompanies silence, for, while it is being uttered, it needs the noises all around and the lips of the other whom it is addressing to be silent; it tends towards silence, which alone can ratify that it has in truth said something and which allows the other to speak, or brings the two interlocutors together in agreement, so that they can peacefully bring together what had been shared out. Uninterrupted speech deafens others and itself, it is no longer listened to, and ceases to listen to itself, it becomes the hum of insignificance.

Thus, one completely misunderstands the phenomenon of silence and its meaning if one defines it as a mere absence of sound, whether the sound be noise or speech – if one defines it, that is, as a privation in the Aristotelian sense of the term. Silence is not a complete absence of sound, as darkness is a complete absence of light. To start out from this definition, even if in order to go beyond it subsequently, is to have started out from a false premiss.1 For light does not come from darkness, and in no way derives from it: darkness is merely its absence, whereas speech is born from silence. The study of the vocabulary of silence in different languages would confirm that it has a positive identity. The merely privative meaning is often the most belated in the history of the language, and the first meaning of silence is often the human act of falling silent, keeping silent – and this is not insignificant. Unless, that is, the same word, such as the German Stille, or the Greek *hèsuchia*, designates calm and silence – which even here differentiates it from a privation, for calm is not merely the absence of agitation. A dead person has nothing calm about him but is neither agitated nor calm.

And a mute man is the only man who cannot be silent, precisely because he cannot speak. The silence that a man keeps does not form the interruption of a speaking machine that has momentarily broken down, like that *Sprachmaschine* into which Kant thought that we are transformed by lying: this alone would require a privative definition.

If we move from human silence, which still rests on positive acts, to the silence, or silences, of nature, the fact remains that even the latter is for us something that we *listen* to, if it is to be perceived as silence, and that it too does not have the status of a privation. Every time that we are attentive to it, it manifests itself as filled with meaning; it calms us or makes us feel euphoric, it causes us joy or anguish, it instils boredom or anxiety in us – in other terms, it never presents itself as the mere perception of an absence of sound, an absence that in any case is never total.

To this must be added the fact that silence does not form the precondition of listening alone, but also of vision. The man of the gaze is silent. All attentive consideration of the visible also requires silence. The painter is not simply a man of silence by virtue of the fact that he is different from an orator, but because he is a painter and so that he may remain so.[2] The visible voice of painting is completely suffused with silence, a silence that it does not merely keep, but gives to us, making us dwell within it.

Far from negating speech, silence is its source. And what arises and springs from this source never exhausts it or drains it dry. Living speech – just as there is living water – does not forget the origin, which loses itself and gives itself away in its affirmation. Only the silences that have become hardened and dead, the petrified silences of resentment and fear, must be 'broken' by speech, which delivers what they had been holding prisoner in secret. As for open silences, they are illumined by the speech that they were already promising, just as, once the speech has been uttered, it will be able to gather itself within them so as to continue to ripen.

In the order of nature as in that of grace, the most varied remarks have borne witness to this silent nativity of speech. Joseph Joubert refers to this in words that are themselves, so to speak, made porous by the silence that they name rather than say. 'Silence. – The delights of silence. – Thoughts must be born from the soul and words from silence. – An attentive silence.'[3] In these last words, it is not a question of a note that would fade away into its own platitude, since the expression 'attentive silence' is so commonplace: it is not a matter of teaching us something about silence, but rather of letting it leave its signature and the trace, as it were, of three steps on the snow of the page. And everyone who writes knows that he is merely the one who ferries words from silence to silence, from the silence in which he meditates and from whence his as yet unuttered speech arises, to the visible silence of the page, which welcomes it and preserves it, without the blank whiteness disappearing.[4] To write is a Passover of silence. The great Argentine poet Roberto Juarroz describes it very well in a poem in which he states what it is he performing and performs what it is he is saying, in his *Twelfth Vertical Poetry*:

> The white page
> is a listening that waits (*es un oido que aguarda*)
> Writing is the voice
> which can be combined with the whiteness . . .
> At certain moments
> the hand senses the density that awaits it
> and its trace on the whiteness
> finds the necessary pressure
> to reach the music from below.[5]

It is beautiful to see how in these words the interlacing of the visible and the audible happens only in the act of the hand, drilling into the silence of the page an artesian well of music. This whiteness is no more a privation of writing than silence is a privation of speech.

These ideas are not confined to modernity. When Aristotle seeks to describe the status of the intellect before it thinks in act and becomes what it thinks, the intelligibles, he compares it to a tablet on which nothing is written,[6] which is at the origin of the *tabula rasa* of the empiricists. But, as Alexander of Aphrodisia noted in rigorous fashion, it 'is, in consequence, merely an aptitude for the reception of the forms and it resembles a tablet on which there is nothing written, or rather what is unwritten on the tablet, and not the tablet itself'. The tablet, like the paper of the page for us, is defined, determinate, and not, as such, the pure openness of potentiality: only 'what is unwritten on the tablet is . . . the aptitude to receive writing'.[7] The silent white of the page is not the page itself, it is rather a passive listening, filled with dawning potential, to the words that will find shelter on it.

This crossing, this translation, which speech accomplishes from silence to silence makes these silences live or die together. The silence after speech is never the same as the silence that preceded it: it ripens and grows within all the words that ultimately come to offer themselves to it and in it. And speech draws its weight and its gravity from the fact that it does not tear open the silence from which it comes. The eloquent meditation of Max Picard on *The World of Silence* gives this 'admirable commerce' its fundamental importance:

> Speech is born from silence in such a natural and unnoticed way that
> it seems it is merely a silence turned over, the other side of silence
> . . . . In all speech, there is something silent that indicates where

41

the speech has come from; in each silence, there is something which speaks and indicates that speech is born from silence.[8]

And when, as Max Picard goes on to show, in poetry speech takes on its full force, 'silence becomes spontaneously present; it is drawn along by speech – we hear perfect silence as an echo of perfect speech'. [9]

The speech of chatter, the speech that speaks for the mere sake of speaking, is completely different: it gives us no silence to hear, nor does it give to silence anything that speech might have illumined. It is no longer speech, being foreign to silence and not even suspecting its existence. When language is thought of on the model of physical transmission, with its 'emitters' and 'receivers', silence is merely background noise; it has disappeared and, with it, human speech. There then happens what Max Picard, in descriptions close to those that Heidegger gives of *Gestell*, calls 'rumour'. Nobody speaks when everyone merely brings their quota to the bucket-chain of words, the perpetual movement of chatter. The disappearance of silence devastates speech and turns it into a desert. It is with this in mind that Kierkegaard gave a powerful definition of chatter:

> What does *chattering* mean? It means abolishing the passionate disjunction between speaking and being silent. Only a man who is essentially able to keep silent is essentially able to speak; and only he who is essentially able to keep silent is essentially able to act.[10]

It is not in this definition a matter of the simple ascetic precept, repeated frequently in the Christian Middle Ages, of the *silentium loquendi magister*, silence as master of speech.[11] Kierkegaard, anticipating Nietzsche, linked silence – like the speech that it summons and makes possible – to great events; it is in a historical and collective dimension that he defined chatter. Chatter lives off the absence of events but also for that absence: it tries to saturate with noise the calm space in which events might be produced. The genius proper to Samuel Beckett is to have given *voice* to this *rumour*, something that appears to be a contradiction in terms, and yet something that a speech nourished on silence, his own, has achieved.

> I know no more questions and they keep pouring out of my mouth. I think I know what it is, it's to prevent the discourse from coming to an end, this futile discourse which is not credited to me and brings me not a syllable nearer silence.[12]

And, in another passage: 'One starts speaking as if it were possible to stop at will. It is better so. The search for the means to put an end to things, an end to speech, is what enables the discourse to continue.'[13]

42

All of this shows *a contrario* the extent to which speech is born from silence. Even divine speech, surrounded by divine silence, requires another silence, that of creatures, in order to be translated. This speech too passes from one silence to another. Catholic liturgy prescribes, at vespers for the Sunday of the octave of the Nativity, this fine anthem, often quoted or paraphrased by the mystics: *Dum medium silentium tenerent omnia, et nox in suo cursu mediu, iter perageret, omnipotens Sermo tuus, Domine, a regalibus sedibus venit, alleluia.*[14] It is a question of the birth of the eternal Word in the crib, surrounded by the silence of the night. The most silent of all hours is that of the Nativity, of the coming of the Word in a flesh that at first is mute, in which the Word loses its power of speech so as to speak to us. But this anthem is taken from the book of Wisdom,[15] where this peaceful silence precedes a terrible event in which God unleashes his anger against the impious, the last plague of Egypt, the death of the firstborn! Passing from what precedes the first Passover to what makes possible the second, these words also translate silence and profoundly transform its meaning. The silence in which omnipotence makes itself impotent is even deeper than the silence in which it manifests itself directly.

In a fine passage, the author of *Moby Dick* gave, albeit not without ambiguity, a universal dimension to this silence of the Nativity:

All profound things, and emotions of things are preceded and attended by silence. What a silence is that with which the pale bride precedes the responsive *I will*, to the priest's solemn question, Wilt thou have this man for thy husband? In silence, too, the wedded hands are clasped. Yea, in silence the child Christ was born into the world. Silence is the general consecration of the universe. Silence is the invisible laying on of the Divine Pontiff's hands upon the world. Silence is at once the most harmless and the most awful thing in all nature. It speaks of the Reserved Forces of Fate. Silence is the only Voice of our God.[16]

This praise of silence, which Karl Löwith frequently dwelt on, plays on many kinds of silence – too many silences, no doubt, for it to avoid being lost in their diversity, for they cannot all be listened to in the same act or with the same attention. But it is good to see that, during the period in which the mechanisms that would destroy silence were being devised, the most widely separated poets and thinkers were able to see, understand and say that from it alone speech could be born, and that speech alone could in truth bless it.

Hence, in Nietzsche's *Thus Spoke Zarathustra*, the last pages of Part II, which ends with 'The Quietest Hour' ('Die Stillste Stunde'), bring into play, in many different ways, silence, listening and speech. The explicit words about the founding power of silence do not form isolated maxims, they are closely linked to the stories and parables in which they appear. There are the people who turn a deaf ear to the sound of Zarathustra's steps over their heads,[17] but there is also the false great man who is now no more than a huge ear.[18] At the sight of his disciples, Zarathustra is overcome by alarm, which gives way to a burst of laughter, which makes him say, after he has heard the noise of their silent thoughts emerging from their speech: '. . .'[19] But there is also the fire dog, which cannot listen to Zarathustra any longer and runs off – and the disciples barely even listen to this story.[20] All greatness, here too, is accompanied by silence: 'The greatest events – they are not our noisiest but our stillest hours. The world revolves, not around the inventors of new noises, but around the inventors of new values; it revolves *inaudibly (unerhörbar)*'.[21] The most decisive thing, in these passages, is that Zarathustra is sent to himself, sent on his most personal mission, to his own most personal speech, by a silence. It is by listening to the silence, allowing himself to be called upon by silence, that he becomes himself.

Such, indeed, is the effect of 'the most silent hour': it 'speaks' to him.[22] When, around him, there forms a silence so deep that he has never head its like, something speaks to him 'voicelessly' (*ohne Stimme*). This voiceless speech speaks to him of his speech, the speech he must utter and is still not uttering. This speech demands that he speak, 'Say your speech and break! (*Sprich dein Wort und zerbrich!*)' To Zarathustra, discouraged that his speech has not been heard by men, this voiceless speech replies, 'How do you know *that*? The dew falls upon the grass when the night is at its most silent'. And it is this very same speech that tells him – when he has lamented that he does not have 'the voice of a lion': 'It is the stillest words which bring the storm. Thoughts that come on doves' feet guide the world.' When this voice withdraws, there is around Zarathustra 'a twofold stillness', as it were. And of that, he says he has 'kept nothing' from his friends before leaving them. It is another such mute dialogue on which, in the third part, Zarathustra engages with the sky, before sunrise.[23] To be silent together may still be a peaceful, friendly dialogue. Another passage had already mentioned the 'silence of all light-givers'.[24]

There is no need to produce any more evidence of this kind: any meditation on speech that is worth the name, however singular it might be, takes place in a fraternity with silence, and it is never a question, with silence, of a pure nothingness or a mere privation. Unprofitable would be a speech that did not undertake to express the silence that sends it out to itself and does not cease to do so. But all thinking about silence has its perils, not the least of which is that of hypostatizing silence, of speaking about silence as if it formed an entity underlying all other silences. No more than others does Max Picard, in his *World of Silence*, avoid this temptation. As Samuel Beckett's *Unnamable* puts it: 'For it is all very fine to keep silence, but one has also to consider the kind of silence one keeps.'[25] The phenomenality of silence brings into play possibilities, dimensions and acts that vary greatly from one another, something that in any case its perpetual correlation with speech makes necessary.

Silence also is said in many various ways, the unity of which, if unity there be, must be sought, and not merely presupposed as if it were self-evident. If this is not the case, we run the risk of relapsing into the gnostic illusion that made first principles of the Silence and the Abyss.[27] This means incurring an idolatry of silence – an idolatry that chatters noisily. We must describe and articulate the different types of silence. In this way, following a traditional metaphysical order, and distinguishing the different silences in accordance with *what* it is in them that is silent, we cannot identify the silence of the origin, of the first principle or of God, with the silence of nature or with human silence, even if these different silences may communicate with or respond to one another.

The witch of Theocritus calls forth, in her rites, the silence of nature, but this silence merely hears all the more clearly the noise of the resentment that inhabits her. 'Lo there! now wave is still and wind is still, though never still the pain that is in my breast.'[28] What we have here is a rite by means of which she is seeking to call forth the love of the man she loves. And a terrible quatrain of Emily Dickinson, which also brings many different possibilities into play, contrasts the devastating passion of human silence with the innocent, vulnerable silence of nature: 'There is no Silence in the Earth – so silent/ As that endured/ Which uttered, would discourage Nature/ And haunt the world.'[29] This silence in us *must not* henceforth be spoken.

However, distinguishing between silences according to the being that is silent in them is not in the least phenomenological, for if there are various silences, they must by and through themselves manifest their diversity to our listening for us to determine whether they are the silence of God, of nature, or of whatever power it might be. It is lacking in rigour to study the forms of silence as if we were ourselves nowhere, and the relationship between man and silence, man and silences, as much as the acts by which this relationship is established, constitute the only possible principle of a typology.

The first distinction that obviously needs to be made is that which separates silence as a dimension from silence as an act, the silence that we listen to from the silence that we make. Although there is nothing absolute about the distinction, the first could be called, in Greek, *sigè*, and the second *siôpè*. When silence is posited as a principle, it is the first word, *sigè*, that is used, from the Gnostics to Claudel or Merleau-Ponty. Plotinus, who is usually considered as a thinker of silence, does not use even once in his whole oeuvre the term *sigè* or the corresponding verb *sigán* whereas he often refers to *siôpè* and all the silences we can fall into or keep. This is philosophically worthy of consideration. Never does Plotinus hypostatize silence. In German, we could distinguish between *Stille* and *Schweigen*. It is always a being capable of speaking that is silent, that keeps silent, that stops talking; but what is – in the same sense, at least – without speech is *silent* without thereby *stopping talking*. Melville, in the passage referred to above, refers first and foremost to silence as a dimension, even if he relates it to human acts. Joubert explicitly posited it as such: 'Among the three dimensions, we must count time, space, and silence. Space is in time, silence is in space.'[30] When we listen to the silence of nature, this is not at all the same act as listening to the silence of a man who is silent. To speak of the dimension of silence, of a silence that is in some degree elementary, does not mean yet again to hypostatize silence, for this dimensionality opens out on to very different possibilities: it draws its rigour from the specific nature of our listening. Silence as a dimension is the other of human speech as a whole, whereas the acts of silence belong to human speech, are moments of it, its modes and possibilities.

When it comes to silence as a human act, we must of course distinguish first and foremost between an *outer* silence and an *inner* silence. Abstaining from uttering words may be a means of freeing or reinforcing our inner speech, or on the contrary it may merely be a preamble to the attempt to impose silence within ourselves as well. Three examples may illustrate this distinction: they are all the more suitable for bringing out clearly the diverse intentionalities of silence in that they are all from the same religious tradition. Referring to 'the ills of language and the good of silence' in his *Principles of Christian Life*, Cardinal Bona, in the seventeenth century, wrote:

> This is why the art of being silent (*taciturnitas*) is a great thing, thanks to which, withdrawing from the company of men, we learn to converse with God. It is in vain, indeed, that the tongue falls silent, if the spirit does not speak with God.[31]

Outer silence is here merely a condition of inner speech, of conversing with God. To be silent is to enter into another kind of speech. From another point of view, Father Grou, a Jesuit mystic of the eighteenth century, invites us to '*keep silent* inwardly and outwardly'. He writes:

> It is not enough to keep silent with others; we have to keep silent with ourselves, have no converse with our imagination, cease to recall what we have said or heard, not occupy ourselves with useless thoughts which roam across the past or the future.[32]

To be sure, this silence of the imagination and even the memory does not form, of itself, a total silence; it may be the condition of a spiritual speech. But Father Grou has in mind a 'spiritual childhood' in which the aim is to reach 'simple, direct operations, which break away, so to speak, from the control of the soul', and transcend self-conscious thought. The intention is that man becomes a child again in spirit and says to God 'without formulae and without choosing his words everything that his heart suggests to him', and finally 'expresses to him all the feelings which grace inspires within him, sometimes in speech, but *most often without speaking*'.[33] The aim here really is to manifest oneself to God in silence, to present in a naked and wordless form one's spirit and heart before him. Silence becomes twofold, becomes a heartfelt childhood, and is no longer a mere vehicle of speech.

In his spirituality of desire and disquiet, St Augustine, for his part, saw in our amorous ardour that which merely breaks open our mute silence, overcoming the contrast between external and internal silence in so far as this contrast itself is too external and thus superficial. Thus he writes, in his commentary on the Psalms: 'For he who desires, even if his tongue is silent, sings from his heart; and he who has no desire, whatever the cry with which he strikes men's ears, is mute for God.'[34] Silence itself sings, when it is the silence of desire. The greatest attention is thus required in order to describe the diversity of silences: what makes silence possible, and what is made possible by silence, must always be considered if its meaning is to be defined.

Another important distinction when it comes to human silence is that which separates the silence of being *dumbstruck* from the silence that is an *art*. Artistic silence is an acquired silence: there are arts of being silent, and all sorts of practices of ascesis, of meditation or mortification through which we learn to keep silent, to contain and discipline our speech for something to make itself manifest or be in a position to manifest itself. But dumbstruck silence is an unforeseen and unexpected suspension of our speech – one that absolutely does not result from an art or a learned skill; our speech is suspended by the event of manifestation or by the encounter with something or someone. Our speech is taken short, overwhelmed by what suddenly arises. What leaves us at first speechless for joy or horror is also what requires the greatest effort and the gift of speech. This silence for which I do not take the initiative, this silence which forms in some degree the breaking open, within my innermost self, of otherness, this silence of sudden emotion has, of course, certain possible forms. What is common to all of them is that they are suffered passively. This passive suffering may be catastrophic, leading to the traumatic breaking of my powers, becoming, quite literally, maddening.[35] But it may also be the site of a deeper transformation than all those that I would have been able to bring about by myself: this is true of mystic silence, in which this passivity higher than any activity corresponds to the moment when God himself acts directly within us and on us. This silence breaks us down only so as to raise us above ourselves: it has the character of an event.

These distinctions are far from being the only ones. How can these various possibilities of silence be analysed and described, when the sheer number of them is so disconcerting? Since what is at stake here is the ark of speech, we will leave aside the purely privative silences, the silences or failure and death in which speech destroys and condemns itself.[36] The first dimension of silence in its relationship with speech is that of silence as *listening*. It is a question of the act, or rather acts, in which we keep silent so as to listen, in which we listen while keeping silent. This silence must be dealt with first of all, for it subtends all the others, and there is no silence that does not presuppose it. It is not, for all that, a simple matter, for I may keep silent in order to listen to silence, or to listen to an inner or outer speech, and this may vary with many acts that are specified by what they are listening to. The second dimension is that of silence as *response*. Here, the suspense of speech is still itself speech, an eloquent silence, a place of encounter and mutual presence. There are silent prayers, and colloquia of silence in many of the places where we live our lives. It is no longer a matter of merely responding in silence to what we are listening to (of being responsible *for* it), but of responding in silence *to* what we are listening to. Speech gathers itself in silence so as to offer itself to it. The third dimension is clearly demarcated from the first two, which are interdependent in so far as in them, silence is a place in which speech can be exchanged. It is silence as *ecstasy* or *excess*, mystic silence properly speaking, in which speech receives, in surprise and passivity, the gift of a higher silence. This typology is of course merely an outline, which must be filled with meaning by the very description of the acts on which it is imposing order.

Silence as listening

It is obvious that we have to keep silent and stop talking in order to listen, even if its very obviousness has some disconcerting features. For when I speak, I am still listening, I am listening with the utmost attentiveness, and in a way that is, as it were, irreparable, to that which I am replying to, even if I am no longer keeping silent. Would the silence of listening remain such if it never led me to give a reply to what I listen to, if it did not already promise that reply? The silence of listening promises speech, in proportion to its very attention, and speech, when it sounds out, lovingly keeps the promise made by silence and is still related to the silence.

The great palace of silence that is, at the origins of philosophy, the work of Plato, may shed light on this – a palace of silence, and a monument of gratitude and friendship, since in it, Plato never speaks of himself or appears in person to have his say, leaving this to others, so many others: Socrates first and foremost. Many silences, often of a quite contrasting kind, are present in it. There is a silence that, far from forming the precondition for speech to listen, refuses to listen – that of Philebus, the spokesman for a life of pleasure, at the beginning of Plato's dialogue that bears his name as its title. Philebus no longer wishes to discuss with Socrates, he no longer wishes to venture into the space of speech, and takes refuge in the obstinate muteness of one who refuses to change, and remains in his 'positions' which from henceforth will be set in stone. He is going to fall silent, no longer wishing to reply to or be responsible for anything at all: another interlocutor Protarchus is now given the task of defending his thesis. Socrates and Protarchus will be the only ones to speak, and Philebus will merely be a mute spectator. Will he listen to them? By withdrawing from dialogue and its shared light, Philebus, even if he allows the words of others to strike his ears, has ceased to be a *listener*, since he no longer takes an interest in what is being said. Socrates and Protarchus, by exchanging words, will for their part never stop listening to each other in order to reply to one another, and in replying to one another in turn.

When it comes to Socrates, it could seem, if we are to believe the beginning of the *Phaedrus*, that he is far from being a man of silence. Even the countryside that is so close to Athens seems unknown to him, to the great surprise of Phaedrus. Socrates does not go out to listen to the silence of nature, he is fond of learning, and 'the country places and the trees won't teach me anything, and the people in the city do'.[37] Then he jokingly shows that only the bait of the speeches that Phaedrus keeps concealed – with reason! – under his mantle has managed to draw him outside the city. But if Socrates gains nothing from this rural silence, his speech, in other respects, lives within the intimacy of silence. At the beginning of the *Symposium*, his lateness is due to the silent meditation that suddenly brings him to a halt in the middle of the street.[38] In the *Phaedo*, even when time is running out and only a few hours remain before he is to drink the hemlock, Socrates on several occasions falls into long silences, either because he is continuing to think about what he has just said, or because he is meditating on what he is about to say. His speech comes from silence and leads to silence,[39] but this silence is none other than the voiceless speech of the soul with itself, which, for Plato, constitutes thought.

More important, when it comes to listening, is the silence into which Plato makes Socrates fall in the great dialogues of his maturity. In the *Parmenides*, Plato first of all has Socrates, a very young man, engage in dialogue with the aged Parmenides. This Socrates has not yet been completely gripped by philosophy,[40] and, in the second part, Parmenides goes on to give a lesson in dialectics, with the help of another character, while the others listen in silence. Socrates listens, Socrates falls silent. In the *Sophist* and the *Politicus*, Socrates, now a mature man, is facing the trial that will prove fatal to him. And here too he falls silent, for a long time, so that he can listen to another voice, that of a man from Elea, who is accomplishing the task assigned to the discussion. This presence of a Socrates who is merely a listener, a Socrates who is prepared to be instructed, just as he says he has allowed himself to be instructed by Diotima, necessarily belongs to his spiritual figure. It is far from demonstrating, as has sometimes been deduced, his effacement or his marginalization in Plato's work. Who would Socrates be if he were not able to stay silent to listen? How could the inventor of maieutics be presented by Plato as the exclusive and jealous proprietor of speech, wherever he may find himself? Philosophy does not become mute when Socrates falls silent. It is also by his silence that Socrates sends the others to speech. This silence is not an absence but a way of bearing witness to the mind, and it invites us to enter, ourselves, into the patient listening of speech, a listening that is both source and resource.

What are the various possibilities of this listening silence? The first, and one of the strongest, is that in which the act whereby our speech is suspended opens us to the dimension of silence in the world. It is then by my silence that I listen to silence, not in a form of introspection whereby I listen to myself being silent but in going out to meet the silent plenitude of nature. Every 'canticle of the creatures' has presupposed such a listening. In the admirable meditation on silence that is the first of the three edifying discourses of 1849 entitled 'The Lilies of the Field and the Birds of the Air', Kierkegaard emphasizes that the silence of nature is not at all a privation, and is not reducible to the absence of sounds:

> The forest is silent, even when it whispers it is still silent. . . . The sea is silent; even when it rages noisily, it yet is silent. . . . In the evening, when silence broods over the countryside and thou from the meadow dost hear the distant lowing, or far from the farmer's house dost hear the dog's domestic voice – one cannot say that this lowing or this voice disturbs the silence; no, this belongs to silence, is in mysterious but again in silent accord with silence.[41]

The background of silence from which all these sounds emerge, and which gives a warm welcome to them as they fade away, is the silence that in them and through them grasps us. Never is this silence broken or interrupted by natural noises, whereas it is violently broken by human industry, which negates it relentlessly. Rilke dwells on the meaning of this in one of the 'Sonnets to Orpheus' in which he draws a contrast between the way that we are startled by the cry of a bird, and the cries of children who 'cry at random'.[42] To listen to a silence such as this, it is not enough for us to keep silent: Kierkegaard also shows how the poet, in the face of nature, may listen merely to himself and to the noise of his passions or his dreams, and thus have no inkling of the great lesson in silence that nature can give him.[43] But what is this lesson, or what might it be? In Kierkegaard's discourse, this silence of nature forms a creaturely silence, it ultimately refers us to the creatures who stand before God, and to the way that they listen to or await God's speech. In his view, nature provides us with the inflexible example of the silence that we have to learn and which is so difficult for us. Listening to nature is thus of no intrinsic worth here, but constitutes, rather, a *propaedeutic* to religious silence.

It is quite another matter when we turn to the fine prosopopoeia of nature in Plotinus' treatise *On Nature and Contemplation and the One*. Here, the silence of nature has a plenitude of its own, full of meaning: it is a silence that shows and lives. The paradox of this prosopopoeia, in which speech is given to an essentially silent power so that it may speak to us of its silence, is given a weighty and rigorous philosophical meaning by Plotinus:

> And if anyone were to ask nature why it makes, if it cared to hear and answer the questioner it would say: 'You ought not to ask, but to understand in silence, you, too, just as I am silent and not in the habit of talking.'[44]

This denial of the terms of the question already forms a reply, for Plotinus's aim is to show that the production of nature has nothing in common with that of human artisans, and that it cannot be explained by a mechanical model. It does not produce by realizing a plan traced out in advance, any more than it makes calculations. Its finality does not consist in setting up an aim for itself.

By developing a critique of the terms of the question, it is the dimension of the *tinos heneka*, of the 'with what aim' that nature rejects. We are on the way to the *ohne Warum* of Angelus Silesius and his rose that blossoms without a why. This silence is far from being that of abstention or privation: it is the harmonious silence of *theôria* , of contemplation. Plotinus's fundamental thesis in this treatise is that all action and all production originate in contemplation, and this is true on all levels of being, including nature. A creature acts and contemplates because it contemplates and so as to contemplate. As if it were immersed and absorbed in its own vision, nature makes the beings and forms that surround us spontaneously emerge from itself. To break silence, for nature, would be to reason, foresee, explain and calculate, and thus to allow deficiency and hesitation to infiltrate its somnambulistic plans, and thus to fall to the same level as an artisan deliberating on what he is to do. The silence of its vision summons forth, according to Plotinus, our silence, calls on us to rise up in silence, with our silence, from natural forms to the fertile silence from which they emerge and do not cease to emerge. Of course, in the *Enneads*, this is merely one stage in the 'return uphill', to use René Char's expression, for the path of silence is long, and nature constitutes merely the lowest form of the universal soul. But there is in this idea a clear sense of how silence listening to silence is fundamental, each silence having a precisely defined tenor of meaning.

This silent listening to silence is also an essential possibility of art and our relationship to it. The plastic arts enable us to hear the silence of nature or of things with an unequalled intensity. In still lives, the most ordinary implements, things we use every day, are withdrawn from the noise of our gestures so as to make available to us the unheard-of aspects they had, and still have – the aspects that we too did not prick up our hears to hear. This silence, so powerful and strange, nonetheless dwells in the greatest proximity to us, in our own dwellings. On another level, the *St John the Baptist* of Leonardo da Vinci in the Louvre shows us a silent listening to silence and invites us, imperiously and gently, to share it. For the Christian tradition, St John the Baptist is the Voice, the Voice that announces the Word that comes. In this painting, this Voice is silent. The splendid and mysterious face of the Baptist, against a dark background, which intensifies the event of his epiphany, by tearing it away from any context, any circumstance, is turned, with a smile, towards us, and with his right hand he points to the heights. The voice shows the Word, but it does so without words or speech, it invites us to listen to the silence.

A second dimension of silence as a form of listening is the dimension in which it allows us to hear a speech that without it would remain imperceptible. The suspense of our speech allows the speech of the other to emerge, either because it was already speaking and the resonance of our voices had made us deaf to its own voice, or because it had been waiting for us to stop talking so that it can start to speak. What is at stake here is indeed silence as an act of our own: it is not only in silence that one listens, as if it were merely a negative and entirely external condition, it is through it that one listens, in so far as it is one with attention and receptivity. When it is a question of an inner silence by which we listen, as in the Christian spiritual tradition, to God speaking within us, it might seem as if nothing distinguishes this possibility from the preceding one, from silently listening to silence, since it is self-evident that this inner voice is without any resonance, and produces no sound. As the *Imitation of Christ* puts it, in entirely Augustinian fashion, 'Veritas intus loquitur sine strepitu verborum', 'the Truth speaks within us without the noise of any words.'[45] But this lack of sonority of the Word's speech within us by no means allows us to identify it with a contemplation of silence. A silence in which we allow ourselves to be said, a silence in which we allow ourselves to be instructed and transformed by the personal presence of the Word is not the silence by which we go out to meet silence as dimension or element, as in that fine line in the poem by Lamartine in which he has a young musician girl say, as she offers her song to the night, 'Come! The loving silence fills space far and wide.'[46] It is not a question of the same phenomenon, or the same act, or the same affection.

This possibility has been described by Angelus Silesius with his usual sobriety: 'One hears through silence (*Mit schweigen höret man*). Speech resounds in you more than in another's mouth. If you can fall silent before speech, you instantly hear it.'[47] This theme occurs much earlier in Christian mysticism. Tauler brings it out forcefully in a Christmas sermon, in which he distinguishes between three births of the Word, its eternal birth from the Father, its temporal birth from Mary, and its birth within us, which can take place at any time if the conditions are met within us, by the grace of God.[48] It is a Christmas within us, in which we have, whatever our sex, to accomplish our own maternity. Silence is necessary for this event.

> This is why you must fall silent: then the Word of this birth will be utterable within you and you will be able to hear it; but be sure that if you wish to speak, it must be silent. One cannot serve the Word better than by keeping quiet and listening. So if you come completely out of yourself, God will enter you entire: the more you come out, the more he will go in, no more, no less.[49]

A little further on, in the same sermon, Tauler mentions the *Dum medium silentium* . . . of the liturgy and interprets it thus:

> It is in the midst of silence, at the very moment when all things are plunged into the greatest silence, where the true silence reigns, it is then that one truly hears the Word, for if you wish God to speak, you must be silent; for him to enter, all things must come out.[50]

Silence and exodus, an exodus outside oneself, here go together. It is not a matter of the cult of inwardness complacently turning in on itself. My silence tears me away from myself and leads me to renounce myself so that within me the Other may come into being and be given birth. This maternity too brings its own pain. The character of event and advent in this nativity is never lost sight of by Tauler. Listening requires that I come out of myself, so as to make room for speech. It is a listening that is freed from everything sticky and clinging in its psychological representations, a listening without glue, a listening that is free and liberating. This speech does not come to souls that are encumbered and full of themselves. True silence presupposes a self-emptying. This silence, of whose necessity Tauler reminds us, is of a mystic order and does not come from ascesis or inner discipline alone.

When Malebranche mentions, as he often does, the silence that we have to impose on our passions and our imagination so as to hear the voice of the Word, which does not cease to be present within us, it is – despite certain similarities in their formulae – a question of a movement that goes in the other direction from that described by Tauler. It is a question, not of coming out of oneself, but of returning into oneself. If we do not hear the Word, this is because, writes Malebranche:

> our passions continuously draw us away from ourselves, and by their clatter and shadows they prevent us from being instructed by His voice and illumined by His light . . . . We must therefore enter into ourselves and draw nearer to Him. We must beseech Him, listen to Him, and obey Him.[51]

The Word is always speaking within us, but we do not pay attention to it, we cover up its voice with our inner tumult.

This presence is not of the same order as the birth of which Tauler spoke, and for Malebranche it forms the basis, in direct descent from the *De magistro* of St Augustine, of the very possibility of human knowledge, because we cannot be our own light, and God alone is the sun of our minds. But here, too, silence is an act: that of imposing a discipline on the passions and the imagination, to be sure, but also, and more positively, that of *desiring* light. If this silence were not one of desire, it would never lead us to hear and understand. Such is the meaning of this admirable formula, often repeated by Malebranche: 'The attention of the mind is the natural prayer which we make to the inner Truth, so that it may disclose itself to us.'[52] By becoming desire, silence calls and questions the Word, it leads to a dialogue – and so does not remain pure silence, except when we are listening to the replies – in which we received light in proportion to our desire, if we truly desire it and if it is indeed the light that we desire. This inner dialogue, vibrant with silence, is also that to which all the dialogues between men must, for Malebranche, be led back, for it is in this dialogue alone that we can be assured, as St Augustine showed, of the truth or falsity of what we have heard from the mouths of other men. Everything leads back to this listening *sine strepitu verborum*.

In the same period as Malebranche, and also taking his inspiration from the Augustinian tradition, Fénelon refers to this silence of listening as having a loving dimension. It is no longer a question of laying the foundations for a theory of knowledge, but of the life of grace. 'God,' writes Fénelon,

> never ceases to speak; but the noise of creatures without and of our passions within deafens us and prevents us from hearing it. We must make every creature stop talking, we must stop talking ourselves, if we are to listen, in this deep silence of the whole soul, to this ineffable voice of the bridegroom. We must listen most carefully; for it is a gentle, delicate voice, which is heard only by those who no

longer hear anything else. Oh, how rare it is that the soul falls silent sufficiently to allow God to speak.[53]

This loving silence rediscovers the possibilities of loss and self-abandonment that Tauler referred to. In a language close to that of Malebranche, Fénelon, nonetheless, is speaking of mysticism. A little later on in the same short work, he remarks that 'when once we have imposed silence on everything inside us so as to listen to God,' then 'all that we had been holding onto escapes, and we care no more about it; we have nothing left of our own; we have lost everything; we have lost ourselves'.[54]

The silence which enables us to hear the bridegroom's voice is a silence that deepens, that desires to grow and burn more clearly, so that it can listen better. The voice that is born from the silence calls to the silence. 'Speak, oh my bridegroom, and let none other than you dare to speak! Be silent, oh my soul; speak, oh love.'[55] Our speech becomes impatient at itself, so great is the weight of the silence it bears. Of course, the statement 'God speaks ceaselessly within us',[56] even if we do not listen to him (which is the reason why it is enough to stop speaking so as to hear him straightaway), is not without its difficulties. There is a phenomenological difficulty, for how can I assert that God speaks within my heart if nothing of this speech is heard or made manifest? There is a theological difficulty, for the speech of God always forms an act, and if we posit an act of God that is totally inefficacious, are we still talking about God? But the truth is that addressing these objections to Fénelon would be quite unfair.

For, if, for Fénelon, God speaks even 'in impenitent sinners' but, 'deafened by the noise of the world and of their passions, (they) cannot hear it', and 'his speech is a mere fable to them',[57] he speaks within each man, and Fénelon develops a differentiated account of this. This speech always already reaches us, we hear it even obscurely, and the noise that we may make to cover it over is the evasive reply we give to it. It is only because God has encountered us, has come to meet us, that we can turn away from him, or try to turn away from him, and forget him. On another level, the insistence on the silence of the soul, which makes him hear the words of God, must not lead to a coarse and, as it were, mechanical representation. It is not a question of a public speaker waiting for the audience to quieten down before addressing them. Even silence has its history, and has to mature if it is to become a form of listening. Fénelon notes this: 'We are ready to fall silent, to gather our thoughts meditatively . . ., but we do not yet dare to risk listening to the inner voice for the sacrifices that God is preparing.'[58]

Indeed, there is no such thing as a first word, and thus listening too has never started: we have already listened to everything. We cannot fall silent to listen unless we are already in a relationship with speech, and with the speech that is about to be uttered – unless, that is, we have, in whatever shape or form, already listened to it, and it has already reached us. Listening always precedes itself. Or, to speak the language of Tauler, it is not because we give birth inside ourselves that we discover the possibility of a spiritual 'maternity'; it is because we are open to this possibility, and only in so far as we are open to it, that we are able to take the decisions that will lead to this generative act. The silence that allows us to listen is the first grace, the initial favour of the speech for which we yearn.

The same structure is also found in another type of attentive silence, that which the Bible refers to on several occasions. 'The earth is silent with dread when God takes his stand to give judgement,' says a psalm,[59] and Isaiah repeats in various forms the imperious invitation to a listening silence: 'Come near and listen, you nations, pay attention, you peoples. Let the earth and its contents listen, the world and its entire population.'[60] Isaiah later writes: 'Coasts and islands, fall silent before me'.[61] We find the same idea in Zechariah: 'Let all people be silent before Yahweh, now that he is stirring from his holy Dwelling!'[62], as in Habbakuk: 'But Yahweh is in his holy Temple: let the whole earth be silent before him.' [63] There are other examples too, including the silence in heaven, according to Revelation, at the opening of the seventh seal, a silence of 'about half an hour'.[64] This Biblical silence, according to one commentator, 'deepens when God is preparing to make a speech of particular importance, affecting our salvation; it reaches its pinnacle when God announces his coming, when man awaits his appearance.'[65] This silence, we should emphasize, is not only the silence of man: the whole of nature stops speaking when God is about to manifest himself, and this sometimes happens in a terrifying way. This silence that precedes and accompanies a divine manifestation is also found in pagan religions. One of the finest examples can be found in the *Bacchae* of Euripides; when the words of Dionysus ring out, 'The high air hushed, and along the forest glen/ the leaves hung still; you could hear no cry of beasts'.[66]

Here too, as is clearly shown by the fact that certain of these passages are invitations to keep silent, listening comes first. Nature must already be listening for God's words if it is to stop speaking so as better to listen to him. This is an aspect of what scholasticism called *obediential power* in reference to the relationships between the creature and the Creator. However, if such silences may present a reverential dimension, which extends from fear to adoration, we must distinguish, phenomenologically speaking, between the silence of listening and the silence of adoration. Attentive listening is not in itself one of adoration, it is not necessarily the Single and Absolute One that it adores, and its silence may prepare it for adoration without already being involved in it. On the other hand, the silence of adoration may dissociate itself from all listening, as what it adores may in fact not be a Speech, even a silent one, as is the case for what are called the Neoplatonic philosophies.

Persian mysticism, with the dignity characteristic of it, has also spoken of this liberating virtue of silence in the face of speech. Thus Farid-od din Attar writes,

> Because it is silent the falcon perches on the king's wrist
> because it sings the nightingale remains in the cage
> If your soul accustoms itself to keeping silent
> every atom will speak to you
> Until when will you continue to murmur like the spring
> if you fall silent you will become an ocean
> Whoever in this ocean seeks the pearl
> must in order to dive down hold his breath.[67]

This held breath is that of an active silence, which is converted into speech.

One decisive question remains: how do these multiple silences, interdependent as they are with the diverse possibilities of existence, relate to speech? Is their attention a pure abstention, remaining outside that to which it is attentive? Does the silence of this listening really form an absence of speech, at least of my speech? Merleau-Ponty wrote, 'There is no silence that is pure attention and that, having begun nobly, remains equal to itself,'[68] by which he meant the impossibility of evading dialogue and the alteration it causes within me. We have always already climbed into the ark of speech, and we cannot evade it. Even silence explains itself, and ends up talking about itself. All listening belongs to speech, from beginning to end. Even silently listening to silence is not an exception to this belonging.

To listen in silence to silence, with all my silence, such indeed is the preface to every speech that is not mere chatter, a preface which is thus always begun again. If we did not listen to silence in silence, what would we have to say that has not already been said a thousand times over? Merleau-Ponty himself agrees:

> We should consider speech before it has been pronounced, against the ground of the silence which precedes it, which never ceases to accompany it, and without which it would say nothing.[69]

Without this silent gestation of speech, we would have to content ourselves with 'the established language', reiterate its insignificant rumour, the all-pervasive tittle-tattle, which 'in effect is a way of silencing me'.[70] But if the silence by which I listen to silence did not condemn me to speech, did not wound me with a burden of speech, if it remained a permanent muteness, I would cease to listen, and I would become empty, even if this emptiness were to be thought of as ecstatic. It is with great rigour that Proclus, in allusion to certain expressions of the mystic silence, says that the One, the first principle, is *epekeina sigès*, beyond silence.[71] One who transcends, or claims to transcend, speech, also transcends the silence that suspends speech.

As for listening to the speech of the other, whatever its nature may be, it allows itself to be said, it allows itself to be inhabited and penetrated by speech, it is, in its silence, densely resonant with words. Here too, Merleau-Ponty has described it well: 'When I am listening . . ., the conversation pronounces itself within me. It summons me and grips me; it envelops and inhabits me to the point that I cannot tell what comes from me, and what from it'.[72] And elsewhere, he adds:

> I am not active only when speaking; rather, I precede my thought in the listener. I am not passive when I am listening; rather, I speak according to . . . what the other is saying. Speaking is not just my own initiative, listening is not submitting to the initiative of the other.[73]

'I hear myself in him, while he speaks in me. Here it is the same thing *to speak to* and *to be spoken to.*'[74]

This eloquent description of the activity of passivity and the passivity of activity in the exchange of speech doubtless requires us, given the equivocal nature of its play of mirrors, to show what is inadequate in these concepts, and the extent to which they still cover over with their constructions the phenomena they aim to lay bare.

The still largely unknown and original meditation of Heidegger on speech goes further and deeper. Beyond the alternation and the interlacing, within dialogue, of speaking and listening, Heidegger sees in speaking itself an act of listening, and before all else an act of listening. Prior to all acts of showing that come about through us, there is a 'letting oneself be shown (*Sichzeigenlassen*)'. Before all acts of saying performed by our voice, there is a 'letting oneself be said (*Sichsagenlassen*)',[75] which is the very listening of speech. To let oneself be said does not come from the metaphysical opposition of activity and passivity, even if it is made dialectical, as it has been for the past two centuries. Not only does this silence of listening belong to speech, but it is the very origin, the perpetual origin, of our speech. Such considerations lead, as if spontaneously, to another dimension of silence, to eloquent silence, the silence that speaks and replies.

Colloquia of silence

In all orders of existence, we come across eloquent silences. Heidegger appeals to them so as to distinguish between speaking and saying, *Sprechen* and *Sagen*: 'Someone may speak, endlessly, and it all means nothing. On the other hand, imagine someone keeping silent: he does not speak and in not speaking he may be able to say many things.'[76] With the forcefulness characteristic of him, Pascal, in his *Discourse on the Passions of Love*, remarked: 'In love, a silence is worth more than language. It is a good thing to be dumbstruck; there is an eloquence of silence which penetrates deeper than language ever could.'[77] Nonetheless, these eloquent silences are multiple and diverse. Silence may mean that I choose to be silent when I could speak: not replying to a question that is addressed to me can show that I consider it null and void, indecent or offensive, etc. Silence can also say, by showing how I have been dumbstruck, as in the example of Pascal: I am silent because my confusion deprives me of the possibility of speaking. And not being able to speak, I go on saying.

To this initial contrast between the voluntary and the involuntary can be added another: silence may be eloquent simply because of its relationship with the speech that it suspends or interrupts, as in the figure called *aposiopesis*. The monastic vow of silence does not destroy or abandon speech, it constitutes its ascesis or purification. To a philosophical eye, the words a thinker does not utter are just as significant as those he does. We can also read his silences. Merleau-Ponty did not merely invite us to hear speech against the background of silence, he added that 'we should be sensitive to the thread of silence from which the tissue of speech is woven'.[78] They are indeed present in it, they perform their own proper duty, far from constituting a mere privation. In this domain, it is possible to construct a rhetoric of silence, or a linguistic description of all the ways in which to keep silent about something may be a way of signifying it, in ellipsis, irony or presupposition.[79]

Silence has yet another eloquence when the interruption of speech makes other dimensions of exchange possible. Silence quivers with meaning when it opens up a new direct partnership. It is not enough that the voice be suspended for the gift to fail to reach its destination. The eloquence of silence is then a shared eloquence. It is a clear silence, a shared silence. Someone who is incapable of keeping silent with someone will never be capable of truly speaking to him either. There are silences as naked as the voice. Karl Jaspers gives a good description of such moments:

A deep silence, which leaves nothing in the shade, a *silence* which is, so to speak, *revealed*, leads, by way of a tacit understanding (albeit one which *could* express itself) to a way of being for each other *which transcends it*. Reserve in reciprocal certainty, the gaze and the hand in place of speech are what is left in the moments of perfection of

59

existential communication. . . . To keep silence then is really to speak.[80]

And he adds: 'Human beings who do not experience communication in silence are incapable of resolute communication.' A common silence of this kind also forms the perpetual resource of dialogue and the proffered words of speech. This silence, of course, listens, but it also speaks and replies, it does not only pay attention, it goes out to meet the other.

It is mystic theology that has the most energetically explored the intimacy of these speaking silences or of this silent speech. And it is St François de Sales who provided the expression that serves as a title for this section, 'colloquia of silence'. For he writes, in his *Treatise on the Love of God*:

> Love does not speak through language alone, but through the eyes, the sighs and the expressions on one's face; yes, even silence and taciturnity represent speech. . . . To be sure, in mystical theology the principal exercise is speaking to God and hearing God speak in the depths of our hearts; and as this talk is performed by the most secret aspirations and inspirations, we call it a colloquy of silence: eyes speak to eyes and hear to heart, and no one hears what is said apart from the sacred lovers who are speaking.[81]

In conformity with the possibility inaugurated and authorized by the *Song of Songs*, the most spiritual contact is expressed and described by all that is most sensual and most fleshly in the loving encounter between human beings. Only love can signify something beyond itself in this way. This silence at once clear and secretive arises from a mutual presence, in which those who are silent give themselves to each other, bearing their gifts at the tip of their intimacy, reinforcing and deepening this intimacy with the very gifts that they exchange.

It is noteworthy that this silent encounter always remains thought of, experienced and described as an encounter *in speech*, as taking place only through a speech higher than any utterance and on its behalf. It is with the Word that we engage in silent dialogue. It is not a question, as in certain possibilities of natural mysticism, of renouncing speech, but of making it realize most fully its possibilities. That is also why there is no contradiction in speaking and writing about such silent encounters. Each of the potentialities of speech can harbour the others in itself. Otherwise, speech could not be the ark.

In this same tradition, that spiritual master, the Breton Jesuit Jean Rigoleuc describes with great precision what he calls 'the prayer of silence'. This is 'a simple and respectful contemplation of God, a loving attention to the presence of God and a sweet repose of the soul in God'.[82] Here is not the place to analyse in all its aspects this mystical ordeal, in which the understanding ceases to reason and relates to God only in 'bare faith', and in which the will, without undergoing any dispersal, acquiesces and consents totally, holding itself in repose in a sort of *Gelassenheit*, but of showing the extent to which this silence is speech. This is Rigoleuc's aim. 'No other means of praying,' he writes:

> has a closer relationship to the greatness of God, and nothing is more appropriate to nothingness than to stand in silence before the sovereign Being. The soul that stands thus before God, confesses by its silence that God is infinitely above all that can be said or thought about him. In this humble posture, and by this tacit confession, it pays him the most perfect homage that a creature can pay him. Without saying a word it says all that it could possibly say to him by way of praise, gratitude, love, trust, and any other affection whatever.[83]

Such a silence gathers in and offers speech. In the eighteenth century, in his writings on prayer, Pierre de Clorivière, another Jesuit mystic, drew inspiration from these formulations to describe what he called 'the prayer of recollection, or of simple sight': in it, the soul stands 'ordinarily before God, but it is an amorous silence, in which it says everything'.[84]

On what conditions can this silence amount to speech? Its own nature and its intentionality are decisive. There is no 'religious experience' that is not supported by a theology, and guided by it. The silence that is here in question is a silence that is offered, and it is offered to the one God, who listens and sees, and not to a blind, anonymous Absolute, lost, as it were, in its own retreat. This silence does not become speech, speech that stands in for other words of speech, unless it is a naked appearance before the Word, a Word that always comes halfway to meet it, and whose grace alone is what has made such dispositions possible in us. Only the divine listening makes of this silence, by acquiescing to it, a speech which 'says everything'. In what sense, finally, does it say 'everything'? This character of plenitude found in the silence that speaks is interdependent on the unification and gathering in of the soul that comes to offer itself to the Lord. But this unification is not the concluding moment of an ascetic method, which is methodically followed and of which we could feel proud. Only a speech wounded by the infinite can give itself in this way. In giving itself by silence, it does not give uniquely, or even first and foremost, any perfection it might lay claim to, but everything that in its voice has remained unfinished, unfinishable, everything that in it has been burned. It also gives all that by which and in which it has not been able to give, in other words the very fact of its own *self*-giving. This speech comes to the bridegroom in the way she can, and not in the way she would like to have come, and in this respect she comes to him lovingly, knowing that it is his gaze that will make her beautiful, and not her own allure.

A comparison with another speaking silence may enable us to describe these features more precisely. In one of his most powerful descriptions of the union of the soul with the One, Plotinus refers to the soul that has 'prepared by making itself as beautiful as possible' and, forgetting itself in this amorous encounter,

> does not still perceive its body, that it is in it, and does not speak
> of itself as anything else (sc. the One), not man, or living thing, or
> being, or all'. The soul enters into the silence of its own effacement.
> 'What it speaks, then, is that, and it speaks it afterwards, and speaks it
> in silence (*siôpôsa legei*), and in its happiness is not cheated in thinking
> that it is happy.[85]

For whom does this silence speak? It has none of the character of a speech addressed to the One who might be able to listen to it. It is not a 'colloquy of silence', for it is not a colloquy at all. The One is without speech, it cannot enter into speech. What the soul says silently is said for the soul alone, just as later it will speak of it, in words, to other people: the indubitable joy of having reached the goal of its quest. The speaking silence of its plenitude is a monologue. It has nothing in common with the silence of Christian mysticism, with the silence that, in a letter, Jean-Pierre de Caussade described to the woman he was writing to – a silence in which it was a question of that interiority

> in which the celestial Bridegroom awaits you and where he has built
> for himself a hidden dwelling-place, a peaceful retreat, where the
> Lover and his beloved can speak heart to heart, in the deepest and
> most loving silence, without the noise of words or the confusion of
> fleeting thoughts.[86]

But this silence does not spring from joy or plenitude alone. It can also be, as it were, the final possibility of prayer in times of spiritual testing, such as periods of drought and nights of the soul – the offering that one can make when one is deprived of everything, and even of oneself. Jean-Pierre de Caussade invites us to make this offering in another of his letters:

> The acts of your self-abandonment and submission (sc. to God)
> are excellent, but if they are lacking in the time of impotence and

stupefaction, there is something yet more perfect, which is precisely to remain in this inner silence of respect, adoration and submission of which I have spoken to you so frequently, a silence which says more to God than all your most formal acts, and this without any return of complacency or any perceptible consolation.[87]

This is, according to Caussade, the 'authentic mystical death', 'that second death which is the death to spiritual consolations',[88] a death brought about by God himself, which forms the condition for entering into a life of grace that is more intimate and more profound, in which we will be united with God himself and not with his gifts – as a constant refrain of the high tradition of Christian mysticism puts it.

This prayer of silence may appear as the summit of mystic life. This is the case for François Guilloré, who concludes his *Progress of Spiritual Life in Accordance with the Different States of the Soul* with considerations *On Silence and on the Inner Sleep*, which follow those *On the Loss of Actions*. What does this silence consist of? It is 'a certain general calm, spread throughout all the faculties, which comes from the cessation of the operations of the soul', whether this cessation comes from the truth, which absorbs us, or from the binding of the faculties, which makes its presence felt 'by a kind of chains, which seem as it were, to garrotte it, and indeed render it powerless, so it is now stirred by no operation'.[89] It is that mystical passivity in which God himself acts in the soul so as to carry it further and deeper than it could do of itself. Such a unitive silence could seem to be beyond speech, like the silence of excess that will be described in the next paragraph. But François Guilloré goes on to present it as an eloquent silence:

> Furthermore, in this silence, speak not so much of coming to an understanding with God, but let your heart speak; the less it does so, the better it speaks; and when it does not know what it has done, it has done something even better; for it is the Holy Spirit who must make it cry and groan, and not you yourself.[90]

This silence may become that spontaneous speech which gives itself to such an extent that it does not return to itself or come back to itself but forgets itself, forgets itself by giving itself, gives itself by forgetting itself.

The extremity of this prayer of silence would consist in God's speech itself penetrating us through and through, dwelling in this silence to speak there in our place and engage in dialogue in us with itself. Tauler presents this possibility in these words:

It is to praise God in a way infinitely superior to the two other degrees (i.e. those he has just described) when, in full awareness of the incomprehensible dignity of God, all particular words and modes disappear of themselves, to let praise lose itself, fall down, plunge and melt in God, so that He must praise Himself and give thanks to Himself. If someone really plunges into this abyss, it need not be feared that God will ever let him perish.[91]

It must however be with the musicality of *our* silence, and taking responsibility for it, that God thus praises himself. Otherwise it would mean the dissolution, and not the transfiguration, of his creature, and we would no longer be talking about a Christian mysticism. The prayer of silence must not take us back to a solitary God from before the creation of the world nor release us, even in exalted terms, from the irreplaceable responsibility of our voice and our silence.

The pure figure of Elizabeth of the Trinity meditated on these things to good effect. Taking up the comparison already dear to patristic theology between the soul and a musical instrument, she clearly brings out the musicality of the prayerful silence. 'Praise of glory is a soul of silence which is like a lyre beneath the mysterious touch of the Holy Spirit, so that He may make divine harmonies come forth from it.'[92] These sonorities that God draws from us, and even from our sufferings when they are offered to him, which Elizabeth also views as one of the strings, have the timbre of our singular humanity. The 'new song' of which the Holy Scriptures speak is seen by Elizabeth as 'that of a soul stripped bare and delivered from itself', in which God can act without encountering obstacles. And with this in mind she takes up the musical analogy again: 'This soul is beneath his touch like a lyre, and all his gifts are like so many strings that vibrate to sing day and night "the praise of his glory".'[93] This music and this song may themselves be the very music and song of silence. On the subject of adoration, Elizabeth goes on to write:

> It is love crushed by the beauty, the force, the immense grandeur of the loved Object. It falls into a kind of faint, in a full, deep silence, that silence of which David spoke when he exclaimed: 'Silence is your praise'. Yes, it is the finest praise, since it is the praise which is eternally being sung in the depths of the tranquil Trinity.[94]

At the very heart of the terror aroused by the divine beauty, our dumbfounded state is turned into an offering, and silence becomes song. This is a transfiguration that Angelus Silesius has described many a time, as in this stanza on the child Jesus, on the Word without a word: 'The best hymn of praise. Sing, sing, angels, sing: a hundred thousand tongues would not be enough to sing worthily this adored child. Ah! If I could be without tongue and without voice! I know I would straightaway sing to him the very best song.'[95]

This song of silence, in the Christian order of things, finds its highest sonority in the prayer of Mary. This has been expressed nowhere better than by Bérulle, who also shows how this prayerful silence of Mary already forms a gift of her Son and a reply to him. She, who more than anyone else could speak of her Son, says Bérulle,

> is in silence, ravished by the silence of her Son Jesus. And it is one of the sacred and divine effects of the silence of Jesus that it places the most holy Mother of Jesus in a life of silence; a humble, profound silence, adoring in a more holy and discerning way the incarnate wisdom than the words of either men or angels can. This silence of Mary is not a silence of impotent stammering, it is a silence of light and ravishment, it is a more eloquent silence, in the praise of Jesus, than is eloquence itself.[96]

For, Bérulle continues, this silence is a grace, 'it is a silence performed by the silence of Jesus, who imprints this divine effect on his Mother, and draws her to him in his own silence.' Such is the highest colloquy of silence that ever took place with the Word.

Silence as excess

The figures of silence I have referred to so far, however different they may be, are all found in a space in which speech and silence belong mutually to one another, and are devoted as if fraternally to one another. Silence is the honour of speech, and speech is the honour of silence. What we have here is something quite different from a mere formal correlation. Without the silence from which it comes, which accompanies it and to which it is at last delivered, speech would lose all its dignity and become an insignificant noise in a suicidal empty chatter. Without the speech that it listens to or that it calls for, without the speech that it keeps by safeguarding it like a jewel box, and without the speech that it itself becomes when it bears it and bears itself even higher, silence would crumble away in its own desert. But all this still does not exhaust the possibilities of silence or those of the human act of ceasing to speak. Its negativity has not, in fact, been explored up until now.

There are two main forms of this negativity: the first consists of thinking of silence as superior to speech, and superior precisely because it withdraws speech (or withdraws us from it), denies it and surpasses it; the second lies, once this first movement has been accomplished, in the discovery that it makes silence still relative to speech, and in the project of overcoming and deposing this silence as an act of our own. This means a self-overcoming of silence, in a sort of vertigo of negation. The Platonic tradition, in its multiple representatives, has meditated long, hard and intently on these two figures. The first stems from *euphèmia*: this is the silence that really pays honour to and really respects that in the face of which our words break and falter. But this silence, unlike the preceding figure, is no longer presented as a form of speech or as something standing in for it – it is no longer an eloquent silence.

It is in this sense that St Thomas Aquinas, commenting on Pseudo-Dionysius the Areopagite, writes: 'What is hidden we venerate by abstaining from scrutinizing it, and what is ineffable by keeping silent about it (*per hoc quod ea silemus*).'[97] Angelus Silesius, in turn, remarks: '*It is through silence that one honours God*. The holy majesty (if you wish to pay him honour) is in the highest degree honoured by holy silence (*mit heilgem Stilleschweigen*).'[98]

If the origin is silence, it may be by silence, by the silence within us, that we may reach it and venerate it. At the beginning of his *Theology of Plato*, Proclus is thus able to extend to silence, in a way that at first may seem surprising and disconcerting, the ancient Greek principle which states that it is through the similar that the similar is known. It is sensation that knows the sensible, discursivity the discursive . . . 'so that the most unical nature must be known by *The One*, and the ineffable by that which is ineffable (*tôi arrètôi to arrèton*)'.[99] It is the transcendent in us that knows the transcendent. Even radical negativity cannot prevent a knowledge of something equal in nature. So it is that in Socrates' silence vis-à-vis the young Alcibiades, Proclus sees an image of the divine silence:

> For the first relationship of man to man is to speak to him; so the failure to have even this communication with the object of his provision reveals him as completely transcendent and unrelated to his inferior. So at the same time he is both present to him and not present, he both loves and remains detached (*askhetos*).[100]

These paradoxical, not to say oxymoronic schemas, of absent presence and non-relative love are however still inadequate as far as Proclus is concerned. For what characterizes the negative concept of the principle in the Platonic tradition is not simply a matter of positing that negations are superior to affirmations, nor of showing that one cannot say of the principle what it is, but only what it is not. More powerfully, it is also a matter of surpassing the negations themselves. After writing that, when it comes to the One, it is 'proper to abide in negations', Proclus adds that we should 'exempt him from the negations also': 'if no discourse belongs to it, it is evident that neither does negation pertain to it.'[101] Even apophasis must be surpassed. So if our silence forms the goal that is reached by the negations, we must go beyond the silence itself. The One is 'more ineffable than all silence' (*pasès sigès arrètoteron*).[102] As Werner Beierwaltes says, in his magisterial work on Proclus:

> If the One were thought only as silence, it would also be necessary, in the silence of the origin as negation of speech, to think at one and the same time the positive sense of speech. But this sense is abolished by the negation of negation in the power of that which lies beyond speech and beyond silence, a power which founds both speech and silence.[103]

In a treatise of which we possess only the Latin translation, Proclus describes in the following terms the place, or the non-place, of the soul that has gone beyond thought itself:

> Having reached superintellection, the soul no longer knows itself or anything of that which it once knew, it enjoys the peace that is procured by its proximity to the One, sealed off from knowledge, having fallen mute, made silence with an inner silence (*muta facta et silens intrinseco silentio*). And how indeed could it be united with the most ineffable of all other than imposing silence on all useless speech within itself? Let her then be one so as to see the One, and even better so as not to see the One.[104]

For if the soul could see the One, it would not yet be the One. These striking lines could nonetheless lead us into error and induce us to believe that our silence constitutes a locus of coincidence with the silence of the principle, as in the preceding figures of silence.

But they stem from what Emmanuel Levinas called 'diachrony': what characterizes this ordeal is that no one is ever or has ever been contemporary with it. We always speak of it elsewhere and belatedly. For the soul, here, is united to the principle only by exceeding itself and surpassing itself; even its silence is outside its control, and the soul cannot tell itself of the action by which it is silent. The soul has thus passed beyond silence in so far as silence would still be an act of our own in which we would coincide with ourselves. If the soul does not know itself, it does not know, either, that it does not know. Its union with the principle cannot be reduced to any metaphysical schema of presence. Everything here is dispossession and loss of self. The soul 'coincides' with the principle only by no longer coinciding with itself: what we have here is a coincidence without incidence. And what is this coincidence? A non-seeing, seeing in not seeing. This excess was already named by Plotinus when he wrote of the soul united to the principle: 'It does not even think that it does not think',[105] a phrase that was in the past corrected by editors who did not understand its rigorous audacity.

All these possibilities were to be sharpened to the point of vertigo – vertigo in the face of the impossible that requires these very possibilities – by the man who was doubtless the greatest 'deconstructor' in the history of philosophy, St John of Damascus. That whole strenuous effort of speech, that whole struggle for knowledge that constituted Greek thought, finds its consummation – and this is something worth dwelling on – in the adoration of silence and unknowing. Or, more rigorously, by a silent and unknowing adoration of what is so far away that it cannot even be adored, for this would mean positing a relation with it and thus make it lose its dignity. The ineffable cannot even be said, any more, to be ineffable, the unknowable cannot be said to be unknowable: these terms are merely harpoons launched into the void, and merely show us ourselves, our own impotent efforts to grasp the ungraspable.

At the period when reason was converted to the one God, who is Speech, and thereby started to listen more attentively than it had ever done before, St John of Damascus, with the genius characteristic of him, renounces thought in thought. Even the One of Plotinus or Proclus is no longer sufficient for the desire for the absolute, we must rise even higher above and beyond it, towards what we cannot name. 'That one must be honoured by a perfect silence (*pantelei sigè*), first of all indeed by a perfect ignorance, the ignorance which considers all knowledge to be unworthy.'[106] The speech without end disowns itself and is turned upside down when it comes to the absolute. 'The best we can do is to keep silence (*hèsuchian agein*) as we remain in the unspeakable sanctuary of the soul without any wish to leave it.'[107] But can silence be a dwelling place? The same passage indeed asks: 'What will be the limit of discourse, if not a silence (*sigès*) which we have no means of leaving and the admission that we know nothing of the things into the knowledge of which, since they are inaccessible, we are not allowed to enter?'[108] Speech is in its death agony. This silence in which we ought to dwell is also a silence which we ought to reach. And St John of Damascus describes in the following terms the ascent back to the principle: 'Beginning with the things which are perfectly sayable and known by the senses, we will rise up to those of that realm, and we will lead as into a port (*kathormioumen*) the birth of truth, into the silence (*siôpèn*) which surrounds the first.'[109]

However, can this image of the port or the anchorage, with its implications of a goal reached and a shelter found, be valid when it comes to something that immediately turns into its opposite – the wide open sea of ignorance? To be silent is to refer to that about which one is silent. But silence for St John of Damascus cannot in truth keep silent about the absolute, for this latter must not be relational. To posit a relation between the absolute and us means to determine it, define it, albeit negatively, and thus make it fall from its transcendent condition, or rather its unconditioned state. Even to call it transcendent is still to place it in a relationship to what it transcends and thus deny the very transcendence one is claiming to affirm. This is why what is beyond everything cannot be the Lord revealed by the Holy Scriptures: what is denied him is the sovereign liberty on which depends any relationship that the absolute may create between what springs from it and its own self, without thereby imprisoning or losing itself in it. For St John of Damascus, in a word, our silence is silent only about ourselves. Even the Logos of philosophy, left to itself, finally calls for its own nirvana.

But is not this absolute, which can neither turn to what comes from it, nor act nor give nor love nor speak, this absolute without power or freedom, the most limited of all absolutes? Is not this radical nothingness, which exceeds all that is human, still an all-too-human representation, the void of our own spirit transformed into an idol? The slightest human speech and the slightest human love are higher and purer, by virtue of their ability to give themselves freely and find a place, than the suffocating nothingness to which Greek philosophy in its final stage would like to offer them up as a holocaust.

This adoration of silence, which is perhaps surreptitiously nothing more than the adoration of the negation that suppresses our speech and thereby also our silence, was to haunt, albeit with less spiritual grandeur than in St John of Damascus, other periods of disintegration. *Fiat silentium, pereat mundus!* The hatred of Christianity and the fashion for an orientalism that arose in pure reaction against it, thereby made the work of Leconte de Lisle into an adoration of death that was accompanied by a hymnic appeal to silence, in which speech, discovering its own vanity, deposed and unmade itself endlessly.

Stream through us, sparkling silence of the skies!

clamours the 'Dies Irae' of Leconte de Lisle, which ends with this paradoxical verse in which death becomes a mother, in which to die is to be born into nothingness. And this is really perverse:

And you divine Death, into which everything returns and vanishes,
Welcome your children in your starry breast;
Free us from time, number, and space,
And restore to us the repose which life disturbed![110]

Death is thus 'divine', but so are nothingness and silence. The famous poem 'Midi' ('Midday'), in which the vision of the splendour of the vision of nature merely constitutes an opportunity for discovering its emptiness and vanity, ends with this grandiloquent invitation:

> And return with slow steps to the lowly cities,
> Your heart dipped seven times in the divine nothingness.[111]

For Leconte de Lisle, the silence of nature is a silence of death, but this death is alone what we should love. Another poem, 'Çunacépa', also evokes, in its last line, 'the divine nothingness'.[112] With brilliant cruelty, Jean-Paul Sartre analysed at length this cult of nothingness and this rhetoric of silence in which Leconte de Lisle 'begins by *positing* what he intends to deny'.[113] The excess of silence here forms the movement in which man jubilantly lays down his speech and his life – an act of *vengeance*.

Less vengeful, but no less idolatrous of the void in the shape of failure, we find Karl Jaspers, for whom this silence in which speech comes to an end is the highest human possibility. He writes, at the end of his *Philosophy*:

> We cannot know why the world is; perhaps we can experience it in failure, but we cannot then *say* it. In the empirical condition, in the face of being, there is no longer, given the extent of the failure, any more thought or speech. Only silence is possible in the face of the silence of reality. But if speech tries to break the silence, it will speak without saying anything.[114]

Does one have to philosophize at such length simply to arrive at Hamlet's last words: 'The rest is silence'? Is it worth working through the figures of the spirit in order merely to justify the suicide of thought and speech? The fact remains that the excess of these silences about speech is an excess that speech alone can say, and speech still bears witness thereby to its own power, the very power it disowns, even when it rejoices in its own destruction. Having been an ark, speech then becomes a raft of the Medusa. And a raft like Medusa the Gorgon, for who can lead a man, instead of keeping silence, to persuade others *that* they ought to be silent? The worst form of despair is that which needs, if it is to continue to exist, to propagate itself.

Christian patristic theology likes repeating this adage according to which 'what is not assumed is not saved', in other words to recall that in order to save the human condition in all its dimensions, Jesus Christ had to take them all upon himself. To every possibility of human speech there thus corresponds a possibility of silence, and all the ways in which speech falls short also bring with them silences that are wounded by sin, whether they be silences of pride, hatred, despair, cowardice. If there had not been in silence, too, something to redeem and justify, why should Jesus have delighted in crossing through silence in all its forms, from the silence of childhood to the silence of death and the descent into hell, by way of those times when he kept silent in the face of certain questions as well as those times when he withdrew in silence to pray? Only Speech Incarnate could redeem human silence. How could evil not attack human speech, and how could speech be attacked without silence also being wounded? The silence that Christian mysticism can extol, without doing insult to human speech or ending up adoring nothingness, is that resurrected silence, the silence that is redeemed and transfigured by the crucified Word. In this cult of nothingness, a cult that has many possibilities, Franz Rosenzweig saw the only place in which one could 'flee from the voice of the true God', for here one is 'secure from his voice'. For, he went on,

> the voice of the living God echoes only where there is life, even if
> that life be intoxicated with gods and hostile to God. But the terror
> of God, which could not muster the courage to become fear of God,
> flees into the vacuum of the non-idea, and there that voice loses itself
> in the void.[115]

The silence of the Platonists finds its Easter with Dionysius the Areopagite, whose decisive historic mission it was to rescue negative theology from the impulse that was leading it towards the idolatry of nothingness, so as to offer it to the incarnate Word. For when his *Mystical Theology* named 'the darkness beyond light of the hidden mystical silence (*ton huperphôton tès kruphiomustou sigès gnophon*)',[116] this was after an invocation to the Holy Trinity, in the domain opened up by the Holy Scriptures, and so as to show in this darkness a place in which mysteries could be *revealed*.

This excessive silence illuminates speech, it makes manifest instead of concealing. It is no longer the silence of the Platonists, even if philosophically speaking it is true that Dionysius the Areopagite owes a great deal to them. St Maximus the Confessor was later to borrow this expression in relation to Jesus and to make it more specific, speaking as he did of a 'silence mysteriously hidden and with many and various voices (*tèi kruphiomustôi kai poluphônotatôi sigèi*), literally a silence 'which is to the highest degree polyphonic'.[117] This silence gives voice, and it does so generously.

The importance of silence in Christian mysticism cannot, furthermore, be derived from a Platonic tradition, such as that of Plotinus or Proclus, for it is an issue from the first generations onwards, and more specifically in the very body of work in which the word 'Christianity' makes its first appearance, namely the epistles of St Ignatius of Antioch, the theologian of the Word and of silence in their mutual inter-relations. And expressions which, taken out of context might seem to lead back to the equivocal expressions of natural mysticism, such as these lines by Mme Guyon, 'O solitary peace which we taste in our nothingness', or, 'O profound silence which we find in Nothing',[118] are quite different from them, referring as they do to Speech, for she writes shortly afterwards: 'It is here that we receive the arrows of pure love/ And that the Word speaks in the soul.' Negative theology and the extolling of silence necessarily come up against both their limit and their supersession when it comes to the revelation of God and of the incarnation of the Word. Hans Urs von Balthasar has shown as much with his characteristic forcefulness.[119]

A Christian mysticism can only be a mysticism of love received and given, as takes place first and foremost in God himself. That this love is the incomprehensible love of the incomprehensible God going so far as to surrender himself on our behalf, and that no speech except his is capable of spelling out its excess, requires a negative theology and the various modes of silence that go with it. Nobody who does not rigorously recognize God's radical transcendence can experience any astonishment or give thanks for the fact that He became man. But silence is a way of adoration of God, who speaks and comes, and not the object of that adoration. It is the ark of speech for which silence is necessary. To leave this ark would also mean making oneself unsuited to *keeping* silent in the true sense.

The highest Christian silence is a loving silence, the silence of union with God. This silence, for St John of the Cross, has nothing acosmic about it. To be listening out for God in silence may lead to one finally hearing the true song of the earth. This is what happens in what the 'Spiritual Canticle' calls 'silent music', *música callada*. Here, the soul is raised to a high degree of contemplation. 'In this repose and this silence of the abovementioned night', writes St John of the Cross,

> and in this knowledge of the divine light, the soul sees an admirable fittingness and disposition in the Wisdom of God in the differences in all his creatures and all his works, seeing all of them and each of them endowed with a certain correspondence to God, in that each in its own manner makes public what God is in it. So that this seems to the soul a very exquisite musical harmony which surpasses all the concerts and melodies in the world. The soul calls this music *silent* because ... it is a calm and tranquil understanding, without any noise of voices, and thus one enjoys in it the sweetness of the music and the quietness of silence. And the soul says that its beloved is this *silent music*, because in him is known and tasted this harmony of spiritual music.[120]

Before the 'unheard melodies of Keats', in his 'Ode on a Grecian Urn', sweeter than those one hears, it is here the whole world that sings God and sings in God. Seeing and hearing are interlaced, as in everything that is human, for only a creature that can see can also listen, and only a creature that can listen can also see. They should not be contrasted, as if one were passing from one order to another. As for St Augustine, each thing here has its 'voice',[121] and this voice is visible, offers itself to the gaze: it is nothing other than its beauty, its own potential for manifestation.

But this voice, intimate and singular, does not sing itself, it sings what is even more intimate than itself, 'that which God is within it'. The voice of things refers to their Creator, it gives thanks. How could this song fail to be eucharistic? For what is more beautiful than 'all the melodies in the world' is the world itself as melody. Only a way of listening that is itself perfectly silent can pick up its sonority. For we hear this world that sings God only in God, and silent music is a loving music. The Beloved, at the end of this passage, is itself that silent music, for it is he who gives both this silence and this song. Max Huot de Longchamp clearly shows, in this respect, that what is at stake is the glory of God, and 'a *real* perception, here and now and in accordance with the constraints attaching to the here and now, of what in the hereafter gives joy to the souls of the blessed: the permanent overflowing, the gratuitous gift of divine life'. And he adds: 'This perception of the divine glory is possible here and now in so far as the life of every creature is sensed by the spiritual faculty to be a flooding of the superabundant life of God.'[122]

Naturally, it may seem as if listening to this silent music, in a cosmic eucharist, is linked to the first type of silence described in this chapter. But this is a truly mystical ordeal and not an attentive silence into which we could of our own volition and by our own efforts gain access: it is really a silence of excess. St John of the Cross alludes to it in other parts of his oeuvre. Thus at the end of *The Dark Night of the Soul*, after many other mystical writings, he draws on the *Dum medium silentium*, and, quoting from memory, transforms it into *Dum quietum silentium tenerent omnia*. It is a question of the 'divine marriage between the soul and the Son of God', when the sensitive part and the spiritual part of the soul have been brought 'to peace and rest'.

> The instant the two houses of the soul are tranquil and confirmed, with the whole household of its powers and desires sunk in sleep and silence (*poniendolos en sueño y silencio*), as to all things of heaven and earth, the divine Wisdom, immediately in a new bond of loving possession, unites itself to the soul, and that is fulfilled which is written, 'While quiet silence contained all things and the night was in the mid-way of her course, Thy omnipotent Word saying forth out of heaven from the royal seats.'[123]

This silence of the dark night, in which it is necessary, as it were, to die in order to be reborn in a purified state, is not in the least a dissolution of the finite into the infinite or of a sacrifice of the creature to the Creator. It is a nuptial silence, the silence in which the Beloved and his lover encounter each other in intimacy. And if it lies beyond our words, it is not beyond the Word, since it is he whom we have to meet heart to heart. This silence utters speech, gives it again and again in its most naked and highest form, since St John of the Cross sings this silence and this night in poems of an unsurpassable purity. Such a silence is at once final and initial: final, because it is the goal of mystical life and constitutes the highest union with God; initial, since it is a sign of future blessedness.

Jean-Pierre de Caussade later said that the 'divine inner and outer silence' is a 'real earthly paradise, where the souls who love God already savour the foretaste of heavenly bliss'.[124] It is in no way a privation or an absence, except an absence from oneself, a self-forgetfulness. This forgetfulness is described by St John of the Cross towards the end of *The Living Flame of Love*: in this calm, he shows, the soul does not realize that it is advancing, even though it is making better progress than ever, for it is God who is bearing it and bearing it away.

> And even though the soul performs nothing with these powers, it does much more than if she were to do so, since God is the workman. And it is no wonder that the soul does not notice this, since the sense cannot understand what God performs in the soul during this time, since it happens in silence. And, as the Wise man says, the words of Wisdom are heard in silence.[125]

Such a self-forgetfulness means that this silence, in which we allow the Creator to work within us, becomes a participation in the silence of God himself, in the soughing silence of the Word.

In their very diversity, the figures of silence that I have described are always turned towards speech, and in no case can be reduced to a privation of speech. Against the tendency to hypostatizing silence, it was necessary to refer them back to the various acts that found them. But these figures of silence are not thereby foreign to one another, for silence, each time, has its own *hospitality*. It is through silence and within it that our existence can truly welcome other silences just as much as other voices. Our voice cannot build the ark of speech, in which everything will be given shelter and received, unless it be in proportion to the hospitality of its silence. It is only by being perpetually translated from silence, to quote the apt expression of Joë Bousquet, that our voice can falter and allow itself to be broken, to give itself to what it has to say in such a way that it is not left intact. For this silence is never merely our own: it is we who belong to it, indissociable as it is from the call that summons us and sends us, sends us by summoning us and summons us by sending us.

Far from enclosing ourselves, in some dark crypt, it is that which opens us, in the only way that anything can be opened: irreparably. Nor is it, even in the highest of its possibilities, a purely spiritual silence. Only what has a body can throw itself bodily into the fray. All attention takes place body and soul. The 'invisible poem' of breathing that Rilke marvelled at is the first hospitality of silence and never ceases to keep open all forms of welcome. To suspend one's voice is not to suspend one's breath. This hospitality that breathing gives to the world, and the world gives to breathing, is broken only when life itself is broken. And then it is another silence that awaits us in the light of its promise, that of the eternal ark.

4

DOES BEAUTY SAY ADIEU?

Human speech forms an ark: it thus sets in motion, incessantly, its potential for gathering, sheltering, and safeguarding, by taking up, translating and giving them new impetus the luminous and inchoate solicitings of the world, its murmured appeals, its silences verging on utterance, its urgent insinuations. The ark lets be what it welcomes, and without this there would be no welcome given to the world, or to what dwells in it or is found there, but an arbitrary fantasmagoria, a disorderly carnival of images. And yet, as Heidegger powerfully shows, this letting-be is an incandescent act in which things are liberated into their being and become themselves as they come into the light of speech.

The half-light of speech is at one and the same time, in the sole trembling of the voice, a half-light of dusk and dawn. Dusk, for it does not in any way create what it names, but lets it come from its long wandering, the uncertain pilgrimage of oblivion and silence, that sudden flicker of mute things for which Leibniz forged the astonishing expression of *mens momentanea*, a mind that disappears the minute it is called into being. In what one names there is always something immemorial. And yet this half-light is also that of dawn, for this 'second time' of speech is really its first time; its belated and retroactive thrust is one that pierces right to the heart of things, and we receive it in our own hearts too. If speech is prepared to risk itself, it always has the clarity of an awakening.

This dialogue between speech and world, in which silence is both broken and consummated, raises many difficult questions, which listening to God's Speech merely renders even more acute and even more questionable. One of my earlier works, *L'effroi du beau* [*The shock of beauty*], described in an, as it were, naked fashion the event in which beauty affects us and arouses our irreparable response, without which it would not have its resonance, nor its future. The present chapter, and the following one, try to examine the conditions of possibility of this drama. They form a diptych, which hinges on two questions. Does beauty say adieu? And: Can one offer the world to God?

These two questions are neither separable nor identical: they explore the same space but in different ways, without however being superimposed on one another like an outward and a return journey. The first question concerns the way in which things are summoned into the ark, the second concerns the destination of the ark itself.

In order for things to be summoned by our speech, they must in one way or another have provoked our gaze and our voice, and, as it were, broken into them in our presence, by rousing our disquiet. Beauty is not the only one of these provocations, but it is certainly the most imperious of them. What does it say, and can it say adieu, in other words send a message to God, call forth a response in which gratitude and thanks are opened up in such a way that they can no longer close again? For a eucharist of speech to be possible, a question the following chapter investigates, a condition must be fulfilled *a parte rerum*, on the part of things, namely that the offering of these things that we make with our breath, from our throat, does not rest on violence, and that speech fulfils the tension of their silence. Does beauty lock us into immanence, and into the somnolent pleasures of mirrors and their reflections – or does it have the power to send us further? Such is the question. In this question, the many different meanings of the expression 'say adieu' must be heard. To say 'adieu' is to commend 'to God' (à Dieu') – to that which lies beyond time and yet is the Lord of time. But to say adieu is also the sign, as sharp as the bevel of a diamond, of separation, of parting, of absenting oneself, the last word, before any definitive exodus. In this second sense, asking whether beauty says adieu is to ask whether there is within it a power which breaks presence, which separates and invites separation, a power of denudation and dispossession, a demand for itinerancy. Can beauty be such a power?

Each of us has, in many ways and on many occasions, experienced beauty in his or her life. A man is someone whose tranquillity has been threatened by beauty, even if he has done everything in his power to ward off this threat and evade it. Intense or discreet, gentle or violent, and more surely both at once, this experience, a gruelling one, has not left us intact and has sometimes decided the course of our entire lives. It calls upon us to exist in obedience to a demand that we cannot addresses to ourselves, of our own free will – in surprise and dispossession. This ray of sunlight may be transmitted to us and reach us through many moons and reflections, and it does not, as such, depend on the history of taste, for it can often affect us through derivative, epigonal, routine, even adulterated works, even if, in this case, they arouse a thirst that they cannot quench. And the distress opened within us by the devastation and growing ugliness of people, places or things is another form of this harrowing experience of beauty: anyone who destroys beauty seems to us to be profaning, in some degree, that by which the world really is a world, containing things that demand that one stop and consider them (in the dual sense of looking at them and respecting them) – not a simple stock of raw material for our vital needs. Even a hatred of beauty, if we remember the multiple figures of Erostratus, recognizes in its own way beauty's surfeit of force, which it attempts to harness in its orgy of destruction.

We do not consume beauty like a commodity – beauty consumes us like a fire, burning us with a flame that lightens and enlightens us, and thus helps us to rise to a state of full being, to our perfection as men, as Schiller so eloquently put it in his *Letters on the Aesthetic Education of Mankind*. To destroy a place is never merely to despoil the world but to attack the humanity of mankind too by destroying a human possibility of habitation. To destroy a thing is also to impoverish man's hand and gaze. A world deprived of beauty would no longer be what the Greeks called *kosmos*, which implies something resplendent. A rich tradition of thinking, which has developed in many ways, has seen in beauty a call, and has derived the word *kalos*, 'beautiful', from *kalein*, 'to call'.[1] But what is it that calls, in beauty, and what does it call to or for?

By calling to us, beauty moves us, in other words touches us, comes to touch us where we are, and sets us in movement, on our way and en route, so that we do not remain where we are or remain content with where we have got to. Can it lead to God? Can it make us pass from the beauty of the world to the beauty of God, if there is such a thing? Is it God who is calling in this call? And if this call leads to God as to its source, to which God does it lead? To the God confessed by the Christian faith, to the crucified Christ? Can there be a path of beauty that leads to Calvary? The possibilities brought into play by such questions seem, right from the start, to be problematic in all sorts of ways, not to say downright incongruous or indecent.

Indeed, beauty as we undergo it in the world – and there is no place other than the world in which we might undergo it – is, in the strictest and strongest sense of the term, phenomenal. In other terms, it is a self-manifestation, it is that which manifests itself of its own accord, and it is only thus that it calls, ensuring that our gaze and our attention are turned towards it as if they had not really taken the initiative, but had been demanded and harnessed by it. We want a beautiful piece of music to carry on echoing, and it is still that music that we hear even in the silence in which it comes to an end and which it blesses. When we see a beautiful face, we want to continue to dwell in its light. For, in the event of beauty, it is not a case of a beautiful object shining out against a neutral or dark background, a background of ugliness: it is the whole world that gathers together to deliver and set free, here and now, the murmuring, singing clarity that it bears within it, giving itself up to its own daylight and opening itself to it.

The appearance of beauty does not *take place*, it *makes space*. It does not occur in a preconstituted place from which it derives its condition of possibility, as if it were coming out on to a stage, in a decor and under a lighting that were there before it. By taking place, it makes space: in other words, it causes this place, *here,* to arise in all its jubilant and heartrending exclamation. The *here* opened up by beauty cannot be found on any map, any more than flashes of lightning flicker in the margins. With all due respect to romanticism, the powerful strangeness of beauty does not reside in the way it is supposed to insinuate a longing for elsewhere, for the most distant elsewhere, infecting us with the desire for 'grand unsatisfied departures', such as those deplored in *L'horizon chimérique* by Jean de La Ville de Mirmont, to whom Gabriel Fauré offered his so very limpid songs. This strangeness is nothing other than that of the 'here', wrenched away from the indifference and interchangeability of places – a 'here' on which the furthest distances converge.

In the *Duino Elegies*, Rilke affirms that 'being here is a great deal' (*Hiersein viel ist*) and proclaims the 'glory of being here' (*Hiersein ist herrlich*).[2] The lordship of being is that of being here – in a 'here' independent of all laws, completely and utterly different from Leibniz's expression 'it is the same everywhere as it is here', by which he understood the universality of laws, valid in each and every region of the world. To make of the beauty an index directing one elsewhere, the symbol of a beyond, is to transform it into a mere allusion, and deprive it of its essence. Its transcendence, its power to go behind forgetfulness and veiling, far from forcing us to leave our dwelling place, constitute the most urgent of invitations, not to say initiations, to the 'here'. So does not the inexhaustible character of beauty lead to its contemplation tying us to the world, and nothing but the world? How can what makes the world really inhabitable and life really liveable lead us beyond the world?

Supposing, on the other hand, that the beauty of God is made the source and foundation of the beauty of the world, will not the very word 'beauty' become altogether equivocal, if it can designate both a manifestation of the creature within the world and the absolute manifestation of the absolute both this side of the world and outside it? What then would be the common core of meaning of these two senses? And if we think of Christ, how can we forget that the man of sorrows prophesied by Isaiah is without 'form or charm to attract us' or 'beauty to win our hearts': 'Non est species ei, neque decor: et vidimus eum, et non erat aspectus.'[3] To which we should add that the Greek noun for beauty, *kallos,* is not used a single time in the New Testament, and if the adjective *kalos is* used very frequently, it is only in the sense of 'good', and not that of 'beautiful', just as we say in English 'a beautiful game' for 'a good game'. Even the accounts of the Transfiguration of the Lord do not speak of beauty, even though it is one place in which we might have expected it to be referred to.

All of this tends to foreclose the questions raised above. But is it tenable, from a biblical point of view, to be forced to choose between a God without beauty and a beauty without God? Is it more satisfactory than a religion of the beautiful, which would have destroyed both God and beauty by transforming beauty into an idol fabricated by one's desire? One of the most explicit pages of Holy Scripture on the relations between God and beauty may enable us to formulate these questions more adequately and at the same time to gauge their difficulty. This passage is found in the book of Wisdom. Chapter XIII refers to the divinisation by 'stupid' men of the elements of the world and the stars.

'If, charmed by their beauty (*tèi kallonèi*), they have taken these for gods, let them know how much the Master of these excels them, since he was the very source of beauty (*ho tou kallous genesiarkhès*) that created them.'[4] A little later, it is stated that 'through the grandeur and beauty of the creatures, we may, by analogy (*analogós*), contemplate their Author.'[5] But what is then proclaimed about this divinisation of nature is rather surprising: 'Small blame, however, attaches to them, for perhaps they go astray only in their search for God and their eagerness to find him; familiar with his works, they investigate them and fall victim to appearances, seeing so much beauty (*hoti kala ta blepomena*).'[6] A clear distinction is drawn between those who go so far as to adore the beauties of nature, divinising the works of God, and those who have 'given the title of gods to human artefacts', the idolaters, who are punished with an immeasurably greater severity. But the fact remains that even where Scripture clearly makes of the world's beauty a path to God, this path will not exactly have been a path but will have interrupted them in their quest for God, arrested and, as it were, stupefied them in the face of the world. Beauty will have awoken them only finally to plunge them into another kind of sleep, peopled by bad dreams. And if they are not put on the same level as the idolaters, it is nonetheless said of them that 'even so, they have no excuse'.

What manifests God may become a veil that conceals him and makes us forget him or fail to recognize him. What leads towards him may become a place where we settle down to build our dwelling place. When the road is so beautiful, the danger that we will stop en route is merely all the greater. Woe to those who are too quickly contented, woe to those who are satisfied straightaway! It is the same situation as in that remarkable parable in which Plotinus compares the manifestation of beings and of their principle to the suite of a great king. The bystanders see the members of the royal suite processing by in increasing dignity and importance, until right at the very end the great king himself 'suddenly' appears.[7] Then, says Plotinus, 'the people pray and prostrate themselves before him – those at least who have not gone away beforehand, satisfied with what they saw before the coming of the king'. The gravest threat, here, resides not in dissatisfaction, but in satisfaction. Those who leave before the end think that everything is already over, that they have seen, as people say of a firework display, the crowning piece. They

81

cannot imagine anything better than what they have already admired, and they go away blissful and contented, without even suspecting that they have deprived themselves of the highest bliss, for it is only when the most beautiful thing that we can imagine has presented itself – something that is on a par with our imagination, and with it alone – that there may arise something that is even more beautiful than what we can imagine, a truly unimaginable beauty, which can only be encountered without its having been anticipated and calculated in advance. This danger, that of departing too early, before the arrival of something quite surpassing our expectations, has a particular intensity in the relationship to beauty.

Chapter XIII of the book of Wisdom raises another and decisive question. Should we say, of this God who is the creator of all the beauty of the world, that he is himself beautiful? Is he of all creatures the most beautiful? How far does he exceed all finite and created beauties? In his commentary on *The Divine Names* of Pseudo-Dionysius the Areopagite, St Thomas Aquinas writes: 'Excess is twofold (*excessus autem est duplex*): the first is excess within a genus, and it is signified by the comparative or the superlative; the second is excess outside a genus, and it is signified by the addition of this preposition: *super*.'[8] So should we say that God is *pulcherrimus*, 'that which is most beautiful', or that he is *superpulchrum, huperkalon*, 'beyond the beautiful'? Can beauty name God in himself or only in his gifts? And does the path of beauty lead to a supreme beauty or altogether beyond beauty?

So as to formulate these questions more adequately, it may seem natural to seek for enlightenment in Christian dogmatics in its form as a science, with scholasticism and its later developments. Now, a rapid overview is enough to show that this enlightenment is, when it comes to beauty, not very impressive and quite hesitant. The attempt made by dogmatics to measure up to these questions was far from being on the level of the questions themselves, and sometimes this attempt was not even made but was avoided or sidelined. It is crucial that we understand how and why. All theologians are agreed on the fact that *beauty* does not, in the Bible, constitute a major and central name or attribute of divinity, unlike *glory*. To be sure, there is no glory without beauty, whereas there may be beauties without glory (this is the question examined in this chapter), but the fact remains that if we are seeking a definition, or a thematisation, of beauty, it is not in the Bible that we will find it (and that is not the Bible's task). To bring the question of beauty into dogmatics will thus require us to appeal, even this involves working over it and transfiguring it, to the language of philosophy. We will need, or would need, an inventive and heuristic translation, a translation that truly crosses the stream and is capable of exploring both shores and what passes or does not pass between them. The swimmer's aim is not necessarily to emerge completely dry from the water.

All things considered, it would even be better to emerge all muddy. So how do things stand?

In modern theology, the very place of beauty as a divine name is extremely variable, just as is the importance granted it. It is thus that Suárez, in his treatise on the divine attributes, does not devote any particular discussion to the question of divine beauty. But in the seventeenth century, the Jesuit theologian Denys Petau, one of the greatest dogmatic theologians of his period, together with the Oratorian Louis Thomassin, does not follow this example. Indeed, he writes in his majestic *Dogmata theologica* a chapter 'De Dei pulchritudine', 'On the Beauty of God'. This chapter is the last of those that study the 'properties' of God, before the author comes to the question of the vision of God. It follows on after the study of the divine goodness and perfection, and its first difficulty is precisely that of establishing a clear distinction between God's goodness and his beauty. Thus Denys Petau reviews, somewhat laboriously, all sorts of definitions of beauty, taken from ancient philosophy or from the Fathers of the Church who drew inspiration from it. The Platonic tradition occupies a central place in this survey. The beautiful is eventually defined as 'that the knowledge of which procures pleasure, because it corresponds exactly to its model and its primordial form'.[9] It is doubtful whether, defining beauty by the adequacy of a being to its idea, we have advanced much further towards the beauty of God himself, whatever Denys Petau himself may say. He goes on to establish that 'God is the primordial idea of all things and their model.' As he can neither depart from nor turn away from himself (*a seipso abhorrere*), he corresponds and conforms adequately, in every respect, with that most perfect model that he himself is (*est exemplari perfectissimo accurate consentaneus*). The knowledge of this immense beauty procures a commensurate joy, and God thus corresponds completely to the definition that has been given of beauty.[10] To think of beauty as a conformity to something else, or as conformity to itself, is still to think of it as conformity and correspondence. What does the beauty of God really signify in this metaphysics? That God, the creator of the world, is identical to himself. God is beautiful thus means: God is God. This rather anaemic phrase becomes a little more full-blooded when it comes to evoking the beauty of God on the basis of his effects, in other words the beauty that he communicates to the world, the beauty of the creatures in it. But this was not the point, as the idea was to see foreground beauty as a divine attribute.

As for Louis Thomassin, he does not tackle beauty, as does his contemporary Petau, only at the end of his treatise on God, as a supplement that we are not quite sure what to do with. But since he does get round to referring to it between truth, on the one hand, and love and life, on the other, and thus places it at the very heart of his theology, his procedure is in many respects analogous. One chapter studies the Platonic philosophy of the beautiful, another chapter goes on to glean quotations form patristic writing, and a third and last section turns to the communication of beauty to the various different creatures, both spiritual and corporal. The philosophical thought of the beautiful still serves as a point of departure, and guides the whole discussion, whereas it has quite evidently failed to take into consideration what it was supposed to question, the beauty of the one God.[11]

These reflections on the part of thinkers, who in other respects are capable of great insight, start to look like an abandoned building site, where all sorts of stones have been assembled for a building that will never be constructed. There are three reasons for this, which have to do with the architectonics of theology and the status, or the stature, of the speech that it can utter. The first reason is related to the systematic organization of theology, which has a treatise *De Deo uno* (*On the Divine Nature*) followed by a treatise *De Deo trino* (*On the Divine Persons*). It is in the first that beauty is discussed, when it is discussed, as one of the positive attributes of the divine nature. This leads to a twofold confusion. First and foremost, since the Bible has little to tell us on this topic, large use is made, openly or discreetly, of philosophical definitions of the beautiful, which were valid either for this-worldly beauties or for the idea of the beautiful, which makes them inadequate for thinking in terms of a name and a dimension that belong to the one God. And, at other points, trinitarian considerations invade the discussion, which contravenes the order it is supposedly following and puts a question mark over its relevance.

This appears clearly in the dogmatic theology of Thomassin: drawing inspiration from admirable pages by St Augustine, of whose light St Thomas Aquinas had already drunk deep,[12] Thomassin takes the unusual step of attributing beauty particularly to the Word, the second person of the Trinity. It is, he says, 'God the Word who is really and properly beauty itself (*pulchritudo ipsa*)'.[13] But if this is the case, if this alone can constitute the guiding thread of the Christian way of thinking about divine beauty, it is in the Word and from the Word that this question must be raised, and thus in the treatise on the Trinity.

These architectonic difficulties lead us to another one that is just as grave, and which brings into play speech itself. Whatever their faith, which is not in question, these thinkers speak *of* divine beauty without standing before it themselves, they speak of it without speaking *to* it, without addressing it in familiar tones, with that intimate and reverent familiarity that is the precise opposite of superficial familiarity. One cannot speak condescendingly of divine beauty, as if one were bending over some object to examine it. One can speak of it only in accordance with its own condescension, in accordance with the movement whereby it comes to meet us before we make any move. We can speak of it, therefore, only if we express our thanks. If patristic theology had more freedom and more force to describe God's beauty, it was not because of a more perfect systematic organization but by virtue of its character, which is, however modestly, hymnic, prayerful, familiar, advancing towards that beauty in the light of prayer and song, and advancing in prayer and song through the light of that beauty, even if its progress is, like that of any of any real progress, limping. When speech tries to unveil God instead of letting itself be unveiled and stripped bare, the loss of its dramatic tension is also a loss of light and intelligibility. If there is a divine beauty, we cannot be its spectators, but only its witnesses. And the witnesses of such beauty speak in proportion to their wound and their sense of being torn apart.

It is striking to see that the theological imbalance we glimpse in the works of Petau and Thomassin is encountered again and again across the centuries, in thinkers who in other ways are quite different. Karl Barth, not of his nature inclined to sing his praises, nonetheless credits the great nineteenth-century Catholic theologian Scheeben with having, in his treatment of divine beauty, performed an important service: 'It is no less surprising that Roman Catholic theology did not return expressly and seriously to this conception until the 19th century with M. J. Scheeben' (though it is not true that Scheeben was the first to do so).[14] But where, and how, did he do this? Does he add anything new to previous theologians? The *Gotteslehre* of the *Catholic Dogmatics* of Scheeben, following the traditional order, studies first the one God, then the threefold God. Still following this tradition, he moves from the negative attributes to the positive attributes, which are transposed from creatures to God: it is among these latter attributes that beauty appears.[15] The horizon is that of the attributes of the being or essentiality (*Wesenheit*) of God, before the attributes of his life or his nature, knowledge and will are tackled.

Beauty is studied after unity, truth, goodness, and before dignity or holiness. God is 'beauty itself', 'the ideal subsisting in all beauty', 'primal beauty' (*die Urschönheit*). It is characterized by its 'absolute simplicity', being an 'absolutely inner beauty', although it also demonstrates a 'unity in multiplicity', in that it contains eminently or radically all the modes or all the forms of created beauty. Nothing in these metaphysical determinations sheds any light on specificity of this attribute in relation to the others. Thus, a little further on, breaking away from his own plan, Scheeben sees in the divine Trinity the place par excellence of this beauty. We again come across the philosophical theme of the unity of the multiple, in a manner that seems displaced, for it makes of the very unity of God the illustration of a general schema: 'In fact there is no unity-in-multiplicity that is greater and more sublime than the essential unity of the different divine persons.' We also again come across the (Augustinian) theme of the image, which forms the basis for the way in which beauty is seen as proper to the Word: there is 'no more perfect resemblance between image and model than the resemblance and the equality between the Son and the Eternal Father'.[16] The same themes and the same aporias are constantly repeated: if the divine beauty can be elucidated only with reference to the Trinity, and is made manifest to us by the Word, why is it discussed outside what is proclaimed to be its most suitable place? Why conclude with what ought to be the point of departure and serve as a guiding thread? It is just as if these thinkers wished to hold together a metaphysical concept, taken from natural theology, with a Platonic tinge, and a properly Christian concept, taken from revealed theology, in their attempt to define divine beauty. It is equally problematic that they do not dwell on the idea that this beauty should be deduced from the divine *life*, even if in other places they affirm that, of all creatures, living beauty is the most consummate.[17]

In his *Dogmatics*, Karl Barth has the merit of making of the divine beauty once more a *question*: can we and should we say that God is beautiful?[18] This question is tackled in the section devoted to the 'perfection of the divine freedom', and beauty is strictly subordinated to glory: 'We speak of God's beauty only in explanation of His glory.'[19] But, in spite of its 'subordinate and auxiliary' character, beauty nonetheless has a radical necessity, if it is true that 'God's glory is effective because it is beautiful', and thus alone unfolds the perfection of its form.[20] But when Barth comes to describing in more detail the nature of this beauty, he follows a traditional plan: the beauty of the divine essence, the beauty of the Trinity, the beauty of the Incarnation. The first is characterized in a way reminiscent of Denys Petau: it is a matter of 'God's being as it unfolds in all His attributes, but is one in itself in them all' – a matter, that is, of its perfect identity. But even if God is everything that he is said to have, to what extent must that be called his beauty?[21] The second appears again as the essential place of these reflections: 'the triunity of God is the secret of His beauty. If we deny this, we at once have a God without radiance and without joy (and without humour!).'[22] The third leads Barth to affirm: 'The beauty of Jesus Christ is not just any beauty. It is the beauty of God. Or, more concretely, it is the beauty of what God is and does in Him.'[23] But, if this is the case, and if this beauty powerfully disconcerts us and strips us bare, do we not have to return to the preceding moments and transfigure them on the basis of this centre that has finally been reached?[24] Can we *conclude* these considerations on divine beauty with Christ in a Christian dogmatics? This difficulty constantly recurs.

Unlike the theologians cited above, that thinker of speech Karl Barth immediately follows his meditation on the divine glory with an investigation of the glorification of God by his creatures, on the act of praising and giving thanks. He refuses to separate the beauty of God from the response that we can make to it, however great in other respects may be the difficulties that in his eyes this response arouses. But, right at the heart of his discussion of divine beauty, a first question on this topic had already made its appearance, concerning theology itself. Any 'proclamation of the glory of God,' Barth showed, which lost sight of his beauty and itself failed to do justice to it, would thereby blind itself to its own ugliness, becoming sad, dull, ineffectual. It would thereby cease to show what it intended to show. 'But where this element is not appreciated – and this is why the question of the form is so important – what becomes of the evangelical element in the evangel?',[25] if it no longer sounds out like a piece of good news, if it does not radiate its joy and radiate with joy. A little further on, Barth recalled the considerations of St Anselm on theology, on the beauty of theology in so far as it is demanded by the beauty that it meditates on. While approving these views, Barth refused to touch on this question otherwise than by 'allusion', leaving it to the personal discernment of each individual: 'reflection and discussion of the aesthetics of theology can hardly be counted a legitimate and certainly not a necessary task of theology.'[26]

But is it really a question of aesthetics? Is it not a matter of our incessant responsories to divine speech? A matter, that is, of the very welcome, within these responsories, of the event of beauty? St Anselm, at the start of one of his greatest treatises, wrote:

> I fear lest, just as I myself am apt to be indignant with bad artists when
> I see our Lord depicted under a misshapen form, so it may happen
> to myself, if I presume to investigate so sublime a subject by rude,
> contemptible speculation (*incompto et contemptibili dictamine*).[27]

What happens in our speech cannot be separated from what passes, or may pass, through and by means of it. Its 'form' is not distinct from its transparency and its ability to transmit what it has to see and show. It is a matter of we ourselves appearing before this beauty. It cannot be placed in question without us too being under examination. The absence of this dimension, which can be called dramatic, makes the treatises on divine beauty, as it were, rootless and vague, and deprives them of the site at which our responsibility comes into play.

These various attempts at objectification by understanding of the divine beauty do not really say adieu. They name, to be sure, the excess and the superfluity, but they do not show it. If we are to shed light on these questions, we need to raise more radical questions. The *excessus* of which St Thomas Aquinas speaks is at the heart of the way Plotinus and Pseudo-Dionysius the Areopagite think about beauty. How should we consider the source of beauty? Is it the height of the beautiful, a maximum finally reached, or is the giving of beauty without itself being beautiful – an eternal *envoi*? Plotinus, for whom the beautiful certainly is a way towards the principle and origin of being, affirms on several occasions that the Good is anterior to beauty, to that intelligible beauty which itself founds and brings into being the sensible beauties that participate in it. 'That which is before it does not even want to be beautiful.'[28] And in another place, Plotinus specifies: 'But he is beautiful beyond all beauty (*huperkalos*) . . . transcending the best (*tón aristón*).'[29] What we have here really is an excess that goes beyond the genus of the kind mentioned by St Thomas Aquinas as even the superlative is left behind.

Another of Plotinus's treatises gives to this idea of the radical transcendence of the Good over beauty its most powerful and most rigorous formulations:

> so his beauty is of another kind and beauty above beauty (*kallos huper kallos*). For if it is nothing, what beauty can it be? But if it is lovable, it would be the generator of beauty. Therefore the productive power of all is the flower of beauty, a beauty which makes beauty (*kallos kallopoion*). For it generates beauty and makes it more beautiful (*kallion*) by the excess of beauty which comes from it, so that it is the principle of beauty and the term of beauty.[30]

The source of beauty is thus not a beautiful thing, not even the most beautiful of all. What makes the beauty that we admire spring forth is nothing other than an excess of beauty itself. The origin that gives birth to the beautiful does not form a reserve from which beauties would in some way be drawn as and when required. The excess of the beautiful over itself, in its manifestation, refers to another, anterior excess, the excess by which the Good surpasses everything that it gives forth. In this eternal gift of intelligible beauty to itself by the Good, we must note the comparative *kallion*: to give beauty is to make it live and shine, to make it something entirely excessive and surprising. The flower of beauty, which precedes beauty, is also the flower that beauty offers us, transmits to us, being itself received by that flower, for how could it not call us to what called it to itself, to what gave it to itself and to us, and which is nothing that one could ever, in any way whatsoever, appropriate?

In the Christian dimension, Pseudo-Dionysius the Areopagite, at the heart of his treatise *On the Divine Names*, was to take up and develop these ideas. To think of God as that which is beyond beauty and gives beauty is to discern that only his excess over and above the beautiful, and over all the formal definitions of the beautiful that we might put forward, makes it possible for there to be a gift of beauty, and for the beauty of creatures itself to be in excess – an excess of itself, which *is* itself in so far as it responds to the call of God.[31] It is no longer an always imperfect resemblance between principle and principiate, a resemblance that makes all beings resemble one and the same essence and thus also makes them resemble one another. On the contrary, the purest notion of the One excludes all multiplicity from the principle so that the multiple can spring all the more purely from the One, spring from it for the first and only time, so that there can be such a thing as a world. To think the multiple without resentment is the yardstick of all notions of the One.

For Pseudo-Dionysius, everyone has to be his or her own beauty, and even love it, for that beauty forms what it is able to shine forth, in a way all the more intense the more singular it is, in response to the unique source of light. On each person, indeed, a ray of this light has shone, and it has transfigured everyone. Beauty, as Pseudo-Dionysius thinks of it, unites and separates at once the different beings among themselves: beauty unites the most diametrically opposed beings in the same luminous exclamation, and it leaves to each one, in the most intimately converging chorus, its own voice, its own timbre. The Greek of Pseudo-Dionysius is filled with dense expressions that can only be paraphrased in French, as when he affirms that by the One, 'contraries communicate, and the united elements escape confusion' (*hai koinóniai tón enantión, hai asummixiai tón hènómenón*),[32] or, a little further on, when he refers to those *asugkhutoi philiai*, those unmixed friendships that Maurice de Gandillac explains persuasively when he says: 'the beings love each other without being absorbed into each other'.[33] For the divine light does not illuminate beings that are already constituted: by illuminating them, it creates them and enables them to arise. To give them beauty is not to add anything to them, it is to give them to themselves, and to each other, in the unity of a world that, as such, has a richness in proportion to its diversity.

Nobody has shown this more clearly than Gerard Manley Hopkins. With the murmured clarity of poetic speech, he abandons without negating it the contempt in which the *poikilos*, the many-coloured, is sometimes held, in his short hymn, brief and sure-footed, even its apparently hazardous moments, 'Pied Beauty':

Glory be to God for dappled things –
For skies of couple-colour as a brinded cow;
For rose-moles all in stipple upon trout that swim;
Fresh-firecoal chestnut-falls; finches' wings;
Landscape plotted and pieced – fold, fallow, and plough;
And áll trádes, their gear and tackle and trim.

All things counter, original, spare, strange;
Whatever is fickle, freckled (who knows how?)
With swift, slow; sweet, sour; adazzle, dim;
He fathers-forth whose beauty is past change;
Praise him.[34]

Here, it is not the uniform, the regular, the symmetrical that refers us to the sole and simple God but, on the contrary, the most varied, the most diverse, the most composite, the most multiple. As for Pseudo-Dionysius, what we have here is a unity of tensions, a heartfelt community of contraries. And it is that which is most ephemeral – for what could be more ephemeral than the fugitive flock of the clouds, the migrating light of dawn and dusk, or the reflections on a fish glimpsed in a river? – that bears witness to the God 'whose beauty is past change'. The ephemeral does this all the more surely in that it does not have the leisure to linger over itself, but sends its message as it passes and disappears. The poem does not invite us to praise God, in its last two words, except in so far as it has itself done nothing else, from its first word, 'Glory', onwards. It does not cease to say 'adieu', in the double sense of the expression: it commends to God and says adieu.

The poem here evokes everything mottled by becoming mottled itself, assuming that very same 'pied beauty' of which it speaks, for what do finches' wings have in common with the tools of human trades? And if this poem exhorts us to praise in turning into a hymn of praise itself, what does it say if not that to obey it and listen to it is to become ourselves, in turn, in our very being as in our songs, 'counter, original, spare, strange'? It wants, itself, to arouse strangeness and dappled hues as the only possible response to the call it has thus answered. Living, inanimate; natural, artificial; ephemeral, durable – everything is here brought into play. But the same is not true of a definition of beauty as mere motley, for then Harlequin's coat would be the best example of it; this diversity must each time be rhythmically unified and must converge in the flash of an event, in which the world itself comes together as one.

While showing that the relationship between the beauty of things and the beauty of God cannot be imagined as one of mimesis or resemblance, Gerard Manley Hopkins inaugurates, here as elsewhere, the drama of speech when it attempts to describe and convey beauty. He speaks of its event in a way that refuses to be theorized. If beauty may be, in whatever sense, theophanic, this cannot take the form of a spectacle offered to a gaze that looks down on it and masters it but as the request addressed to an existence that is denuded, transported, drawn out of itself, and thus truly existing, by virtue of this manifestation in act. In every manifestation of God, direct or indirect, there is adventure and advent: God comes to me, God happens to me, and I am affected by his arrival. To speak of this beauty is to speak to it also, to respond to it and become responsible for it, just as it means becoming responsible for my own transfiguration at its hands and thus being responsible for myself more than is really possible – for it is not I who have transformed myself in this way; I would not have been capable of it. To this act of presence the only response can be an act of speech.

This drama of beauty attains, in a celebrated passage of Book X of St Augustine's *Confessions*, its greatest and most blazing intensity. It is necessary to listen to him so as to gain a more precise idea of this *drama*:

Sero te amavi, pulchritudo tam antiqua et tam nova, sero te amavi!
Late have I loved you, beauty so old and so new: late have I loved
you. And see, you were within and I was in the external world and
sought you there, and in my unlovely state I plunged into those
lovely created things which you made (*in ista formosa, quae fecisti
deformis inruebam*). You were with me, and I was not with you. The
lovely things kept me far from you, though if they did not have their
existence in you, they had no existence at all.[35]

God is invoked by the name of *pulchritudo*, 'beauty'. But this name, which
arises in the vocative, this name, which is you, is not in any way defined,
founded or justified in an argumentative way in this passage. The beauty
that is God himself is in no sense described, and St Augustine does not wax
eloquent about it as if it were a divine attribute that he had the leisure to
contemplate or scrutinize. The self-evidence with which this name sounds out
here is rather the self-evidence of a kind of catastrophe: to express this beauty
is to say that we have been astounded, thunderstruck, staggered by it, as by an
avalanche of light. The urgency of this event, which completely overwhelms
us on every side, is not something that can be described from the standpoint
of a mere onlooker.

The first dimension of this excess is temporal: eternity is expressed through
the words of our speech and through our lives – and thus in temporal terms
– as being 'so old and so new'. It is for us a past more ancient than any past,
any past that might belong to us, any past that we would have constituted
or posited as such. Eternity is always already there, always already there
within us, in our most intimate being, like the heart of otherness within
this intimacy. In this respect, the belated nature (referred to twice over) of
Augustine's love for this beauty may indeed be related to his conversion and
have an autobiographical relevance, but these latter do not exhaust it. The
Sero te amavi has something universal about it; it is a matter of principle, too,
for the response of our love is necessarily belated with regard to the splendour
of God. It was there within us and for us, before we could become aware of it
and reply to it. We cannot be contemporary with what is always already there.
Giving it the name *diachrony*, Emmanuel Levinas has, with great profundity,
developed the idea of an analogous level. So at whatever moment of our lives
we are able to love this beauty, and however early it is placed, it would always
be possible to say 'Late have I loved you.' When this beauty manifests itself, it
thereby manifests also its precedence, the fact that it comes before us and that
it was shining forth long before we opened our eyes to it.

This belatedness of our gaze in relation to the light, and of our hands to the
richness of the offering that is already pouring down on us and within us, is
not, however, revealed by a patient and slow introspection, but by the shock

of its newness. *Tam antiqua et tam nova*. Where is this beauty new, and how? The eternal present is in itself neither old nor new. This beauty is old wherever we discover that it has gone before us, even in the depths of our being, and it is new wherever it renews us, and forces open our doors and wounds us with its clarity. It is its newness, in fact, that manifests how old it is, for when all of a sudden it discloses itself to us, it thereby discloses to us its immemorial character. For this newness is not the newness of an event in time, a newness that little by little ceases to be new: it is the radical newness, safe from all ageing, of eternity springing forth into time – an advent.

When it is not a matter of finding and taking something we did not have but of letting ourselves be found and taken by that which already dwelt in us, the very act of seeking may put its seal on loss and perplexity. Malebranche, following St Augustine, thought at length about this. It is what is at stake in his words, 'You were within, and I was in the external world and sought you there'. This should be compared with the passage shortly after: 'You were with me, and I was not with you' (*Mecum eras, et tecum non eram*). In order to be present to what already dwells within us, to what has already approached us in the depths of our being, we need only open ourselves to its presence and bid it welcome. The welcoming we give to what is already there is the true welcome, the one that never ends. The opposition between inside and outside does not so much distinguish between two regions in which we can embark on a quest for God, two dimensions in which to seek him, but rather, on the one hand, a direction in which to seek where God is lost precisely because we are seeking him as if he were not already there (but we were), because we always move further and further away both from him and from ourselves when we think we are getting closer, and, on the other hand, a space in which it is not a question of seeking an absent or distant God, but of letting him, already there as he is, find *us*. And this can happen only if we hold ourselves available for him to take hold of us.

How can St Augustine call himself *deformis* when he rushes *in ista formosa,* deformed and ugly when he hastens towards the beautiful forms? This is by no means a way of denying the reality of the world's beauty, which is so often evoked by him as a witness to the Creator and an *envoi* to him. The person who asks individually created beautiful things for what, on principle, they cannot give him, namely the capacity to make himself beautiful, can only end up deforming himself through his very love of the forms. It only needs him to be absent from himself for his procedure to be erratic and discordant. As he says a little later, 'There is a struggle between joys over which I should be weeping and regrets at matters over which I ought to be rejoicing.' This painful self-division deforms him.

The end of the paragraph, which I have not yet quoted, is of particular importance.

You called and cried out loud and shattered my deafness. You were radiant and resplendent, you put to flight my blindness. You were fragrant, and I drew in my breath and now pant after you. I tasted you, and I feel but hunger and thirst for you. You touched me, and I am set on fire to attain the peace which is yours.

In this evocation of what theology would later call the spiritual senses, there is a fivefold wound, which is an essential part of the manifestation of God's beauty. God breaks in, he comes towards us and upon us as the Lord, by creating the conditions of possibility of his own manifestation. He alone can take the initiative, he opens the doors that we have closed behind ourselves, and he does not come to fulfil or satisfy a desire that is already ours, but he himself comes to rouse its flame within us.

What is here being said of the divine beauty? We do not so much speak of it as to it. This prayerful and vocative speech addressed to God never loses sight of the fact that he is as God always greater. And what is offered up to this beauty is nothing other than the desire it has opened up within us, the wound it has inflicted on us. There is in speech of this kind something agonistic, which forcefully recalls the intimacy of Jacob wrestling with the angel. This theophanic beauty is a theopathic beauty: the manifestation of God can be expressed only through a suffering of God, an enduring of God. Nothing else is described but the event of the encounter, the imperious and generous way that God comes: there is here none of the pride and presumption of the person who would claim to define and determine the beauty of God as he is in himself. That is why this passage from St Augustine allows us to grasp clearly the *drama* of speech: it does not recount an event unless it itself constitutes an event, and thus delivers us from aestheticism rather than threatening us with it. Beauty here says adieu and commends to God because it arouses, as the only possible response to its manifestation, a prayer, a speech that itself says adieu and itself turns towards God.

These characteristics of failing and excess can be found, albeit in a different style, in another decisive passage from Latin patristic writing that discusses the divine beauty, in the first book of the great work of St Hilary of Poitiers on the Trinity.[36] Quoting the book of Wisdom, St Hilary sees, in turn, the beauty of the world as an opening up to the beauty of the Creator: 'And since the work (*operatio*) surpasses even our comprehension, so the worker (*operator*) must far exceed our comprehension.' The sense of beauty is that it exceeds our sense, always gives itself in addition. The world's beauty refers us to God's beauty in the way that something elusive refers us to something even more elusive, and not in the way that a copy refers us to a model, both of which would fall, in a banal way, within the compass of our minds. St Hilary brings out again, within his Christian and Latin way of thinking, the

Greek sense of *kosmos*: 'The heavens, the sky, the earth, the sea, and the whole universe are beautiful, therefore, because of its splendour (*ex ornatu suo*), as even the Greeks agree, as it appears to be called deservedly *kosmos*, that is, the ornament.'

Such a preamble is not going to lead to any self-assured description of that splendour of creation; on the contrary, the rest of the chapter goes on to interlace speech and silence, thought and that which exceeds thought, in a meditation on the possibility or the impossibility of praising beauty. We relate to the beauty of creatures, St Hilary shows, by a 'natural instinct'. If the language we use to describe it is not up to the level of the feelings it inspires in us, if, to some degree, beauty leaves us speechless, nonetheless our inner sense engages in a dialogue with itself as it directs its thoughts to beauty. These lead us back to its source:

> Should not the Lord of this beauty itself be conceived as the most beautiful of all beauty, so that, while the form of His eternal adornment eludes the mind's power of comprehension, the ornament is not withdrawn from the mind's power of comprehension?

If beauty here forms a way to God, this is not because it provides the opportunity for an apologetic argument in favour of his existence, but because it is one of the figures of excess, and surpasses our intelligence without being completely independent of it. It is to faith that it is disclosed, out of respect for its transcendence.[37] This leads to the formulation, at once balanced and taut, that brings the chapter to an end:

> We must acknowledge God as the most beautiful of all in this manner, that He is not included within the thoughts that we comprehend nor is He beyond the comprehension of our thoughts (*neque intra sententiam intelligendi, neque extra intelligentiam sentiendi*).

This chiasmus, which defies translation, is an attempt to signify that the experience in which we undergo the divine beauty really is an ordeal, and does not leave us separated from it, even though this ordeal tries to match up to that beauty without measuring it, and even though it cannot appropriate it in such a way that we can grasp it entire. It is yet again a question of the drama of speech: beauty says adieu, to God ('à Dieu'), it does not say God himself.

Speech cannot say adieu in response to beauty unless 'song is existence'. *Gesang ist Dasein*, this is the imperious demand made by Rilke in the *Sonnets to Orpheus*.[38] Song is existence, the existence that is most ours, but also that which we most share in common, when it remembers to sing in forgetfulness of the singer and ceases to be our own expression.

Song, as you teach it, is not desire,
Not the striving for a good that is finally achieved;
Song is existence.

This is why, in the same sonnet, to the young man in love whose 'voice forces open his mouth', Rilke says:

Learn
To forget that you struck up your song. It flows away.
To sing in truth is another breath.
A breath about nothing. A breeze blowing in God. A wind.

The pressure of our own need to sing listens too much to itself, it is in fact not urgent enough, for it does not measure up to the urgency of the things themselves. When we read the end of this sonnet, how can we fail to think of the revelation of God to Elijah on Mount Horeb, in which God is neither in the great and strong wind, nor in the earthquake, nor in the fire, but in the 'light murmuring sound'.[39] Except for this: by an inversion, it is our own voice, in so far as it is responsible for the world, that must be such a still small voice in God if it is to become existence and an authentic song.

But how can this take place? At first glance, one might be tempted to think that if song becomes existence, it is by reaching a dimension of harmony and reconciliation, in which the singer would no longer be anything other than his song and this song a wayside altar, a dwelling place for the beauty that it sings. A dream of peace, a dream of all tensions being finally resolved, a luminous and radiant sphere. But is this really possible? The lofty, pure poetry of Jacopone da Todi, in thirteenth-century Italy, collected under the title *Laudes*,[40] shows with characteristic vigour the illusory nature of such a vision. Song is existence only when it is wounded to the heart by what it sings, and breaks down, shattered by the radiance of what it sings – and yet still continues to sing. If praise by definition excludes a complacent reflexivity that turns us right round back on ourselves, this does not thereby mean that it is unreflective and naive. How could a speech in which we have to pay with our whole person, pledge our own life, remain devoid of lucidity with regard to its procedures and its movement?

Thus it is that Jacopone, at the heart of a hymn to divine light and love, addresses this objection to himself:

O proud tongue, how have you dared
To speak of holy Love?
Human speech cannot rise to such heights.
In speaking of this love

The tongues of angels falter –
And you feel no misgivings and shame?
You reduce love
To the measure of your words;
This is not praise, but blasphemy.[41]

To which Jacopone replies that one must 'shout the praises of love', and describes the suffocation, the asphyxiation in which the person unable to sing of his love would perish. But what is the status of this reply? To what extent does it counter the legitimate objection that praise that is not appropriate to the object of its praise turns into its own opposite and, unable to say kind things, comes out with unkind gossip instead? To point in excuse to our own inner necessity, the need we have to utter the things that weigh on our chests, may seem a way of ignoring the question rather than answering it adequately. But to think as much would mean altogether failing to grasp the dimension in which speech such as that of Jacopone da Todi works.

The centre of his poetry is the 'sickness of love' of the *Song of Songs*, referred to by an entire mystical tradition.[42] The one who is thus wounded in his most intimate being cannot describe the beauty of the Beloved as in some tranquil contemplation in which he would be at perfect leisure to weigh his words: he cries out his wound in urgent alarm, and in uttering his cry he makes that wound deeper, allows it to grow deeper within him. This wound forms an event: it overwhelms existence in such a way that in us is created an opening that we have not ourselves opened, and that there is given to us, in a joy that tears us apart, more than anything we could give ourselves, more than anything we can receive or contain. Jacopone speaks of a wine so strong that it makes the hoops of the barrel burst.[43] To speak of the wound of love, and because of that wound not to speak of oneself first and foremost, it is to speak of the other. And it is not to speak of the other as if one had an opinion about him, some personal point of view, but to speak of the other in so far as he makes us other to what we were or could even try to be. The praise of lovers does not claim to measure up to the beauty it sings, it is borne into the immeasurable excess of the event in which that beauty has encountered it, countering and overcoming as it does so any pre-existing image.

Furthermore, praise knows better than anyone that there exists no standpoint from which one could compare the beauty of the song and the beauty of what it sings, so as to show up the exact measure of its failure to match up to it. Who could look down from such a panoramic height? We would need to see beauty better than the one who is singing its praises; in consequence, either this vision would be silent, and in not responding to beauty it would not really see it (for to see without this vision committing us in the slightest way to anything at all is merely a form of empty curiosity), or else it would sing its own self, and such a song could not take as its object the criticism and devaluation of other songs.

For Jacopone, the 'jubilation' of the heart, at one and the same time with one and the same movement, withdraws speech and gives speech, withdraws it so as to give it in reality:

> O heart's jubilation, love and song,
> Joy and joy unceasing,
> The stuttering of the unutterable –
> How can the heart but sing?[44]

Only a wounded speech can express the wound, only a speech expatriated from self-certainty can express the wrench that has flung it outside itself:

> O Love of the Lamb, vaster than any sea,
> Who can dare to speak of You?
> He who has drowned in You,
> And no longer knows where he is.[45]

In another poem, Jacopone alternates two voices that both express their relationship to the event of the cross, but in inverse fashion. The first clamours: 'Once I was blind, now I see', and the second replies: 'The light has blinded me.' The first goes on to say: 'Now – I can speak, though once I was mute', and the second: 'And I who once could talk am now made mute.'[46] What is decisive in this dialogue is that it does not contrast these two voices like truth and falsity: neither of the voices refutes the other. What we have here are two relationships to the wound of love, and they are together equally true. But, for Jacopone, it is the voice that is most wounded that has gone furthest, for what has wounded that voice has gone furthest within it, to the verge of the intolerable, the intolerable that bursts open a song that we are no longer alone in singing, a song that is broken, torn, paradoxical, in love.

Among the paradoxes of this poetry, there is one paradox that brings beauty into play. There appear, in one and the same poem, two opposite movements. The first is that whereby the way we are seized and ravished by divine beauty seems to reduce to nothing the beauty of creation, so that the latter merely arouses a kind of violent impatience:

> I can no longer see any creature,
> My whole soul cries out to the Creator;
> Neither earth nor heaven have any sweetness for me any more;
> Compared with the love of Christ, everything for me is foul.[47]

The sun itself seems dark in comparison with the divine glory. But, three verses further on, Jacopone writes:

> For heaven and earth cry and all things
> Do not cease to proclaim that I must love thus;
> They all tell me: With all your heart, love
> The Love that has made us, and burn to embrace it![48]

How are we to understand this tension? If the beauty of creation is nothing compared to God, how can it direct us to him? If it really says adieu, how could its adieu be forgettable?

This drama of speech has to be grasped in the unity of its act, without its different movements being fixed and isolated. Beauty says adieu when the excess of its manifestation calls out, in our own voice which it causes to falter and seizes with urgency, a name higher than all names, which we alone, albeit in fear and trembling, can pronounce. This adieu is an *envoi*: we cannot in God himself contemplate the beauty of things created, for of this beauty we are the only lieutenants and the only mouthpieces. It is our voice that carries to God and into God the adieu of things and of the mute world. If things in all their radiance are charged with a mission to us, we too have the mission of welcoming them, gathering them in, carrying them by means of our voice to a place that they cannot reach of themselves. But this merely intensifies the question: Can a beauty which makes all other beauty ugly still be beauty? Is beauty a divine name?

The *Treatise on the Love of God* of St François de Sales opens up some far-reaching questions in this domain. To be sure, he evokes the 'most excellent beauty' of God, his 'sovereign beauty', without lingering too long over the question as to whether this name can be justified.[49] But when, referring to the beatific vision, the vision of God face to face, he comes round to thinking about the place where this beauty will be truly seen, what does he say?

> The blessed spirits are ravished by two forms of admiration: the one, for the infinite beauty they contemplate, and the other, for the abyss of the infinity which remains to be seen in this selfsame beauty. O God, how admirable is what they see! But O God, how much more admirable is what they do not see![50]

a little further on, in the words that end the chapter, St François adds:

> They feel a sovereign joy when they see that the beauty they love is so infinite that it cannot be totally known except by itself: for in

this consists the divinity of this infinite beauty, or the beauty of this infinite Divinity.[51]

The first question that arises is that of knowing whether the word 'beauty', repeated several times, still has a specificity proper to itself. Indeed, it clearly appears that what is central, here, is nothing other than the divine infinity, and what St François de Sales affirms of beauty could be said, in the same terms, of absolutely any divine attribute, such as justice or wisdom. The second question brings into play the idea that the full vision of this beauty can only be the vision it has of itself. This feature means that it is radically different from finite beauty, which only ever allows itself to be seen by the other. Neither the beauty of nature nor the beauty of art see themselves. They are beauty only for our gaze and our voice. And even the beauty of a face is only really made visible to the other – otherwise, as the fate of Narcissus shows, it would be more harmful than joyful, and would disappear. Can we use the same term to name something that can be seen only by itself and something that can be seen only from the point of view of another? The third question bears on the inexhaustible character of the vision of the beautiful and on the nature of this inexhaustibility. Every vision is a vision with a future. We never exhaust or will exhaust the visible. And this inexhaustibility assumes, in beauty, a particular intensity: that is beautiful which offers to my gaze, as if tremulously alive already in the present, the future of that gaze. Not a future merely dreamt of, but a future already there, which is the very excess of beauty in its manifestation. This future does not form some 'other' visible realm, of the kind we mean when we speak of an 'other' world: it is the jutting prow of the visible itself. And already, in the vision of the finite, it is not correct to say that what we do not see is 'much more admirable' than what we see, for to see is precisely to see this 'much more', to see it as that which fills my gaze with futurity, making it a permanent apprentice and yet at the same time sated and satisfied once and for all. The consequence of all of this is that we cannot help but think that the biblical term *glory* would be much more appropriate than 'beauty' to what St François has in mind. When 'beauty' comes to designate the very divinity of God, it loses its community with what we can admire and praise by this name in ordinary creatures.

But this question bounces back, transformed, if we consider another place in which it raises its head. There is, in the history of thought and art, a decisive area in which the status of beauty and its adieu is a topic of meditation: the question as to the beauty of Christ. Where the glory of God, in the incarnation, comes in person to dwell in humankind, body and soul, can we also talk of beauty? In what sense can we speak of the beauty of Jesus, and – first and foremost – should we? What about the way art depicts his body and his face? Does Jesus's perfection require bodily beauty? These questions were and are disputed, with the most widely different replies being given. We need to set out in essence the various possible answers.

In the eighth book of his *De Trinitate*, St Augustine remarks soberly that we know nothing and can know nothing about the physical appearance of Jesus, Mary or the apostles. We have neither description nor portrait of them. 'But', he continues, 'what concerns our faith is not a matter of knowing what face these men had; it is knowing that by the grace of God they led the life and accomplished the actions attested by the Scriptures.'[52] Of course we can imagine the faces or the places of sacred history. But these images are arbitrary, and we can take it as a given that, here as elsewhere, reality, if we could see it, would be completely different and would totally dispossess us of those images.

> The face of the Lord itself is infinitely varied, depending on the different representations of it each person forms: and yet he was unique, whatever his appearance. But what is salutary in the faith we have in the Lord Jesus is not these imaginative representations, far-removed from reality as they may be: it is what we think of the man, of what in him answers to our idea of man.[53]

And when, in his commentary on the Psalms, St Augustine speaks of the *magna pulchritudo*, the great beauty of the incarnation, a theme that then develops into a sort of hymn to the beauty of Christ, in which the word *pulcher* is repeated several times over, he is not talking about Christ's physical appearance, but of the radiance of his justice: 'Supreme and true beauty is justice . . . If someone is just in all respects, it is in every respect that he is beautiful.'[54] The vision of this spiritual beauty is inseparable from faith: 'For us who believe, it is everywhere that the bridegroom presents himself in his beauty.' This beauty resides in the performance of his acts – all his acts. Beauty is the justice that comes: the occurrence of beauty. We grasp it as and when it happens. Such a conception to some extent rules out the question of knowing whether Jesus was or was not endowed with any particular physical beauty.

In his own style, Bossuet later paraphrased and extended these ideas of St Augustine in his 'First Sermon for the Feast of the Circumcision of Our Lord'.[55] The paradox of a beauty of horror, or within horror, is there taken to a sublime level:

> Although those cruelly torn limbs and that poor mangled flesh almost sicken those who approach him; although the prophet Isaiah predicted that in this state he would not be recognizable, that he would have neither grace, nor even any human appearance . . ., nonetheless, it is in these effaced lineaments, it is in these bruised

eyes, it is in this face which inspires horror, that I discover the features of an incomparable beauty.[56]

The beauty of Christ in the Passion is conveyed through its opposite: the perfection of the human face lies in its being able to offer itself on behalf of justice and truth, even if, in this offering, it is, as it were, obliterated or disfigured. And yet, Bossuet addresses to himself the following objection:

> But perhaps you will say to me: What a strange imagination it is that seeks his beauty amid his sufferings, which do not even leave him with the face of a man! Why do you not much rather contemplate it in his marvellous transfiguration, or in his glorious resurrection?

For Bossuet, this beauty is none other than that of God's gift: it sounds out in the *pro nobis* of faith. To those who 'find deformity in his wounds', Bossuet replies:

> For me, assured as I am that it is for love of me that he was thus bruised and beaten, I cannot share their opinion. The true beauty of my master cannot be taken away from him: no, no, those cruel bruises did not disfigure that face; they embellished it in my eyes . . . . The love my Saviour King has for me, the love which opened all his wounds, spread over it a certain grace that no other object can equal, a certain radiant beauty which transports the souls of the faithful.[57]

We have here, so to speak, a slippage from one possibility to another: we move from an indifference to the fleshly appearance of Christ, his only beauty lying in justice, to the contemplation of supreme beauty *within* supreme horror, even in the disfigurement of the Passion. This tradition leads to Léon Bloy's *In the Darkness*. God, he writes, 'seems to have condemned himself to the end of time to exercise over man no immediate right of a master over a servant, or a king over a subject. If he wants to win us over, he has to seduce us.' That God can seduce was already the astonishing turn of phrase of the prophet Jeremiah.[58] And Léon Bloy continues: 'He will not defend himself by his power, but only by his patience and by his Beauty.'[59] What beauty? 'Infinite Beauty and Strength are those of the Man of Sorrows.'[60] 'We do not understand that we are the members of the Man of sorrow, of the Man who is supreme Joy, Love, Truth, Beauty, Light and Life only because he is the eternally distraught Lover of the supreme Pain, the Pilgrim of the ultimate sacrifice.'[61]

If the extreme character of this thought, in which the crucified Jesus becomes, as it were, the black sun of beauty, does not avoid running the risk of an indefinite rhetorical expansion, it is also, spiritually speaking, somewhat ambiguous. Is this beauty in horror imagined on the basis of the unique event of Jesus's passion, in which faith alone can discover it and open itself up to it, or does it arise from a law of inversion, in accordance with which opposites reveal and reinforce one another? Beautiful ugliness, *formosa deformitas*,[62] has been a source of constant and unending fascination through the centuries, and it has given rise to all sorts of works of art. To speak of the beauty of the disfigured Jesus is either an example of the cult of oxymoron, of an inverted aestheticism, which is always a little murky, or else it supposes that we highlight the fact that beauty too dies and is resurrected, that the incarnation, by making all things new, renews beauty also, and opens it up to new dimensions. When Bossuet speaks of the 'grace' and the 'charms' of pain, is he not illegitimately mixing up two different levels and two different languages? The beauty of the crucified must be thought within the dimension opened up by the event of the resurrection, and not on the basis of the concepts of aesthetics.

Before we can formulate this question more adequately, we ought to examine the sense, the scope and the foundation of the various traditions that mention the beauty of Jesus as a man. In the preface to his masterpiece, the *Dialogues on Metaphysics and Religion*, Malebranche justifiably waxed indignant that an obscure polemicist should have accused him of having decided for metaphysical reasons to attribute a certain bodily appearance to Jesus, thereby accusing him of heresy. So that author had written:

> According to Tertullian, one of the principal errors of the Marcionites and Apelletians and Valentinians was to believe that Jesus Christ was beautiful before his passion. Father Malebranche, who sometimes follows their opinions . . ., has declared his entire agreement with them on this point.

To which Malebranche retorts: 'The fact is that I have never spoken on this question, neither in the *Treatise on Nature and Grace*, nor in any of my books.'[63] The debate on the beauty or ugliness of Jesus, which goes back to the early Church, was reignited in the sixteenth and seventeenth centuries.[64]

Numerous Fathers of the Church insist, if not on the ugliness of Jesus, at least on the absence of physical beauty in him. There are two reasons for that. The first is that they apply to Jesus, not for his passion alone, but for the whole of his earthly life, the prophecy of Isaiah on the suffering servant, his absence of beauty and charm.[65] The second is that it belongs to the truth of the incarnation, to the assumption by God of the human condition, that

Jesus is a man like other men, a man in a quite ordinary sense, and that he does not at first attract attention by any visibly exceptional status. Tertullian pronounces with his customary trenchancy:

> In fact it was only for his words and works, solely for his doctrine and power, that they were astonished at Christ as man: whereas a new kind of flesh in him [like the heavenly flesh attributed to him by certain gnostics] would even have been remarked upon and taken for a marvel. But it was precisely the non-marvellous character of his terrestrial flesh which made the rest of his activities things to marvel at . . . . So far was his body from being of human comeliness, not to speak of celestial glory.[66]

As does Justin, Clement of Alexandria, or Irenaeus of Lyons,[67] Origen goes so far as to speak, as if it were self-evident, of the ugliness of Jesus:

> By general agreement, the Scriptures say that Jesus' body was ugly (*duseides*), but not commonplace, as Celsus has explained, and there is no clear indication that he was short . . . . Isaiah announces that he would not come to the multitudes in a pleasing shape of superior beauty.[68]

It is within this tradition, whether he was aware of it or not, that Kierkegaard placed himself when he criticized the aesthetic relation to the Christian faith, following which the divinity of Christ would have been, during his earthly life, directly recognizable, thanks to his beauty or his mildness. Faith, he says, has as its sign 'the crucifixion of the understanding and of fantasy-perception, which cannot have direct recognizability'.[69] And Kierkegaard says elsewhere: 'it is characteristic of an idol to be known directly'.[70] We all know how far an allegedly religious art has been able to go in what Kierkegaard calls a 'repellent sentimental frivolity'.

At the other extreme, another tradition insists on the beauty of Jesus. Dürer follows it quite naturally in his theoretical writings when he asserts that art, which is 'great, grave, and good', must be employed 'for the glory of God'. How?

> In the same way that (the pagans) gave their idol Apollo the proportions of the most beautiful human shape, we want to use the same measure for our Lord Christ who is the most beautiful in the world. And as they considered Venus to be the most beautiful woman in the world, we want to attribute, chastely, the same graceful form

to the purest of virgins, Mary, Mother of God. And from Hercules we want to make Samson, and likewise with the others.[71]

This strict correspondence is all the more surprising because, in the same passage, Dürer observes that this ancient science of proportions has been lost, and that it is therefore time to found a new one. Of course, this is part of the plan to make the beauty of art say adieu too, but would the transposition of ancient art be enough to achieve this? However this may be, many theologians share Dürer's views. Thus, the great contemplative Luis de León, in his masterpiece *The Names of Christ*, attributes to Jesus the greatest possible bodily beauty, and invites us 'with the eyes of faith' to gaze at:

> his lovely face, his grave and mild attitude, his eyes and that mouth, the latter always imbued with gentleness, the former of a brightness even more dazzling than the sun's gaze, too at the whole harmony of his body, its aspect, its movements, its members conceived in the very womb of purity and endowed with incomparable beauty.[72]

The contemplation of this 'perfect beauty' goes so far as to include an encomium on Jesus's complexion! It would need little more to turn this into a *blason* of Jesus's body, praising his body limb by limb. Is it the crucified and resurrected Christ who is being contemplated here? Is it really faith that inclines one to sing praises of this kind? Suárez, too, indulges in such considerations, affirming that 'Christ assumed a perfect corporeal beauty' and rising in wrath against a certain Medina who 'dared to deny it', 'without reason, and with great presumption'.[73]

Imagination and hyperbole are here allowed to run loose. When art starts to follow a path such as this, has it not ended up confusing different levels, and producing (as André Chastel says of a strange *Christ with Angels* by Rosso) 'something equivocal', 'something suspect'.[74] By virtue of what article of faith should the Crucified be as handsome as Apollo, indeed handsome in the very same way? In the nineteenth century, a critic cast doubt on the orthodoxy of an overwhelming *Crucifixion* by Jordaens in the name of the following arguments:

> How can we recognize this great, sublime drama of the suffering of Christ in this crucifixion scene with its three characters all equally banal? How can we discover in this painting the admirable figure of Jesus Christ, the Virgin, the holy women, the beloved disciple, amidst all these models taken from the taverns of Antwerp?[75]

Since these faces are, in his eyes, neither beautiful nor distinguished enough, he deduces that this painting, which he recognizes to be, in other ways, 'a masterpiece of colour and execution', is 'void of any religious feelings'. When he attacks the 'paganism' of 'recognizability', Kierkegaard is clearly not fighting against fictitious opponents.

What are we to think of this debate and this confrontation between two traditions? Should we not question the very question that asks whether Jesus was beautiful or ugly? Is the question adequately formulated? And are not the two theses, as so often, basically in agreement on the immediate character of the beauty or ugliness of a human body and face? Is not the affirmation of the ugliness of Jesus just as aesthetic as that of his beauty? Is not imagination just as much at ease, in its element, with disgrace as much as grace? What does it mean to assert, without further ado, that a man is beautiful or ugly, if not that such an assertion forgets the character of an event comprised by the manifestation of spirit in the body, on its surface of skin – an event that decides, in each case, whether we see beauty or ugliness? Can all this be deduced from canons of beauty, from proportion and measurement? The question of the beauty of Jesus can have a meaning only if it is formulated in Christian terms.

In his *Sermons on the Song of Songs*, St Bernard of Clairvaux dwells with great insight on the extent to which the beauty of Christ is veiled for us, being discerned by faith alone.

> The words he speaks are 'spirit and life'; the form we see is mortal, subject to death. We see one thing and we believe another. Our senses tell us he is black, our faith declares him fair and beautiful. If he is black it is 'in the eyes of the foolish', for to the minds of the faithful he is wholly beautiful. He is black, then, but beautiful: black in the opinion of Herod, beautiful in the testimony of the penitent thief, in the faith of the centurion.[76]

For St Bernard, this beauty is hidden and veiled by taking on itself our own ugliness and deformity, so as to free us from them. If this beauty is taken away, it is so as to restore to us our own beauty:

> that he who surpasses all mankind in beauty should be eclipsed by the darkness of the Passion for the enlightening of mankind; that he himself should suffer the ignominy of the cross, grow pale in death, be totally deprived of beauty and comeliness that he might gain the Church as a beautiful and comely bride, without stain and wrinkle.[77]

Light turns itself into darkness so as to illumine us, strength becomes weakness so as to make us strong, beauty makes itself ugliness so as to make us beautiful: such is the way this sermon of St Bernard develops. But this beauty hidden within its opposite is still being thought of as beauty, as the source of all authentic beauty and so it must be in some way accessible.

And it is accessible to listening, and not to sight. Referring to the centurion, the one later called St Longinus, St Bernard says that he:

> certainly perceived how great his beauty was . . . . For supposing he considered only what his eyes beheld, in what way was this man beautiful, how was he the Son of God? What did the eyes of the beholders see but a man deformed and black . . . . How then did the centurion see the beauty of the Crucified? . . . It was the sound of his voice that inspired his belief, it was by the voice that he recognized the Son of God, and not by the face. . . . The hearing succeeded where the sight failed.[78]

It is not for St Bernard a matter of merely contrasting listening and sight, for anyone who has heard, listened, listened to the unheard-of, will also be given the ability to see – to see the unimaginable.

What is decisive here, in this beauty that we hear and that we welcome within ourselves without seeing, is its character as an event and an advent. Anyone who sees this beauty does not remain untouched by it but is radically transformed and renewed by it. And the very act whereby he discovers this beauty against all appearance is inseparable from the act whereby he himself, against all expectation, becomes beautiful. It starts to give him a form and to reform him wherever he has welcomed its form into himself. What we have here is a beauty that does not keep itself to itself, but gives itself: it is impossible to distinguish in time between the moment when it is grasped and the moment when it gives itself, in other words embellishes us. This is its way of saying goodbye.

On this level, an unusual but deeply meaningful possibility is repeatedly encountered in the history of painting: that of painting one's self-portrait as Christ. The painter offers Christ his own features, which does not mean that he takes himself for God made man, but that he allows the latter, of whom we have no portrait, to dwell in his face, limn his own countenance. The most splendid and famous is the *Self-portrait* of Dürer, in 1500.[79] In it, Dürer follows the iconographic type of the *Salvator mundi*, and represents himself full face and frontally, in a gesture of blessing. 'It is undeniable,' says Panofsky, 'that Dürer deliberately sought a stylisation of his features in the image of those traditionally attributed to Christ.'[80] But Dürer is, all the same, perfectly recognizable, if we compare this work with other self-portraits.

Werner Beierwaltes, without claiming to find any certain historical correlation, has drawn a parallel between the spiritual horizons of this work by Dürer and the thought of Nicolas of Cusa, especially as it is found in his *De visione Dei*.[81] Even as a mere possibility, this confrontation is powerfully revelatory. For Nicolas of Cusa, the face of Christ is, indeed, 'the truth of all faces':

> Thus I understand that your face, Lord, comes before all faces that can be formed, that it is the model and truth of all faces, and that all faces are images of your irreducible face, which participates in no other. Every face which can gaze into yours thus sees no otherness, no difference from itself, because it sees its own truth.'[82]

We see ourselves, in truth, in Christ. But gazing towards Christ and allowing him to gaze at us, with that creative gaze that, literally, envisages us, we do not thereby become identical copies of the same empirical face: far from it. Nicolas of Cusa emphasizes the fact:

> O Lord, how admirable is your face which takes a young form in the imagination of a young man, an adult form for a man and an aged one for an old man! Who could conceive this the single model for all faces, the truest and most accurate for every face in particular and for all of them at once, so perfect that it seems to represent nothing other than each one of them?[83]

This living exchange clears of any suspicion of narcissism a self-portrait such as that of Dürer, which is none other than the self-portrait of an image of Christ, that image that we are all called upon to be, according to the Christian faith. 'If I must love myself in you through my resemblance to you, I am all the more strongly bound to do so when I see that you love me as your creature and your image', says Nicolas of Cusa.[84] Dürer's example is far from being unique. In a more pathetic and immeasurably less vivid way, the English painter Samuel Palmer, in 1833, also painted his self-portrait as Christ.[85] And Van Gogh, in 1889, when he did two copies of Eugène Delacroix's *Descent from the Cross*,[86] gives his own features to the dead Christ,[87] as he does for Lazarus when he copies a resurrection by Rembrandt in 1890. It is dizzying, of course – the possibility of doing one's own self-portrait as a dead man, or as if one were dead, even if this dead man is to rise again.

At all events, in these works, painters say adieu twice over: by the religious and, as it were, prayerful character of these paintings, and also by the act of offering their own features so that Christ may come and transfigure them and bring them into conformity with himself. They do not paint icons, they offer their faces so that they may become, really or potentially, icons. To the invisible they hand over the obolus of their own visibility. These dimensions often disconcert and embarrass art historians, who present what amount to excuses for something that seems to them to verge on blasphemy or megalomania. They thus completely fail to see their meaning and scope. To see, or try to see, Christ means, first and foremost, welcoming, one way or another, his face into ours, allowing it to work on ours. This vision is not a spectacle. It is transformative, and it transforms us in our inter-relations with others. A beauty that says adieu does not leave us where we were.

That Christ's beauty is a message, that it summons us and passes on, lighting up every human face with a new light at once furtive and definitive, that it gives to the body and its dignity a status unheard of amongst the Gentiles – this is what iconoclasm forgets. The vision of this light calls for our response, an active response that sets us to work, for only in the way we perform our task is this light made more intense and deeper. The imperfection of this response does not relieve it of its irreplaceability: the two characteristics are interdependent, and relate to the excessive character that comes looking for us. It is not because no one can ever think, say or paint divine beauty in all its plenitude that we can avoid the task of praising it every way we can: quite the opposite is true – it is an essential aspect of its radiance that it demands our hands and voices.

Iconoclasm paradoxically rests on a maximalist attitude towards the image: by supposing that the image could or should be a reproduction and, as it were, a double of its model, take its place, replace it, it emphasizes, in a victory without either risk or glory (being analytically contained within its premisses) the impossible and sacrilegious character of making a portrait of God made man. But who has ever claimed to make such a portrait? The only people who believe in portraits of Christ are those who believe in miraculous images not made by human hands – which, precisely, is no concern of art. Christ in art does not have one face, he has a thousand, and these thousand faces, in their power to disquieten us, are not claiming to reproduce anything: they are one way among others of discerning, of trying to discern, the passage of the light of the Spirit on a human face, which is something we have to do just as much out in the streets. When these faces really speak, they presuppose – just think of Grünewald, Rembrandt, Rouault, and so many others – an attention of an almost prayerful kind to man's face. If there is a Christian art, it does not rest on the pride of claiming to represent God but on the humility that bears witness to the fact that no one can prescribe limits to what the human face can show, in its joy as in its suffering. The Spirit alone decides on its manifestations, as it decides on the extent to which they may go. No one owns the divinity of God in such a way as to assign to it its possible places of appearance or non-appearance.[88]

The question asked repeatedly by Christian conceptions of beauty is this one: if Christ makes all things new, does he not also make beauty new? If in him all the dimensions of the human condition die and are resurrected, must not beauty do likewise? If he recapitulates all things in himself so as to lead them to God, can the beauty of the world and that of man be excommunicated from this recapitulation? Is not this message, that things deliver to us and invite us to deliver in our turn, transfigured by the light of the resurrection? Where the divine summons sounds out in its definitive clarity, it is certainly not so as to silence the song of the world, reduce it to muteness, but to raise it up, bring it to a dawn of which it could have only an obscure presentiment. Malebranche says profoundly that through the incarnation, the Word 'simultaneously became united to the two substances, mind and body, of which the universe is composed, and . . . through this union He sanctified the whole of nature.'[89] This was also the view of St John of the Cross in the Spiritual Canticle:

> He quickly walked across
> These woods, and turning his face on them
> Enriched them again
> By imbuing them with his beauty.[90]

And St John goes on to explain his words thus: this transient communication of beauty, 'occurred when he made himself man, exalting him to a divine beauty, and in consequence all creatures in him, having united himself to the nature of all of them in man.' Thus it is that he 'left them entirely clothed in beauty and dignity'.

There is nothing so humble that it does not receive some of its radiance. What in English is called 'still life' and in French, misleadingly, *nature morte* ('dead nature'), shows how the most common and everyday things also have a share in this light of dawn, and thereby bear witness to the Spirit. If the body can be recognized as the temple of the Spirit, its dialogue with things does not fall outside that by which it is able to cry and sing adieu. What of beauty dies is what was mortal in it: its self-sufficiency, its autarchy, everything by which it might become an idol by ceasing to be an event and an advent. And what of it is resurrected lives with a life more intense than ever, with a beauty so beautiful that it surpasses all norms, codes, and canons.

Where the face of the Word has deprived itself of beauty, it is quite simply any human face that has become theophanic, a place in which the divine is made manifest. Where the Word has been made flesh, it is the flesh of every man that has been given the responsibility and the glory of bearing Spirit, and with it all the things that surround it, among which it dwells. Beauty is a way (*voie*) only when it is a voice (*voix*), when to see it is to hear it and to reply

109

to it by giving and showing oneself. And it is also then that it sends us out on our human tasks. But we must be wounded by it, we must pay with our own persons, be there as present and praising: so we must be the contrary of an aesthete. Yes, beauty can say adieu, but it says adieu only when we offer our own adieu, and all of our voice, so that beauty can break it, and make it all the surer for having been broken, and make it remain trembling, with the trembling of the person who knows that all the sonorities of the song of the world, without a single one being forgotten or left by the wayside, will have to be given by him, in the eternal dawn, to God, who alone made them arise from silence.

5

THE OFFERING OF THE WORLD

There are silent gifts. There are none that are mute. Speech alone opens the dimension of the gift, for without speech I could never be assured that something is being given, or that it is indeed to me that it is being given, or, by accepting it, take cognizance of the way that someone else has renounced it so that I can benefit from it. Every gift (*don*) is an abandonment (*abandon*), but not every abandonment is a gift, for if the gift has the irresistible and definitive character of abandonment, it requires a destination that the latter does not possess, and the humility of what can be accepted or refused. What I abandon becomes *res nullius*, and it is in so far as it no longer belongs to anyone that the first person to come along can seize on it and make it his own, as a piece of unclaimed property – which is not the same as having received it from someone. To be sure, there may be circumstances in which the speech that gives does not necessarily need to be proffered, but there is none in which we can be relieved of the obligation to listen to it, that is, to respond to it, and thus to thank the giver – or refuse the gift.

After all, a gift that imposes itself and to some degree forces a *yes* would not be a gift at all, having in fact foreclosed and silenced the *yes* that could respond to it, having spoken in the stead of the other to whom it is supposedly giving. It would thus have stolen the speech of the other, and spoken all alone. The fact that the gift requires speech means that it requires two speeches, the one that gives and the one that receives. For the gift begins only where it finishes, where it is received. What has not been received has not been given, merely abandoned. And this is equally true of the speech of the gift. This speech begins to speak truly when someone begins to reply to it, it begins by replying – as does all speech. The speech that gives and the speech that thanks are both obedient, in other words they are both listening out for something. A gift that does not listen to the person to whom it is giving would be a gift only by inadvertence: could anyone thank the 'giver' for it?

The speech that gives is already listening, and the speech that receives is still giving, for to thank is to register the fact that there has been a gift, and only the recipient can give to the giver the status of a giver. The Stoics saw and said this clearly. Seneca, in his treatise *De beneficiis*, which speaks in such detail about debt and exchange, because he is trying to think of a gift without debt, writes: 'This, in my opinion, is the least surprising or least incredible of the paradoxes of the Stoic school: that he who receives a benefit gladly has already returned it.'[1] The one who receives has thus already given his joy to be shared. At its very first instant, the gift already has a past, it has already circulated without our thought being able to arrest this circulation on the pretext of defining more closely what in fact it destroys.

The preceding considerations concern that form of the gift in which speech accompanies and, in truth, founds the transfer to another of some good that is not itself an act of speech. What would the situation be if speech never gave anything but itself? Would the giving and the gift, that which gives and that which is given, end up being confused, in a pure and transparent transitivity? The poem of Stéphane Mallarmé which he finally entitled 'Gift of the Poem' ['Don du poème'], after having borne several other titles, lends itself to a reflection on this possibility.[2] Of course, 'Gift of the Poem' gives a poem, the very same poem that it is. But as an earlier title, 'Dedication of the Nocturnal Poem' ['Dédicace du poëme nocturne'] shows, what it gives is not the same as what it is, it is offering another poem,[3] the 'Nocturnal poem', which is merely a 'relic', the 'horrible birth' of which it evokes. It is an aborted offspring of 'the blue, sterile solitude', which is offered to the mother so that she can 'welcome' and 'nourish' it. The completed poem that we have been given to read is the offering of an unfinished poem to a woman, someone quite different from us. And this offering is an offering that, far from satisfying, continues to make demands: the voice is proffered 'from lips that the air of the virgin azure starves'. So concludes the poem that had begun with the words 'I bring you.'

Far from being transparent, the gift is full of meanings that fly off at a tangent and dense ambiguities. Is it a bequest or a request? Is it gift or poison? What does it mean to welcome a 'horrible birth' and what Mallarmé calls in a letter a 'baneful scion'? This gift (before it bore this title) met with a reception in proportion to its strangeness, from Villiers de l'Isle-Adam – one that he describes in a letter, with the mixture of naive humour and grandiloquence characteristic of him. Roused to transports of enthusiasm by a nocturnal reading of this poem, he rose from his bed, got dressed and, having availed himself of a child's drum, recited it in his stairwell, accompanying each hemistich with 'a drum roll that imposed itself on the attention and gathered everyone onto the landing'. This way of making the inner silence in Mallarmé's poetry echo aloud is an unusual way of receiving it. But Villiers does not stop there: 'Out of modesty, I declared that the poem was by me, but that the drum rolls had been sent to me, *in musical notation*, by you.' In respect of which he adds that he will have to buy, ' for two francs, the silence of the cook', as she has discovered the 'deception'.

Is there not a certain truth hidden behind this scene, burlesque and out of place as it may seem? How can one avoid parodying a poem that parodies the gift? How can one fail to be jubilant at a poem that jubilantly recounts the drama of writing? And is it not equally true that a poem which is given away is one whose words can be appropriated by everyone, but that the author remains the one who has noted its silences, the silences that in one way or another we cause to echo? 'I wrote down silences and nights, I noted the inexpressible', said Rimbaud.[4] When speech gives itself because it sings itself and sings nothing other than itself, as the modern idea of 'writing' has it, this gift that it makes of itself is laden with a thousand ambiguities and rests first and foremost on the withdrawal of the world whose place it has taken, leaving us nowhere to dwell but a palace of mirrors or a library of Babel. The indefinitely parasitical muffled noise of 'intertextuality' has always imposed silence on any voice that might give or receive. Deprived of its own being, the anonymity of the 'text' listens to itself writing, merely signing itself, signifying itself, making itself insignificant, with all the greater obstinacy. The *translation* performed by all speech on other acts of speech, which it listens to even as it replies to them, constitutes a phenomenon of a different order,[5] which concepts such as those of 'textuality' make it their profession to fail to recognize.

If speech is really to give itself in what it gives, it must *give* – and not be the mere incantation of its reflexivity, drawing us into its vain crystal. And what could speech give if not the world? Such is, in the religious dimension, the intention of the 'Canticle of the Creatures' (to confer a generic scope to the Franciscan title), the intention of uttering a prayer of cosmic praise: *offering the world to God*. It is a matter of thinking through, on a Christian level, its conditions of possibility. This thinking may illuminate how things stand with speech and how things likewise stand with the world, the world that gives itself to speech, the world that gives itself through speech. But, even before we can study how this intention is realized, the question arises of knowing whether it has the least sense.

For a number of damaging objections, both philosophical and religious, seem to rule it out. Philosophical objections first of all: if it is true that every gift is sealed by words, the fact remains that whatever we give by means of it must one way or another belong to us, be ours – and what we are not and do not have cannot, it seems, be given by us. Is not giving *the world* by speech a merely magical operation, in which we grow intoxicated on our imaginary omnipotence? Where philosophy has dwelt on the possibility of giving what we do not have, as was the case with Plotinus, it was in a sense quite opposite to that intended here: the first principle, the Good, gives what it does not have in so far as it is radically transcendent to everything that it produces. That it gives what it does not have means that it is not anything that belongs to the world, or the worlds, of which it is the origin. It gives the world to the world without this gift being a communication, a sharing, a transmission of the principle, since the principle is nothing and has nothing. And this unique gift does not take place in speech but in silence: it is not, as in the Bible, a creating Word, nor indeed a creation. This possibility, where it was rigorously thought out, is distinguished from every human gift and cannot be transposed, even analogically, to man. If the intention to offer the world can have any meaning, two conditions would have to be met: it would have to be ours and our speech would *really* have to be able to give it – and this does not seem to be the case.

But – and this is a second philosophical objection – even supposing we can indeed offer the world, would this be an offering to its origin and its principle? Do not the task and the dignity of human beings consist, rather, in giving to each other this world as a place to live in? And is this gift not solely, or even principally, a speech of praise but a labour of transformation? Does not the real gift consist of constructing, each of us with the others and each of us for the others, a world fit to be our dwelling place, and devoting our works and days, our hands and our thoughts, to this task? And if we accept that this world comes from God, is this not the mission that he has assigned to us? Is not everything that diverts us from this task mere *Schwärmerei*, the product of an overheated imagination, distracted and distracting – something which, in singing all that lies beyond the human, would end up denying what is properly human? The word *ethical* comes from the Greek *èthos*, which first and foremost means abode and dwelling place. To make of the world an authentic dwelling place for mankind – is this not the first and last moral task? If the intention of offering the world to God is to have a meaning, this offering would itself need to be that which makes it inhabitable, and impels us to labour so as to make it such. And this seems to have no relation to praise, and the prayer of praise.

To these philosophical objections can be added religious objections, which overlap with them and reinforce them at the same time. The intention to render cosmic praise seems simultaneously vain and presumptuous. Vain, for the Lord of the world, who with his own word brought it forth from nothingness, and who is its omnipotent master, certainly has no need of us offering it to him – this seems obvious. Can we give someone that which already belongs to him, and is entirely his? When it comes to God, this belonging is more total and intimate than in any human example, since no creature can sustain itself in being for an instant without the Creator, whereas human works can, once they have been produced, subsist without their author. If anyone could offer the world, it would be God offering it to us, as he has done, so that we can live in it, rather than us offering it to its author. Furthermore, this intention seems to be presumptuous and steeped in pride, for we have enough to do, being responsible as we are for a task that requires our entire lives (that of converting ourselves, offering ourselves to God, knowing – and never ceasing to learn – about everything that within us resists this offering and rebels against it) without us having the arrogance to offer to him, to imagine we can offer him, anything other than ourselves, let alone the entire universe. The very thought seems derisory.

A full reply to these objections cannot come from rational argument, but from the very plenitude of the phenomenon constituted by prayer, which we have gradually to discover, with its conditions. The first of all praises is the praise that God himself utters at his creation. To this silent praise all human words of speech, whether profane or religious, will always be a reply. In the account of creation given in the first chapter of Genesis we see brought into play, so that the game of the world can be played, a word and a gaze – and they are inseparable. The creative word, which causes beings to arise from nothingness and constitutes the world by ordering it and differentiating it, and the gaze that God brings to bear on his creation as it springs forth from his word and stands before him: 'God saw that it was good', are repeated several times. The creative word is as such strictly incommunicable and cannot be shared: whatever human arrogance may have thought since the Renaissance, no human word can call what does not exist into being, it can only forget being so as to indulge more comfortably in the belief that it is conferring being. To name, to say, to gather, to promise: such is its *poetic* greatness, on a different level from that of creation. But while it is true that God's gaze, resting on his creation, is one that our own gaze can never coincide with, since the world is not our work, God's is nonetheless a gaze that in analogical fashion offers itself to sharing, which once and for all opens up the space in which will awaken our gaze, and the words in which we will express what we see.

The first exclamation that greeted the world was uttered silently by God who, as he looked on it, looked on it to look after it and keep it in safekeeping. His silence means that our words do not repeat it in the way one might copy a model. We are entirely responsible for taking the initiative for those words in which it is the world itself which for the first time each of us is *learning by heart* by becoming adepts of the one and only gay science. With regard to this gaze in Genesis, St Augustine wrote: 'God delighted in the thing made with the same benevolence that inspired him when he made it. For there are two aspects to God's love for the creature: he loves it so that it will exist and so that it will persist in being.'[6] This gaze, in his view, constitutes another act of the Creator, in which he blesses time, and all that unfolds in time, in 'the beauty throughout all ages' of the creature that from now on exists; it is not the gaze of a spectator, but a gaze which maintains and seeks to maintain, in all the ways it can be.[7] And we also can rejoice that the world is, and is such as God created it, we also, in our own way, can enter into this gaze, which can only be described as a gaze of praise.

To see that this is good can surely be nothing other than to praise what one sees by gazing at it. The fact that this praise is inseparable from a safeguard, a benevolence, a blessing of the time in which what we see is transformed and develops, teaches us exactly how urgently we are requested to praise. What would a praise be if it did not watch over what it praises, which would not keep vigil over it? All human praise for the world as God's work is inscribed and accomplished in this first gaze, this gaze that follows the behest of the Spirit, which does not show itself but shows other things. To evade praising the world, however imperfect our praise might be, would mean leaving, as it were, the divine gaze without reply and without a future, leaving God as the only one in the world who sees things, as if no mind could see in its turn what he himself sees and shows. God's gaze is always a word: it calls for a response, a sharing, even if the nature of this latter still remains to be defined.

It is not only the faith of the Bible that asserts that we are given the task in our words for responding to the world's beauty and taking responsibility for it. Nor is it a merely religious task. Jerusalem has its gratitude, but Athens has its gratitude too. It is called philosophy. The response that the philosopher makes to the world is to think out its order and beauty (this is part of the meaning of the Greek word *kosmos*). Of course, not all gratitude performs a task of philosophical thought, but all true labour of thought is an act of gratitude. Certainly, such thought does not have to express itself in pathetic exclamations or in sentimental outpourings, it comes into its own the more able it is to reach, as the ancient phrase taken from Philo puts it, a sober intoxication. 'The words *denken* and *danken*, to think and to thank, have, as Paul Celan was not the first to say, the same root in our language.'[8] These words are not Greek, but the idea itself is. In what way? In celebrated passages, Plato as well as Aristotle see in *thaumazein* the very origin of philosophy.[9] In contemporary translations, this word is sometimes rendered as 'to be astonished', which provides a pretext for holding forth about philosophical astonishment. But astonished merely means profound unsettling and shock, without showing what produced those effects, and one can also be astonished by evil and horror. *Thaumazein*, in this case, would be more accurately translated by 'to marvel' or 'wonder' (a *thauma* is a marvel or a wonder), or, as formerly, by 'to admire' (in the sense of 'to gaze in wonder at').

This admiration is desire, and Aristotle states that 'the object of wonder is an object of desire',[10] and 'scientific wisdom is the knowledge of many wonderful things'.[11] There is nothing neutral about this disposition (as if it was open as much to evil as to good): it is joyful, even if its joy includes the disquiet that is desirous of knowing how and why things are as we see them. Philosophy is a quest imbued with admiration, an inquisitive marvelling. And the principle *thauma*, for thought, is nothing other than the world itself. Philosophy as such does not pray, but it accomplishes, in its very own way, an exercise in admiring the world.

Commenting on Aristotle, St Thomas Aquinas writes:

> It is also by admiration that the philosophers themselves were led to philosophize. And because admiration stems from ignorance, it is clear that they are led to philosophize in order to overcome ignorance.[12]

The knowledge of the causes of what we were admiring suspends that first admiration, which is inseparable from ignorance. This is how numerous thinkers envisaged it. But this was not Aristotle's view. The treatise *Parts of Animals* asserts explicitly:

> Every realm of nature is marvellous (i.e. there resides in it something marvellous, *ti thaumaston*). For if some have no graces to charm the sense, yet nature, which fashioned them, gives amazing pleasure in their study to all who can trace links of causation, and are inclined to philosophy.[13]

Far from abolishing admiration, a knowledge of causes, the consideration of natural organization and purpose here constitute for Aristotle that which increases it and makes its joy deeper. A first admiration is abolished in a second admiration, one that is higher and more intense in that it can see more; it is like a second wind of thoughtful gratitude.

All too often, modern thought would unlearn gratitude by unlearning admiration. Thus Descartes, before the *Nil admirari* of Spinoza, wrote, in the *Treatise on the Passions*: 'But more often we wonder too much rather than too little, as when we are astonished in looking at things which merit little or no consideration. This may entirely prevent or pervert the use of reason.'[14] And if admiration may initially be useful, 'we must attempt to free ourselves from this inclination as much as possible'.[15] Malebranche was less reserved about admiration and its possible role, but he always allotted it (quite misleadingly) to the same domain as a psychophysiology of the passions. In the same century, St François de Sales, on the other hand, was able to let admiration shed its own light on things. He took over and developed the Greek idea that proclaimed that 'admiration caused philosophy and the attentive investigation of natural things', but admiration is not, for him, an astonishment that questions itself, it is the very joy of *théôria*: far from ending with knowledge, it *is* knowledge. He writes:

> Admiration arises in us when we encounter a new truth that we did not know or expect to know; and if to the new truth that we encounter are joined beauty and goodness, the admiration that results is delightful in the extreme.

Ignorance finishes with admiration, instead of giving rise to it. Admiration constitutes the very joy of discovery, a desire that is at once satisfied and forever being renewed. St François continues:

> The admiration of agreeable things attaches the mind strongly, like a glue, to the thing admired: as much by reason of the excellence of the beauty which it discerns in it as by reason of the newness of this excellence; the understanding cannot be sated with what it has not yet seen and which is so pleasant to see.[15]

The *gaudium de veritate*, joy at the truth, by which St Augustine had defined blessedness, is in a certain degree granted us in this life, in the form of admiration.

If St François de Sales insists on the insatiable character of admiration, he places it in relation with the unexpected newness of the truth that is disclosed to us. Kant, in several passages, later distinguished between astonishment (*Verwunderung*) and admiration (*Bewunderung*), using the differential criterion of newness: admiration persists and renews itself ceaselessly because it does not depend on the newness of what is affecting us, unlike astonishment. And we should also note that, for him, unlike the metaphysics of the seventeenth century, it is a matter of *affections*, and 'there is a specific distinction between *affections* and *passions*.'[16] Thus astonishment is 'the affection attending the representation of novelty exceeding expectation', whereas admiration is 'an astonishment which does not cease when the novelty wears off'.[17] Admiration remains open to the excess of what happens to it. And the third *Critique* goes on to propose these definitions, with regard to final purpose:

> *astonishment* is a shock that the mind receives from a representation and the rule given through it being incompatible with the mind's existing fund of root principles, and that accordingly makes one doubt one's own eyesight or question one's judgement; but *admiration* is an astonishment that keeps continually recurring despite the disappearance of this doubt.[18]

Even if Kant does not, for all that, make it into the principle of his philosophy, he confers on it a role in the constitution of Platonism.[19] And the *Anthropology from a Pragmatic Point of View* returns to this distinction, in reference to the sublime: admiration is 'a judgment in which one's astonishment is undiminished'.[20]

Developing these Kantian considerations with more indulgence than usual, Franz von Baader, in an essay just a few pages long, 'On the Affect of Admiration and Respect', writes:

> The knowing mind here reaches a source of knowledge, from which it can always draw, where it can always know anew, without ever exhausting the source; and after it has cut a path through to such a *principle* (from *incipere*, 'to begin again always anew'), it ceases, indeed, to be astonished, but it begins only then to admire the inexhaustibility of that source.[21]

Elsewhere, Baader, quoting Plato's *Thaeatetus*, claims that 'admiration is an affect of the intelligence',[22] and he reproaches Spinoza for having confused the affect of admiration, which lifts and liberates the mind, with that of stupefaction or blind stupor, which lowers it and weighs it down.[23] Baader thus clearly distinguishes between true admiration, which fortifies and activates the power of knowing, from just being dumbfounded (*Angaffen*), which arises from a lack of understanding and paralyses knowledge.[24]

These considerations on the *thaumazein* of philosophy, responding to the *thauma* of the world, to the marvel of marvels, shows that already in the natural order, man is, by and in thought, the one who praises the world, for, ever since Plato's *Symposium*,[25] every philosopher knows that the task of praise is nothing other than the patience of truth. To think is to thank, but for this to be true, to thank must be to think really and truly, in other words to see. Philosophical gratitude is in no way a prayerful gratitude and it is not to God that it proposes to offer the world, but that does not mean that it is parcimonious, for in thinking the world, it also offers it to us so that we may dwell in it with a clearer and freer gaze.

Remaining within the natural order, and referring first of all to profane cantatas, another dimension of human speech brings into play the possibility of offering the world. This is love poetry. This would soon have run out of things to say if it were reduced to repeating its declarations of love, drawing up the *blason* of the loved body and singing its beauty indefinitely. What gives it a broader scope and confers on it its resourcefulness and its capacity for renewal is the way it approaches the beloved, not in a vacuum but amid the far horizons of a world in perpetual influx. By singing the beloved, the lover allows himself to be summoned to all the beauty of the world, illumined and disclosed by love itself, and illumining it and disclosing it in return. The love song becomes the song of the world. Love shows the world and reveals it as a place where we could live in a different way. This is shown *a contrario* by the famous line by Lamartine, 'One single person absent from my side, and all is waste and void.' And it is not merely oneself but the whole world, in its splendour at once immemorial and sudden, that the lover would like to offer in speech to the beloved. *How* speech can assume such a function still needs to be determined, but it is clear that it never ceases to give itself this task and that it would lose its inspiration if it did not.

Charity does not form a prolongation of *érós* any more than the speech of prayer is an appendix to poetry: they are from radically different orders, and the difference concerns the very root of the acts. But, following the theological adage, grace does not come to abolish nature but to perfect it; and the lofty height and the freedom that charity takes and receives with respect to *érós* certainly do not mean that its speech is meaner, more skimpy, less generous with itself and with everything else. Quite the opposite: the illumining of the world, which belongs to poetry as a possibility, must belong, a fortiori, to the speech of prayer. If there is a profane song of the world, there must be a gracious canticle of the creatures, a place of prayerful speech on which converges the world's beauty. We cannot tear ourselves away from the world to offer ourselves to God: if this offering is possible, it will necessarily include all those far horizons from which alone we come into our own, just as immediately to set out again. To exist is to be outside.

This was how the young Teilhard de Chardin put it. 'We are more out of ourselves, so to speak, in time and space, than we are in ourselves, at the moment we are live: the person, the human *monad*, is like every monad *essentially cosmic*.'[26] If we could no longer speak of the world, we would no longer have anything to say, not even about ourselves, since, in describing our exhausted void, as so many people like to do, we are still speaking of the world, of the world's withdrawing. The Holy Bible itself speaks of God only by speaking of the world, of its creation, its history, the human beings who live in it, the animals, the rivers, the mountains and the deserts, the winds and the bushes, of God giving the world and giving himself for the salvation of the world.

All these considerations already cast light on the over-hasty and fallacious character of the damaging objections laid at the door of the intention of offering the world to God in speech. The fact remains that there is an essential difference between giving thanks for the world, by attention, by admiration, by song, of whatever kind they may be, and the *offering* of the world: how can I offer that which I have only received, that in which I am received, that by which I never cease to receive myself? And the fact remains, too, that there is another essential difference between the way speech can only ever sing of the world, or the things of the world, and the intention that speech should be the place where the world returns to God. For speech to offer the world, it must not merely belong to the world, but also and above all, the world must belong to it and gather itself together as world within it. And speech must also, in giving itself, give the world.

To see more clearly what is implied by these demands, and whether they can be met, we must listen to the thinkers who examined what praise means. Philo did this as profoundly as anyone. An admirable passage in his treatise *De plantatione*[27] needs to be read attentively, forming as it does one of the summits of his eucharistic thought, in other words the action of thanksgiving, which is the meaning of the Greek word *eukharistia*. To the generosity and beneficence of God, says Philo, the *eukharistia* of man can and must respond. This gratitude forms the most essential and highest possibility of man. Man is before God, through his speech, a being of hymns and praises. 'Each of the virtues is a holy matter, but thanksgiving is pre-eminently so.' The highest of all duties, and the one that alone is valid as a response to God, to his work and his gifts, has the very same affirmative gratuitous and spontaneous quality of praise that gives thanks. A *thank you* that we wrest violently from ourselves, that is conquered by sheer force, that is uttered simply because we ought to utter it – would such a *thank you* still be eucharistic? The negation of that which within us denies, the no to what says no, will never enable the day of yes to break. That our *yes* to God for the world is for Philo the very hyperbole of virtue (the Greek text has *huperballontôs*), and that the highest summit is reached when on it one can joyfully turn to what is even higher, make of the only Jewish philosopher of antiquity whose works have been preserved a great thinker of the gay science.

But how are we to give thanks? Not, says Philo,

> by means of buildings and oblations and sacrifices, as is the custom of most people, for even the whole world were not a temple adequate to yield the honour due to Him. Nay, it must be expressed by means of hymns of praise, and these not such as the audible voice shall sing, but strains raised and re-echoed by the mind too pure for eye to discern.

These first statements cannot be understood in isolation. If Philo seems to begin by ruling out the voice, preferring a purely spiritual song, a silent act of the mind, as Richard Rolle was later to do in the Christian Middle Ages,[28] this is to exclude a hymn that would be a purely external labour and task, which we would carry out as mere lip service. The hymn must be heartfelt, it must spring from the depths of the heart. But it does want eventually to burst forth and make itself manifest, and, at the end of this passage, Philo goes on to say explicitly that our praise must pass 'through all the expressions of the voice which have fallen to speech and song'.[29]

That the world itself cannot be a temple worthy of God, on the other hand, marks a difference from pagan ideas, and underlines a fortiori that nothing of what we can do with our hands will ever be sufficient for the eucharist. But this eucharist will in no way be acosmic: it is indeed in singing the world that we give thanks to God. The world will be the very material of our eucharist as it sounds forth. And it will itself be honoured by our song as will its creator.

After these considerations, Philo adapts to his own use an old pagan story. When the world was finished, God asked an angel if there was any creature missing.

> He, it is said, made answer that all were perfect and complete in all their parts, and that he was looking for one thing only, namely the word to sound their praises, which should make the surpassing excellence that marked even the most minute and inconspicuous among them the subject of announcement rather than of praise, seeing that the mere recounting of the works of God was in itself their all-sufficient praise.

As with the Socrates of the *Symposium*, the eulogy takes as its yardstick nothing other than truth. And Philo continues: 'the Author of the universe on hearing this commended what had been said, and . . . it was not long before there appeared the new birth, the family of the Muses and hymnody', sprung from the womb of Memory, *Mnèmè* or *Mnèmosunè*.

As long as the speech that sings the world is absent from the world, the world lacks nothing and everything. It lacks nothing, for the very terms employed by Philo bring out how the unsung world is not in the least an unfinished, incomplete world, in which there are empty spaces or lacunae that need to be filled belatedly. The word is not some extra item in the world, as if it added something to it, as if it conferred on it a supplementary perfection, as if in creating it God were putting the final touches to his work. Nothing is added to the world by the speech that magnifies it, and speech does not form a new world. And yet, everything is changed by the speech that expresses the totality: the world really does become a world when it comes into the light of speech. It is the same, unique world that is made new by having someone to recite its qualities. Song adds nothing and, if one may borrow an expression from colloquial language, it does not hype it up. It has the sobriety of the clear-eyed gaze. But the totality shines as a totality, sends itself and addresses itself as totality, when it has a witness to welcome and receive it in his song.

Naturally, the speech of praise can be such only when it is a speech of truth. But here we need to turn the Platonic idea round: when it comes to the works of God, the speech of truth can only be such when it is a speech of gratitude. The gaze must be clear-eyed, and the eucharist does not constitute an intermission of enthusiasm slipping in between our other tasks, but this clarity is joy and praise, for otherwise a shadow would dwell within its heart. The very drift of the story, in any case, confirms this: before praise comes into being, and when he resolves to bring it into being, God 'commends' or 'praises' the speech that proclaims praise necessary. It is always praise that calls for praise, in an affirmation that is always being repeated and deepened. Every *yes* is in full spate. God sings that song that will be. And he already remembers Mnemosyne, before she comes into the world, he remembers memory itself. He promises memory.

And so Philo concludes:

> The work most appropriate to God is conferring boons (*euergetein*), that most fitting to creation giving thanks (*eukharistein*), seeing that it has no power to render in return anything beyond this; for, whatever else it may have thought of giving in requital, this it will find to be the property of the Maker of all things, and not of the being that brings it. Having learned, then, that, in all that has to do with shewing honour to God, one work only is incumbent upon us, namely thanksgiving, let us always and everywhere make this our study, using voice and skilful pen.

Nothing before God belongs to us as our own, if not our ability to say *thank you*. What may appear as the most tenuous, the most slender of all possibilities is in truth the highest and most extensive: the praise that *responds* to the divine giving is the essence of human speech. It is in speech that the gift is received, and that we can give something of our own, in other words ourselves. The speech most proper to man is thus the speech which is turned to the other, given to the other, a speech of transmigration that crosses boundaries, a speech that is eccentric. What belongs to us is the possibility of uttering a speech that ceases to belong to itself. It is, like love, irreplaceable, and nothing can stand in for it; no other work can replace this speech, and nobody can replace us in this speech. Anyone who asked another to love in his place would not love. Anyone who asked another to give thanks in his place would not be giving thanks. This speech has the strength of its weakness, for the voice that praises always has something tremulous about it, knowing at one and the same time that it cannot be enough and yet that nothing other than it *can* be enough.

Other treatises by Philo point out that this human eucharist forms the place of a veritable cosmic liturgy. We give thanks *for* the world in the twofold sense of the word *for*: we sing of the beauty of the world, and we sing on its behalf of what it cannot itself say. The human voice is that by which the world offers itself to God. Philo sets out these ideas with special reference to the costume of the high priest: by its different elements, this costume symbolizes the world: '[The Law] expresses the wish first that the high priest should have in evidence upon him an image of the All . . . (so) that in performing his holy office he should have the whole universe as his fellow-ministrant (*sulleitourgèi*)'.[30] Having described in detail the meaning of these vestments, another treatise concludes:

> Thus is the high priest arrayed when he sets forth to his holy duties, in order that when he enters to offer the ancestral prayers and sacrifices there may enter with him the whole universe, as signified in the types of it which he brings upon his person . . . . For, as he wears a vesture which represents the world, his first duty is to carry the pattern enshrined in his heart, and so be in a sense transformed from a man into the nature of the world; and, if one may dare say so . . . be himself a little world, a microcosm (*brakhus kosmos*).[31]

The theme of man as a microcosm here ends up taking on a liturgical function: we offer the world in offering ourselves. The world becomes a priest when the priest becomes a world. This eucharist of the world itself is something that Philo sees as symbolized by the sacred perfumes that are consumed:

> Surely it is a fitting life-work for the world, that it should give thanks to its Maker continuously and without ceasing, wellnigh evaporating itself into a single elemental form, to shew that it hoards nothing as treasure, but dedicates its whole being at the shrine of God its Begetter.[32]

But only man can compose and burn these perfumes in which the world offers itself and breathes out, and his voice alone forms the true perfume, since it is that voice that releases its odour. If the tunic of the high priest mirrors the sky, it is, says Philo, so that 'the universe may join with man in the holy rites (*suniérourgèi*) and man with the universe'.[33] The world concelebrates with us.

Christian thought would take up and develop these themes. As for Philo, the idea of man as microcosm, as the epitome of the world, an idea so rich in scope and with multiple meanings,[34] can become the foundation of a cosmic liturgy. Man can, in his song, offer the world to God because his own song can be the very song of the world, in the 'subjective' as much as the 'objective' sense of the word 'of'. A vivid and powerful passage by Cardinal de Bérulle dwells on this possibility. His definition of man here depends on the adaptation of the myth of Epimetheus by Pico della Mirandola, in his discourse *On the Dignity of Man*. Man is created by God after all other beings, and there is, so to speak, no other model to follow in making him. 'The perfect craftsman,' writes Pico della Mirandola, 'finally decided that to man, who he could present with nothing that would be proper to him alone, would be common that which had been proper to every creature.'[35] Thus it is that man is 'every creature',[36] and Pico assigns to him the task of admiring and praising the perfection of the world as a divine work.[37] Pierre de Bérulle explicitly takes up these thoughts. 'Having no distinct and particular place to give him in his works, since he was created after all his other works, he found a place for him in the heights of his wisdom, and gave him a being which participates in all his works, and communicates with all his works.'[38] This participation in everything in the world makes man 'as it were a centre of the world', in which all its radii converge and meet.

He is not merely a little world, but 'as it were a God visible on the earth, paying homage to the invisible God, and relating himself and all that is created to God.' Man, Bérulle continues, is 'so to speak the soul and intelligence of the universe: *Mens universi.*' In man, considered in all the dimensions of his being, it is the whole world that opens up to the possibility of God and offering itself to him. He is the centre, where all turns back to God. He who 'looks on everything' can bring it about that the whole universe looks on God. This really is a cosmic liturgy. His work is to relate everything to God:

> his mind being the mind of the universe, to know God and adore him; and his tongue, the tongue of the universe to praise him, and his heart, the heart of the universe to love him; God wishing to receive praise from his creature, a praise and a knowledge that is at once sensible and spiritual, just as he had endowed it with a being that is at once spiritual and sensible.

A rigorous foundation is thereby given to the prayer of praise: it is not a gloss on the world, an admiring exclamation added to it, it is the decisive place in which the silence of the world is broken in our voice, which delivers it and transfigures it in song, making manifest in this silence the obscure advent of our psalms. But, in this obscure advent, these psalms will have drawn the breath of inspiration. The fact that not only our minds, but our tongues and voices too, are required, also shows the irreducibly human character of this task. The angels lack a body, and so cannot make an offering of the body of the world when they offer themselves. Jean-Jacques Olier, another great figure of French spirituality, took up such thoughts from a Christological point of view. The divine Word cannot adore the Father whose equal he is – for to adore presupposes 'worship that involves respect and religion, which requires inequality and dependency' –

he seeks the means to do it and finds it in his humanity. It is in this humanity that he praises God; it is also in this humanity that every creature adores him, because the entire creation is included in man, which would not have been the case if he had taken on an angelic nature, which does not contain within itself, as does that of man, the full diversity of created beings.

And Olier goes as far as to write, thereby inverting the theme of the microcosm, that 'the world is the supplement of man, and the creatures in it are like the limbs that enable him to subsist.'[39] The world is associated with man's fall as well as with his salvation. With our voice the world grows brighter or darker.

However fine and strong this tradition of thought may be, taking it into consideration must not however lead us to yoke inseparably together the indefeasible religious task of a cosmic liturgy on the one hand, and the acceptance of a well-defined philosophical anthropology, that of man as microcosm, on the other. This anthropology constitutes merely *one* of the ways of founding the possibility of a prayer of praise offering the world to God. It is not necessary for man to be a summary or epitome of the world, even in his body, for him to be able to sing it. The vacuity of the voice, open to all things, may be sufficient. The profound idea of Aristotle, developed by St Thomas Aquinas, which claims that the human soul is in a certain way all beings, as it can, through sensible as well as intellectual knowledge, become all of them (a thought in which Heidegger saw an anticipation of what he called *Dasein*), may serve to establish this possibility with a rigour no less, and indeed even greater.[40] Furthermore, Pico della Mirandola and Pierre de Bérulle also signal that such a direction might be followed when they insist, in their interpretation of the myth of Epimetheus, on the fact that man can participate in all other natures because he has in himself no particular and definite nature.

We need now to dwell on an important passage in the *City of God* by St Augustine, which clearly brings out an essential characteristic of the *act* of praise. For it is not enough to reflect on the conditions it must fulfil if it is to be possible: we should also consider what it actually does, and what in our existence it can transform or transfigure when it takes place. It is in its last words that this passage is relevant to our present purposes. But their persuasiveness becomes intelligible only when seen as part of the whole movement of thought, of which it constitutes, as it were, the *Aufhebung* which surpasses, suppresses and maintains at one and the same time. St Augustine first of all develops a central theme of his reflections, a theme that would meet with a wealth of developments in the Middle Ages, and is prominent also in the *De Genesi ad litteram*: the distinction between the knowledge of things in the creative Word, which contains their models, ideas, and archetypes, and the knowledge of things in themselves once they have been created. Here we encounter a contrast between the way things are known in the morning and the way they are known at night, between the knowledge of things in the divine *art* that creates them, and the knowledge of the works actually produced by this art. The whole passage is built up on the basis of an antithesis between these two kinds of knowledge, between their respective natures, modes and perfection. And to sing the praises of the angelic contemplation associated with morning at first seems like an evasion of our condition as men who always think and speak in the evening, as Hegel would later say of philosophy. But St Augustine concludes with a perfect description of what praise can be: 'Yet when all these works are referred to the praise and worship of the Creator, then there is the light as of morning sunshine in the minds of those who contemplate them (*tamquam mane lucescit in mentibus contemplantium*).'[41]

So the speech of praise, considered as an offering and a thank-offering, does not allow morning and evening to remain exterior to one another, in a state of mutual indifference. It leads the evening back to morning, and brings it about that the evening is a remembrance and a sign of the morning. And this is not just a simple relation that would relate the effect back to the cause and what is derivative back to what is original: it does not simply trace the sign back to the signified. Bringing the evening back to the morning, in other terms the creature to its Creator, *itself becomes an activity of the morning*. Morning breaks in the very evening. It is not a matter of denying or abandoning the evening, in other words the existence of creatures according to their own mode of being. If it praises, the evening song becomes a song of dawn, and makes the person who sings it a creature of the morning. This paradoxical morning is of great significance if we are to understand praise. As Philo had already shown, it thereby adds nothing to the world, it merely says it and also says its origin, the origin to which it brings it back as it sings. It also brings it to its truth *by bringing itself to the truth*. Praise makes itself an activity of the morning without ceasing to be an activity of the evening too. In other words, it does not presuppose that we transform ourselves into pure spirits, that we forget or lose from sight the limits of the human condition and of human speech – something that is never without great danger; it also discloses its powers to us. This suppresses everything unilateral and abstract that there might have been in the mere antithesis of the two ways of knowing: that of the morning and that of the evening.

The possibility of offering the world to God, in praise, involves another requirement, no less essential, on the part of the world itself. I cannot offer a thing unless it lends itself to being offered, and I cannot offer it in speech and through speech unless it lends itself to being offered in this way. These propositions seem at first sight useless banalities, since everyone knows that singing the praises of bread has never fed the hungry, and can indeed only make their hunger worse. But these propositions are, nonetheless, decisive, for the offering requires that its 'matter' be appropriate to the gift. Nobody has ever *given* themselves death, as in suicide, or *given* death to another, which is another euphemism for murder. Only life can be given, and, in sacrifice, it is life which is given, without return. For the world to be offered in speech, not only must its beauty and its perfection render it worthy of being offered, but it must also in some measure ask to be borne into the light of the voice. Only that which already sings, in whatever way it might be, can be offered in song. It must be the mute speech of the world, awaiting its utterance, that our speech delivers.

Holy Scripture explicitly and repeatedly expresses the reality of this condition. It may be in the mode of invitation – the meaning of which will be discussed later on – but also in that of affirmation:[42] 'The heavens declare the glory of God.'[43] 'All your creatures shall thank you, Yahweh.'[44] In his *Old Testament Theology*, Gerhard van Rad comments on these verses:

> Since it [the world] was so wonderfully created by Jahweh and is so wonderfully preserved, it has a splendour of its own, from which praise and witness issue: in other words the world is not only an object which calls forth praise, but is at the same time also the subject which utters it.[45]

And in another of his works, he says:

> We encounter the idea that the world is not dumb, that it has a message, in the hymn. The world proclaims itself before God as a created thing; the heavens 'tell', the firmament 'proclaims' . . . This speaking by part of creation appears here as an accompaniment to the divine self-revelation. But it is improbable that the heavens were empowered as witnesses only in the context of this occurrence and that they were previously dumb.[46]

Another psalm sings: 'Let the sea thunder, and all that it holds, the world and all who live in it. Let the rivers clap their hands, and the mountains shout for joy together.'[47] Or again, in the canticle of David: 'Let the countryside exult, and all that is in it, and all the trees of the forest cry out for joy.'[48] All these utterances are perfectly clear, and only those people who, being deaf, cannot themselves hear what they say, think they can get rid of them by asserting that they are 'poetic', as if this relieved them of enquiring into the rigour of their meaning. The theological controversies between Protestants and Catholics on the possibility of a natural knowledge of God have, in any case, obscured rather than illuminated the scope of these words, for they are then used in an argumentative and quibbling way, instead of taking into account the phenomenon of this mute voice of nature as such.

The world itself is heavy with speech, it calls on speech and on our speech in response, and it calls only by responding itself, already, to the Speech that created it. How could it be foreign to the word, when it subsists, through faith, only by the Word? It is not a matter first and foremost of knowing if nature 'proves' or 'does not prove' the existence of God, but of being able to listen to its silence as a 'visible voice', as St Augustine did.[49] The speech we utter about the world does not come from beyond the world, it is no more a stranger to the world than we are. And what this speech sets out to do is not to impose on it from the outside, through our own initiative, an arbitrary meaning: it wants to make the meaning of which it is itself the bearer ring out, a meaning that it cannot without our aid bring to its conclusion. To sing the world is to try and concentrate its profuse and confused choir in the tremulous clarity of our human voice. If this were not the case, the offering of the world through speech would merely form a simulacrum and a dream. When St Augustine, in Book X of the *Confessions*, questions the elements and the creatures of nature, he is clearly taking up themes from the book of Job: 'You have only to ask the cattle, for them to instruct you, and the birds of the sky, for them to inform you.'[50] This is not, of course, some puerile animism, for only a being of speech can listen to nature in this way. By questioning it, he is already responding to it and taking responsibility for it.

Listening in this way is by no means exclusively religious, even if the intention of offering the world to God is religious by definition. Lyrical poetry as a whole wants to give voice to what it hears of the world, and translates its immemorial odes in an antiphonal fashion. Thus Baudelaire, in his sonnet 'Correspondences',[51] refers to the 'confused words' of Nature. These words are the words the poet translates and restates – for it is only when they are restated that they are really and truly said. But this confusion, far from forming an unintelligible disorder, is the polyphonic richness of what never ceases to echo in response from one order to another within the world's unity. It is confused only in the same way as

Long echoes which merge together from afar.

The world sings man before man sings the world, and so that he may sing it. This is why Baudelaire can say that certain perfumes 'sing the transports of the mind and the senses', and that the 'forests of symbols . . . observe us with knowing gazes', in a complicity for which we have not taken the initiative.

A few years earlier, Victor Hugo, launching out on his song of apocatastasis[52] like a hymn, in the *Contemplations*, with 'What the Mouth of Shadow says', had written:

> No, all is a voice and all a perfume;
> Everything says, in the infinite, something to someone;
> A thought fills the superb tumult.
> God has not made a sound without infusing it with the Word.
> Everything, just like you, groans, or sings like me;
> Everything speaks.[53]

This visionary song, with its gnostic and manichean accents (nobody has expressed more eloquently than Hugo the suffering of light imprisoned in matter), is an appeal for compassion – compassion for all that lives, in other words, everything, even inanimate, for 'everything is full of souls'[54] – and an appeal for the redemption and deliverance of all things. For Baudelaire, in 'The Lighthouses', art is 'the ardent sob which rolls from age to age', but for Hugo, it is the whole world that sings and never ceases to sing a threnody:

> The wind groans, the night complains, the water laments,
> And, under the eye which, filled with tenderness, gazes down from above,
> The whole abyss is no more than a huge sob.[55]

God sees the 'huge vastness mounting towards him, stammering its praise'.[56] Here the world offers itself to God, or tries to do so, in a prayer of supplication.

This is a vast gnostic variation on the Christian theme of the suffering of creation: 'We are well aware that the whole creation, until this time, has been groaning in labour pains.'[57] For the act of breaking away from Christianity does not open up new and unprecedented possibilities of existence and thought, but in one way or another leads to a relapse into old-fashioned ideas that Christianity had closed off – in this case, gnosticism.

Hugo's broad strains in various ways interlace summons and response; the poet is supposed merely to be restating a revelatory speech addressed to him, which calls on him to listen to the speech of things, their cries and whispers, and to pray for them. But it is the whole world that brings its songs of suffering and hope converging on the hymn. It is a cosmic listening, right up to the final phrase, the last word of this long poem: 'an angel will cry: Beginning!' [58]

With a quite different poetic intention from that of Victor Hugo, Francis Ponge, in his *Proëmes*, also invites us to exercise that 'occupation which is at every instant reserved to man', and reserved to him alone, 'the-gaze-as-it-is-spoken', which is of course a listening that responds.[59] This gaze, he continues, leads us to recognize 'immediately the importance of each thing, and the mute supplication, the mute demands they make to be spoken, at their true worth, and for themselves – irrespective of their usual value of significance – without choice and yet in measured tones, but measured by their own standards.' This demand is an indication of the scope of Ponge's work, and his *Le Parti pris des choses* [*Taking The Side Of Things*] is nothing other than a series of eulogies, all the more Socratic in that they form merely an attempt at description, in league with the mobility or immobility of things. Here too, our speech is antiphonal, responds by listening, listens by responding, by translating the silence.

In a voice that is, admittedly, less self-assured, Guillevic, in his poem *Le chant* [*The Song*], listens in laconic words to the hymn of all things. Across the silence of the world, 'Mount towards the one/ Who listens to them/ Milliards of songs/ Which in the end/ Find in him/ A point of convergence.'[60] He evokes, over a landscape, 'A total silence/ Amounting to an appeal – / And you would like/ To transmute it into song'[61] – a transmutation already under way by the very uttering of this wish, since the poem is already responding to the appeal that it names. There is no need to quote any further examples. Poetic speech is an attempt to gather within itself and give voice to the word scattered in and among things. It wants to be, in the expression of Henri Maldiney, 'the legacy of things', a legacy that is not at all in mourning but opens up to the future, full of promise. The poet wants the world to concelebrate its praise with him, and he with the world. In this multiple *yes,* which the world bears in it and which we bring to song, men offer the world to each other, make it inhabitable. For a world without poetry is uninhabitable.

Questions such as this are at the heart of the poetry and the thought of Paul Claudel. For him, it is a matter of bringing it about that 'the whole of creation can enter the ark, as did Noah of old.'[62] What ark, if not that of speech? Our hymn is a supplement to the hymn of things, it stands in for it; it is for them too that we speak. Evoking the earth, Claudel addresses God in these terms: 'Deliver the earth, through my mouth, of the praise it owes to You',[63] and elsewhere he affirms of the liturgy: 'The Office said by a priest is the duty of the whole of nature/ He pays off the homage owed by the Creation.'[64] He wants to 'speak, in continuity with every mute thing', and make 'a poem which will no longer be Ulysses among the Lestrygonians and the Cyclops, but the knowledge of the whole Earth'.[65] For our integrity does not reside in breaking away from the world, but in our community and our communion with it.

> I am not whole and entire unless I am whole and entire with this world that surrounds me. It is me in my entirety that you require! It is the world in its entirety that you require from me.[66]

This possibility of welcoming things into our song cannot rest on violence or disrespect. It presupposes a dialogue with things – a dialogue that our kinship renders fraternal. 'Let me see and hear all things with speech/ And greet each one by its own name together with the speech that made it.'[67] Things must offer themselves to us so that we may in turn offer them by offering ourselves, and both of these offerings will be made possible by speech: 'Created speech is that in which all created things are made such that they can be given to man.'[68]

We are being invited to understand what things mean, what they 'want to say': each creature, says Claudel, 'comes towards us with its name: it gives us its name so that we may use it. Each creature tells us that it is, and that it is for and through something other than itself.'[69] This is how Claudel interprets the praise that created beings other than man are enjoined, by Holy Scripture, to sing. 'How could they praise Him otherwise than by existing in relation to Him? What other means do they have available?' It is thus by manifesting and signifying God that they praise him. They 'carry out His word . . ., perform His will: the expression of God, the act of God, the language of God are his creatures. Such is His first Revelation.'[70] They are not asked to voice a speech that they do not have, or that they obtain only from us, but to exercise the gift of speech that they have always already received. This speech provokes and calls to ours to respond. We cannot sing the world unless the world itself sings already. But even a detailed enumeration of things does not make a world. It is by being sung that the world is properly a world, grasped in its unity. 'The world ceases to be a scattered vocabulary, it has become a poem, it has a meaning, it has an order . . . .. We have our place and our role within it. We are associated with a liturgy.'[71]

This elucidation of the world, of the poem of the world, takes place for Claudel in a mutual cross-reference from visible to invisible and vice versa. The visible leads to the invisible, but, he says, 'more often, from the love and the knowledge of invisible things we are induced to know and to love visible things.'[72] This cross-reference makes the song and the light grow and increase. The visible is not merely a path towards the invisible: if it leads to it, it returns from it clarified and enriched, and not destroyed. Even before the medieval theme of the two books, nature and Scripture, this interlacing has theological precedents, of which Claudel was probably unaware – namely the thought, both profound and difficult, of St Maximus the Confessor. Hans Urs von Balthasar, in the fundamental book he devoted to the saint, himself draws the comparison with Claudel.[73]

For St Maximus, God transcends the spiritual as much as he transcends the material, and the invisible as much as the visible. Having emphasized the transcendence of God over *every* creature, 'the more the mind's hope of reaching him by climbing the degrees of cosmic being, the more the world too must close itself in on itself so as to become in its totality, and no longer merely in its most elevated parts, a place of praise and service of the Infinite', writes von Balthasar.[74] The seventh chapter of the *Mystagogics*[75] renews the theme of man as microcosm: the world can call itself man just as much as man can call himself world. Man is not the soul, as in the *Alcibiades* of Plato, he is composed of body and soul, and subsists only as the unity of the two: in the same way, the world, which is only ever *one single* world, is composed of sensible and intelligible aspects. The sensible and the intelligible world are not mutually exclusive, they envelop one another, so as to comprise *the* world. 'The soul of the sensibles is the intelligibles, and the body of the intelligibles is the sensibles.' This is the basis of the 'cosmic liturgy', powerfully organized around a Christological and eucharistic axis (the *Mystagogics* is indeed nothing other than a meditation on the Christian eucharist).

As Alain Riou writes with regard to St Maximus, 'man is thus destined, not to melt into a sacralized nature and lose his personality in a divine impersonality . . ., but on the contrary to bring the universe to its consummation by love.'[76] St Maximus hopes and waits for an ultimate 'Easter of the world':

> The world of visible things, such as man, will die and be resurrected, once again as new as once it had been old . . .. Then the man who is in accordance with us (i.e., the man that we are, as opposed to the world as man) will rise again with the world like the part with the whole and the little with the big, having received the potential to be incorruptible.[77]

The cosmic liturgy, in which we offer, on the altar of ourselves, the world to God, thus has an eschatological future. It is in conformity with a religion of incarnation, of which Maximus truly was the confessor – to the extent of suffering the martyrdom proper to a thinker of praise: having his tongue torn out – not to privilege the movement by which the visible, like a path, leads to the invisible, but the gift of light from one to the other, visible and invisible 'making each other mutually manifest' (*allèllôn dèlôtika*), as Claudel later repeated.

The world is for St Maximus, writes von Balthasar, 'the mirror of God in so far as in his inner space there is ceaselessly brought about the immense reflection (*Ineinanderspiegelung*) of mind in matter and matter in mind'.[78] So it is that Maximus can state, in what von Balthasar calls 'what is doubtless the most astonishing words he ever wrote':

If what does not appear shows itself through what appears . . ., then much more through what does not appear will those who rise to the contemplation of the Spirit gain understanding of what appears. For the symbolic contemplation of the intelligible through the visible is a knowing and an understanding in the Spirit of the visible through the invisible. For the beings who make each other manifest must reflect each other in all truth and clarity, and maintain an intact mutual relationship.[79]

The song of the world returns to the world the light it took from it, but now made even brighter, in an increase of prayer and hymn.

Before going into more detail in our study of the religious status of the cosmic hymn, we have to ask whether it can merely be poetic or religious, or even poetically religious. In other terms, can philosophical admiration become a song of the world? Is there a *philosophical* hymnology? Yes: one that was thought through and brought to completion by Stoic materialism. The 'Hymn to Zeus' of Cleanthes sets out in its first lines mankind's unique responsibility in the universe, that, namely, of singing the divine in which the latter participates, and from which he himself issued.

I salute you, for it is a right for all mortals to address themselves to you,/ Since they are born from you, those who participate in this image of things that is sound,/ Only among those who live and move, mortal creatures, on this earth./ Thus I will sing you (*kathumnèsô*) and celebrate your power for ever.[80]

This right also constitutes a duty, and is our most essential task. To sing the cosmic Zeus is indeed to sing the world, its law and its perfection. And the hymn of Cleanthes ends with the very word *humnein*: it is a question of honouring Zeus 'by singing (*humnountes*) continually (his) works, as it befit/ Mortals; for there is not, for men or for gods/ Any higher privilege than that of singing for ever, as is right and proper, the universal law.'[81]

In the period of imperial stoicism, several centuries later, Epictetus was to emphasize this hymnic duty as the philosopher's real mission. We are, he says, like the soldiers of the commander of the universe:

I obey, I follow, lauding my commander, and singing hymns of praise about His deeds. For I came into the world when it so pleased Him, and I leave it again at His pleasure, and while I live this was my function – to sing hymns of praise unto God (*humnein ton theon*), to myself and to others, be it to one or to many.[82]

This hymn, for Epictetus, should accompany all our activities, they should all end in an act of gratitude towards providence: 'Ought we not, as we dig and plough and eat, to sing the hymn of praise to God?'[83] But 'the greatest and divinest hymn' that we should sing would be to give thanks for our reason, which enables us not merely to enjoy the benefits of providence but to grasp them and understand them as such. Philosophical admiration must give thanks for its own possibility. And, by doing this, it also performs the task of standing in for those who do not sing.

> Since most of you have become blind, ought there not to be someone to fulfil this office for you, and in behalf of all sing the hymn of praise to God? Why, what else can I, a lame old man, do but sing hymns to God? . . . I am a rational (*logikos*) being, therefore I must be singing hymns of praise to God.[84]

This task, one that falls on humanity as a whole, is performed by the philosopher in particular.

There is thus a philosophical eucharist or act of thanksgiving. And it is noteworthy that it was a materialist philosophy that formulated the demand for it with the greatest rigour. This 'eucharist' gives thanks for the world before God, in response to the criteria of sober truth that belong to praise. Various Stoic themes treating of the beauty of the world were to be taken up, furthermore, by Christian thinkers.[85] But there is nothing in this eucharist that has the quality of an offering: the God to whom it is addressed is himself part of the world, he is a worldly god to whom the only thing that can be offered is our consent, and the plenitude of the world of the Stoics has no void within it that the naked voice, giving itself as well as other things, risking things and venturing itself, would need to cross. Immanence feeds itself, in our voice, on its own self-sufficiency. There is nothing to save, nothing to give (*donner*) or to abandon (*abandonner*). The hymn, which for Cleanthes was sung, becomes the dry and brutal prose of Epictetus, the conclusion of a quibbling theodicy rather than the place in which any cosmodicy can become possible. It is not a cosmic liturgy, for here speech merely travels in an endlessly repeated circle, from the world to the world, from the one who understands the law of the world to the that law itself. What can we offer to destiny, if not our consent, which it can in any case manage very well without? Only a free and personal giver can be freely and personally thanked. Whatever may be its own dignity, the philosophical 'eucharist' of the Stoics cannot in truth *offer* anything.

If this offering is to be hymnic, we need to define the hymn. St Augustine does so clearly in his commentary on Psalm 148:

Do you know what a hymn is? It is a song which praises God (*cantus est cum laude Dei*). If you praise God, and you do not sing, it is not a hymn that you are uttering. If you sing, and you do not praise God, it is not a hymn that you are uttering. If you praise something unrelated to the praise of God, even if you praise it by singing, it is not a hymn which you are uttering. The hymn thus has these three (characteristics): song, praise, and praise of God.[86]

The hymn brings into play body and soul, it does not require a merely mute act of our minds, an intimate thank you, but the deployment and resonance of our voice. It is in this respect that it is properly human. But if the hymn is vocal, it always has, as well, the scope of an act of witness – the irreplaceable witness of man as such, but also the *taking as witness* of the entire creation, which itself bears witness in our song. We have to speak on behalf of things, and not only on behalf of one another, as if the world were merely human. Man has a responsibility for creation, a responsibility with which God has entrusted him.

This theme has assumed great importance in contemporary philosophical and theological thought, but it is rooted in the Holy Bible itself, and its only novelty is the novelty that our speech must each time confer on it, with each new human existence. It would be over-hasty and superficial to see a tension or a rivalry between our responsibility for things and our responsibility for men. Every devastation of the world also constitutes a devastation of man, and if we take care of another, we always need to take care as well that he can really live in the world, exist in a human way as he dwells among things. Without quoting Philo, the Protestant theologian Jürgen Moltmann takes up his fundamental idea:

> The human being . . . is destined to be the eucharistic being. It is his destiny right from the start and for all eternity. As God's gifts, all his creatures are fundamentally eucharistic beings also; but the human being is able – and designated – to express the praise of all created things before God. In his own praise he acts as representative for the whole of creation. His thanksgiving, as it were, looses the dumb tongue of nature. It is here that the priestly dimension of his designation is to be found . . . .. Through human beings plants and animals adore the Creator too. That is why in the praise of creation the human being sings the *cosmic liturgy*, and through him the cosmos sings before its Creator the eternal song of creation.[87]

Such a hymnic possibility of offering the world to God *in such a way that the world offers itself in our song* resolves the initial aporias. The world *states its presence* in the hymn of praise. But it is thereby itself *transfigured* by the song that resembles it. The Socratic alternative between a false eulogy that is an ornamental and flattering compliment and the sober praise that merely tells the truth yields to a new possibility. A face that offers itself has a light and a beauty that it does not have when it refuses itself and closes in on itself. Everything that offers itself shines. If the world really offers itself in song, it will not be left untouched in the process. The splendour of what abandons itself comes back to it from the Land's End of the voice. Speech is not merely an ark, but also an altar on which the world is offered as a *sacrificium laudis*, a sacrifice of praise. St Augustine calls it a 'free sacrifice': 'I have not even purchased what I offer, but it is you who gave it. . . . And such is the sacrifice of praise: giving thanks to Him from whom you hold everything good in you, and whose mercy remits all the evil.'[88]

An overly analytical theology would later go so far as to criticize the language of Holy Scripture, asserting, with Suárez, that:

> although it is true that all the works relating to divine worship are sometimes called 'sacrifice' in Scripture, such as inner contrition . . ., and vocal praise . . ., nonetheless this whole interpretation is metaphorical, and derives from the preceding sense, which is its proper meaning.[89]

St Augustine did not draw such contrasts between literal and metaphorical when he saw true sacrifice (*verum sacrificium*) inherent in every work which makes us cleave to God in holy society,[90] or when he wrote: 'Thus the visible sacrifice is the sacrament, the sacred sign, of the visible sacrifice.'[91] Sacrifice by or in the voice cannot be a derived or improper meaning of sacrifice, for all sacrifice offered to God is established only by the voice itself and by divine or human speech, or a speech both human and divine. The voice alone manifests the meaning of all sacrifices of whatever kind, whereas in itself it does not need the others to give itself to God. Without the voice, nothing is ever given. Even if I put 'my hand on my heart' as we say in colloquial English, my lips would still need to utter the words which show that my heart is bearing witness. If not, my heart would be involved in deceiving, or laying a trap. But this offering of the world in our speech is, in Scripture, a demanding, provocative offering, one that issues a summons. It does not merely praise: it summons others to praise as well.

Thus does Psalm 148 invite every creature to praise God. To be sure, it invites the heavens and the hosts of angels and the shining stars to praise, but also sea monsters and all the depths, fire and hail, snow and mist, storm winds, mountains, and trees. The canticle of the three men in the fiery furnace, in chapter III of the book of Daniel, which exists only in the Greek translation, the Septuagint, and for which we do not possess the Hebrew text, follows the same movement, calling on creatures from ever widening spheres, with the refrain: 'Bless the Lord . . . praise and glorify him for ever!' Nothing escapes, and nothing should escape, this summons, which takes no account of the human, all-too-human differences between what we find helpful or harmful, beautiful or ugly, benevolent or disquieting. This is the first Canticle of the creatures. How are we to interpret this imperative, this urgent invitation: *Praise*? It often happens that the object of an order or of an exhortation is distinct from what I myself am currently doing, but here *praise* is itself an utterance of praise, it invites us to praise only by first offering praise itself. Thus it is that one says *see* or *behold* only when one has already seen for oneself and is still looking. And this invitation to praise, in which nothing is left out, does not form a supplement, an appendix, an accident of the praise that man performs. It belongs to its very essence. Song wants song to increase, it wants to become a wider and wider chorus. It wants song to take to the open sea, as we say, in order to sing. It wants this so that it may continue to sing – but only because it wished to do so right from the start. And it wished to do so only because it had itself been desired by the open sea, drawn out into it. Song summons the universe only because it was itself provoked to sing by it. The imperative *Praise* does not constitute a wish left unperformed, it is born from its own performance.

How are we to interpret this paradoxical act of praise sung forth by mute or inanimate beings? In his commentary on Psalm 148, St Augustine writes:

> They do not praise God by themselves, with their voice and their heart; but when they are considered by intelligent beings, it is through them that God is praised; and as it is through them that God is praised, in a certain fashion they too praise God.[92]

And a little further on, he continues:

> Why do they praise God? Because when we see them, and consider the creator who made them, it is from them that is born in us the praise of God; and as it is by the consideration of these beings that God is praised, all of them praise God.[93]

This 'praise' becomes, later in the commentary, a 'confession'. As in a crucial passage of Book X of the *Confessions*, the beauty of things is, in a certain manner, their voice.

> The sky cries out to God: it is you who made me, and not myself.
> The earth cries out to God: it is you who made me, and not myself.

How do such beings cry? When we contemplate them, and this is laid bare; it is by your contemplation that they cry, it is by your voice that they cry.[94]

Many other theologians, from Cassiodorus to Roberto Bellarmine, interpret this psalm in the same way.[95] As for St Jerome, he first emphasizes the anti-manichean dimension of the psalm's words ('The sun praises, it is not the object of praise'), then goes on to see the divine service of beings deprived of intelligence as consisting rather in the everlastingness of their nature, in the way they continue in the function to which God has assigned them.[96] The Augustinian notion of beauty as a *voice* is in itself more persuasive than the idea that the things of the world are an occasion for us to praise God.[97]

In its essence, the speech of praise is a hospitable speech, since it first had a hospitable gaze: it gives voice within itself to the polyphony of the world. Far from surveying what it sings from a remote height, it allows itself to be moved, affected by it. Human speech alone forms the link in which the praise of God for his creatures and the praise of God by his creatures meld together into one single hymn. Issuing from the Bible itself, this hymnic and cosmic dimension, sometimes fading, sometimes gaining new life, has never ceased to dwell in the Christian tradition. One of its most incandescent moments is surely the 'Canticle of the Creatures' by St Francis of Assisi. Is it for 'Sir Brother Sun', 'Sister Moon', 'Brother Wind', 'Sister Water' that he praises God, or *through* them? Father Vorreux writes on this subject:

> Does *per* mean *for*, or *through*, or *by means of*, or *in the name of*? . . .
> For Francis and his listeners, it was at one and the same time . . .
> *for* and *through*: the user's way of saying thank you, the canticle of
> admiring witness, and the translation, by the one who makes himself
> its interpreter, of the song that voiceless creatures wish to offer to the
> One who made them.[98]

As a Franciscan, St Bonaventure thought through the conditions of possibility of such a hymn, but also, in his lives of St Francis, dwelt on the meaning of such praise. Franciscan poverty and bareness are enriched by the richness of the world:

> Every time he saw an object, he would in his meditation relate it
> to the Sovereign Artisan; it was the Creator whom he set out to
> discover, love and praise in each object. Thus he succeeded, by a
> favour of heaven's goodness, in possessing everything in God and
> God in everything.[99]

When we no longer have anything in the world, it is the world itself that one receives. And St Bonaventure continues: 'By returning up to the first Origin of all things, he had come to give the names "brother" and "sister" to creatures, even the humblest among them, since both they and he had sprung from the same single principle.' In fact, the only really new turn of speech that St Francis introduced into the language of the psalms of cosmic praise was precisely that of the *brotherly* relation between creatures. This gives to the song of the world a completely new dimension: man stands in for mute creatures, and this act is rooted in their kinship. How could a brother not speak *for* his brothers? The one who, according to the creation story, was the last to arrive raised his voice in the name of all his older brothers and sisters.

Of St Francis, St Bonaventure also says that he made from:

> all things a ladder by which he could climb up and embrace him *who is utterly desirable*. With a feeling of unprecedented devotion he savoured in each and every creature – as in so many rivulets – that Goodness which is their fountain-source. And he perceived a heavenly harmony in the consonance of powers and activities God has given them, and like the prophet David sweetly exhorted them to praise the Lord.[100]

Nonetheless, considerations of this kind would, if they were to be viewed in isolation from what lies at their basis, rapidly become ambiguous or misleading. The man who bore the stigmata on Mount Alverno, in conformity with the cross of Christ, was certainly not a distant precursor of Walt Whitman: listening to the polyphony of the world is in no way an unmediated exaltation verging on pantheism, but here springs from faith in the one sole Mediator. For Christianity, no one comes to the Father but through the Son. Who is brother, who is sister? 'Anyone who does the will of God, that person is my brother and sister and mother.' [101] This is the first meaning of Christian brotherhood: a human brotherhood in faith, made possible by brotherhood with the incarnate Word. We can be brothers of the wind and the moon only through this brotherhood founded in the Speech that was itself made flesh. Any *immediate* relating of nature to its author, in a mirroring in which there would in truth be nothing to *hear*, would merely lead, after a few cries of jubilation, to a silence of disenchantment and death, a *vanity*, of the kind certain still-life paintings (in French, *natures mortes* or 'dead natures') sometimes are, images of the decrepitude of things. It is not enough to sing the world, this song must have a meaning, it must say something, it must make sense.

It is characteristic of St Bonaventure's genius that he managed, in his theology of the Word and expression, to provide a rigorous foundation for the possibility of offering the world to God: 'It is through the same Word by which the Father says himself that he says all that he can say and all that can be said in divinity.'[102] As a perfect expression of the Father, and the light of origin, the divine Word is the exemplar of all that may be, it contains its models or reasons within itself. 'It is here that the truth of the creature is found, and the lowest creature just as much as the highest are represented by the Word.' The angel is more noble than the worm, but, in the creative Word, 'the reason of the angel is no more noble than that of the worm in the reason of exemplary status.'[103] The divine Speech can never cease to be Speech: in other terms, all the actions of the Word are manifestations, declarations, expressions. God expresses himself by creating, and in his creature:

> The first principle made the sensible world to make Himself known (*ad declarandum se ipsum*) so that, as it were, by a vestige and a mirror man should be led back (*reduceretur*) to loving God the artificer and to praising Him.[104]

The world in its entirety merely forms one immense declaration of love, the declaration which the God who is Love makes to us.

This is the extent of the way the world is identified with a *book*: it has a meaning, an inexhaustible meaning. But, within the book, God has created readers: us. Reading must of course be learnt, and requires, in our present condition, effort and patience; the fact remains that this book is not written in an unintelligible language. 'In the state of innocence,' writes St Bonaventure:

> man had a knowledge of created things and he was impelled by their representations to praise God, to honour him and love him. Creatures are ordered to that and are led back (*reducuntur*) to God in this way. But when man had fallen and lost his knowledge, there was no one to lead man and his knowledge back to God (*non erat qui reduceret eas in Deum*). The book, in other words the world, was then as it were dead and effaced, which is why another book was necessary by which man was illuminated in order to interpret the metaphors of things (*metaphoras rerum*). This book is the book of the Scripture which brings out the resemblances, the properties and metaphors of things written in the book of the world, and reorders the whole world to the knowledge, praise and love of God.[105]

In passing from the world to God, as St Bonaventure says elsewhere, 'we shall be true Hebrews passing over from Egypt to the land promised to their fathers.'[106] What we have here is a Passover. In this Passover, it is not just a question of passing over just by ourselves, we must give passage to other things too, and, far from being entirely naked, we must carry with us the whole world and its glory.

Few notions are so profoundly Catholic, in the Greek sense of the word, which means 'universal'. Drawing a distinction between the thought of St Bonaventure and Neoplatonism, Alexandre Gerken emphasizes the fact that the Word is not for him a distant origin, the external manifestations of which are, so to speak, exiled. The Word is 'in direct contact with each individual creature, without the intermediary of any other being, and is closer to it than is this creature to itself'. This is why 'accepting that every finite creature . . . replies to God with a full-hearted Yes is possible only if we accept a Christian conception of exemplarity.'[107] It is in man that this *Yes* can be uttered. He who is not merely a *vestige* of God, as are merely material creatures, but a Trinitarian *image*, must return towards his living origin. But, as Alexandre Gerken continues in the course of a remarkable analysis, 'man entrusted with this task is not dealing with himself alone: as an image of the Word, he is not called merely to reunite with himself . . .; the world . . ., a creation around man, is waiting to be assumed by man' and led back to the Holy Trinity.

> What the world, as a trace of God, cannot thus accomplish by itself, must be effected by man, so that nothing subsists in creation which does not receive praise and love in return for its conscious journeying towards its resemblance with God . . . . These creatures, reduced to their own bare strength, cannot express their authentic being as *vestigium Dei*, and wait for man, by his return to God, to help them to effect their own return . . . . Man is thus a mediator between the creation and God.[108]

If all comes from the Word and constitutes an expression of it, with greater or lesser degrees of clarity; the song of the world uttered by the human voice is nothing other than the completing by the world of its own end and its own destination. We do not confer a meaning to the meaningless, we gather the meaning that things bear and cannot utter. Both profound and rigorous, the thought of St Bonaventure is Christological from beginning to end. It is through the Word, not just uncreated but incarnate, that we can offer the world and lead it back to God. The Letter to the Ephesians asserts that God's intention is to bring everything together under Christ as head (*anakephalaiôsthai*), everything in the heavens and everything on earth.[109] It is only in this dimension that the song of the world becomes a full eucharist, an authentic offering to God, and a canticle of redemption.

For it is not a matter of saving the world through our song, as in the modern projects of a religion of art, in which the artist believes himself to be a redeemer, but to sing the salvation brought about by the Word – to respond, that is, for the world to the salvation that God offers us.

> Man, to be whole must make himself (and hence the total cosmos, which is whole in him) the answering word . . . He must express himself toward God as he whom God has created in love and addressed. He can do this only if beyond his separated possibilities he lives in the area of the riches of God and draws on them in order to be himself.[110]

The Christian song of the world brings man's responsibility to a culmination in the place of grace where the two branches of the cross, horizontal and vertical, intersect. In responding to God, man does not respond all alone, he responds on behalf of the world and takes responsibility for the world that never ceases to accompany him and which he never ceases to inhabit, in his fall as in his redemption. And this song is possible only if it is exceeded twice over by the disproportionate magnitude both of that which is its task to bear in its speech, the vast and various world, and of the one to whom it addresses that speech in antiphonal response, the God who is always greater. This is the breathing of the song: the fact that there is always more air than our lungs can contain. It would be entirely different if we had to stand between a world foreign to the Word and an ever-silent God.

Thus it is that, for St Bonaventure, admiration does not merely form the beginning of philosophy, but also the end of theology.[111] In a passage in which he at first seems to reserve his admiration for temporal life and what theology calls the status of the traveller (*viator*), St Bonaventure nonetheless ends up writing, with regard to the human soul of Christ, that it:

> contemplates the divine Wisdom and as it contemplates it grows ecstatic in it (*excedit in ipsam*), although it does not understand it. For admiration is not reserved to temporal life, it also exists in eternal life; it does not exist merely in the angels, but also in the soul assumed by God.[112]

Jesus is not merely admirable but also a master of admiration, an admiration that will never be able to fade or disappear. He who invites us to admiration brings this admiration to the highest radiance by virtue of the very fact of his unique perfection as a man.

If the meaning, the possibility and the extent of a canticle of creatures and an offering of the world to God have been established, the fact remains that several objections can be raised against the description that has been given. First of all, is it not the case that presupposing an equivalence between offering the world to God and singing it means restricting oneself to an overly contemplative dimension? Is there not, too, an *operative act of praise*? Why should the *Yes* to God for the world not also issue forth from our hands that labour, and not just from our voice that sings? Of course, to praise is not merely to gaze. As St Gregory of Nyssa profoundly put it, man would be voiceless if he had no hands. All speech comes from a manual creature. And all manual work is that of a speaking man. We cannot contrast speech and hand, for they always collaborate. The work of our hands is of course an offering, but it cannot be born from silence. In his meditation on Adam's work in Paradise, according to the account in Genesis, St Augustine showed how work too praises and speaks in its fashion.

> It was not by some laborious effort, but with a joyful spontaneity (*exhilaratio voluntatis*) that man collaborated, through his work, in divine creation, the earth producing abundant and exuberant harvests: an opportunity to praise more fully the Creator, who had given to the soul placed in an animal body the art and the faculty of working.[113]

St Augustine wishes first and foremost to draw a distinction between human work itself, which is one of the elements of the goodness of creation, and the curse that may weigh on it as a consequence of sin. God did not merely give the world to man as a spectacle that he is merely to contemplate but as the place of his operations and works. And St Augustine refers to 'the dual operation of Providence, the one natural, the other voluntary':[114] the latter includes the arts, the labours and operations of reasonable creatures. Human know-how is not something to be wrenched away from the gods, conquered or stolen from them in a hostile manner, as in the myth of Prometheus: it is part and parcel of the divine plan. So there assuredly is an operative praise, a manual praise. But it presupposes speech, as in any case its social character confirms, and it cannot be seen as its opposite. St Augustine thinks of agricultural labour as a dialogue with nature: 'Human reason can in some degree speak with the nature of things (*cum rerum natura humana ratio quodammodo loqui potest*).'[115] The cosmic liturgy is not merely contemplative, and everyone, whoever he may be, can join in, with his hands and the works of his hands. It is not a virgin forest that is to be offered to God.

But then a second objection arises: does the offering of the world to God in praise not find itself in a supralapsarian position, as if the world were not violated and was not filled with evil, suffering and sin, as if its murmur were not also that of the cries of wounded humanity? If it is as it has been described, would not Dr Pangloss alone be capable of singing it? This is to forget that, for the Christian faith, offering the world to God means offering the real world to the true God: the real world, and not a world of fairytales, to the true God, who is not merely the creator God but God the saviour and redeemer. The 'Canticle of the Creatures' belongs neither to paganism nor to naturalism, it does not worship the world: it also offers what is wounded to the one who alone can cure. Demand, plaint, supplication, all enter essentially into its polyphony too. This song is offered to God only because he calls it to him. The Letter to the Colossians says of Christ that 'God wanted all fullness to be found in him and through him to reconcile all things to him, everything in heaven and everything on earth, by making peace through his death on the cross.'[116] There is no eucharist without Passion. And it is in this way that Franciscan brotherhood with nature is a brotherhood *in redemption*, a supernatural brotherhood with nature, and not a vague pagan sense of complicity with natural forces.

The nature that participates in man's fall and salvation has all the more need of being offered to God in that it is itself wounded and torn. The 'Canticle of the Creatures' is not merely full of jubilation: it has its cries and its tears, it also bears cries and tears to God. And it springs no less from praise. 'Only in the space of praise can the lament come forth,' says Rilke.[117] And if, in fact, as gnostics and dualists have asserted throughout the centuries, the world were completely and totally bad, ugly and horrible, by virtue of its very origin, we could indeed dream of fleeing it, but to complain about it would be as absurd as it would be useless, since evil would be part of its very constitution. Only praise can make lamentation possible, for only love can really suffer. If there were nothing in the world for which we could give thanks, a lament would merely form an empty vociferation. Only the light shows the darkness as darkness, only beauty can be the index of ugliness. If the song of the world is a Paschal song, it necessarily includes the lament of everything that is, in whatever way, imprisoned. The 'Canticle of the Creatures' can only be a canticle of hoping, and all true hoping goes against all hope. The speech that expresses hoping also expresses the darkness of this 'against all hope', a darkness through which it advances, strong despite its fragility, with all the strength of its fragility.

A song that offers the world to the light of its origin, which illuminates it by virtue of offering it, and illuminates itself as the place where it comes to offer itself – such is the horizon of all human speech, and already the horizon of the air that we breathe in and out. Every *yes* that was not uttered by reluctant lips, taking itself back, refusing itself, was always filled by the desire and the hope for this oceanic acclamation. But the world 'horizon', which first of all is the Greek name for everything that defines and limits, expresses at one and the same time the opening up of possibilities and their radical, irremediable limitation. Our voices live only by virtue of such an aspiration, and at the same time break against it and finally fall silent, when they are not transformed, as they fail and fail again to utter this *yes* in all its fullness, as voices that curse, or speak only of themselves, which is the first curse, and the last as well. What haunts the human voice at its very heart as what it senses to be its highest possibility is also its impossibility.

For the Christian faith, this song is possible only by an *event* that precedes our own possibilities, and springs from the loving divine freedom alone. The only song that irreversibly says *Yes* is the Paschal song: it takes place only by the passion and resurrection of the incarnate Word. The incarnation of God transfigures both speech and silence. The silence of darkness and death, the silence of failure and isolation, and even the great glacial silence of hell that Georges Bernanos tried to imagine, are no longer a threat to speech, hemming it in on all sides like an obsession, as if laying perpetual siege like a chaos ever ready to re-emerge, but what it has gone through in order to become itself, that in which it has been baptised. No one participates in resurrection unless they have truly participated in death. Speech does not fear that in which it has been *steeled* – that silence in which it has died to be reborn, and which it has caused to die, depriving it of its sting, by arising.

The recapitulation or bringing together (*anakephalaiôsis*), 'under Christ as head' of 'everything in the heavens and everything on earth' spoken of in the Letter to the Ephesians[118] is the very event, the very advent, of the offering of the world to God, the site from which the song of the world becomes possible. The world that we can henceforth sing, created by the Word and saved by it, is of course no stranger to speech: being its origin, its end, and that which never ceases to sustain and guide its movement, it is more intimately bound up with it than it is with itself. But how can we sing it? How can a singular voice, even if transfigured by this unique event in which a *Yes* without restraint and without return has been uttered, fully sing the world, and make itself the ark in which nothing has been forgotten, left out, abandoned, except for that which is not: evil?

Only the Mystic Body of Christ gives the voice its full strength, and its power to affirm. Affirmation forms the sole place of the struggle against evil. To say no to the no means to say no again, leading back one way or another to what one is opposing and making one dependent on it. To resist evil is to carry with one, permanently, the Trojan Horse that contains it. To struggle against it can only mean attacking it, and only the diamond of the *yes* can really attack all negation, at its heart, without having to deny it.

It is in a twofold sense that the affirmative voice can only be choral. It must be choral in its very solitude and its tenuousness, by virtue of what it sings: the silent polyphony of the entire world to which it offers its nakedness so that it can finally rise up to the Lord. But it must also be choral on the part of those who sing it. St Augustine expresses this admirably in his commentary on the words of Psalm 149: 'Sing a new song to Yahweh.' The new song can only be that of the new man, and it is the song of love and peace. Thus, it can only be the song of communion, and not a song that is isolated and separated from the choir. 'He who does not sing with the whole earth sings an old song, for the old song, whatever may be the words that come from his mouth.'[119] And it would be better to stay silent than to sing an old song, for the old song is, as St Augustine says, that of the 'cupidity of the flesh', the new one that of 'the charity of God'.[120] We cannot say *yes* except in unison, and the speech that expresses the unity of the world can itself be nothing if not unifying.

One difficulty arises because of this very fact: if it is self-evident that no voice can sing alone the song of the world and take itself for Atlas, if it can sing only with others, does it not also, as it melts into the choir, lose everything most beautiful and naked that it can give, all that is unique and irreplaceable in its timbre and its grain? Does it not thus risk becoming the voice of an anonymous member of the choir, one that is no different from all the others? And does this not by the same token imply lessening the value of the gift? A fear of this kind has misunderstood the nature of this choir, which is to form the Mystic Body of Christ.[121] The limbs of a body each have their proper and irreplaceable function. And this is all the more the case here. For the singular place that each one occupies in the Body of Christ does not form a singularity that is added on belatedly to all those singularities that constitute it, as yet one more feature of its identity. It *is* its identity, or more precisely its ipseity, that by which it replies 'Here I am' to the call of the Lord of the world, who by this very call brings it about that he can inhabit this world. We have been chosen in Christ 'before the world was made', says the Letter to the Ephesians.[122] This calling is also our mission, that which sends us on a mission to the world. Whether we respond to it or betray it, which is still a mode of response, forms the very heart of our story in its uniqueness. And this story can be brought to its consummation in its irreplaceable capacity to receive and to give (for receiving too is unique, and something required by love), only where it is possible for us to receive from each other and to give to each other: in the choir.

Far from effacing its singularity, our voice, as it joins in with the choir, discovers, accomplishes, exercises and activates that singularity. It does not need to seek to differentiate itself from others in order to become singular, for its difference is already given and offered to it (even if seeing it may take a whole life, and an eternity too), its difference is that of its vocation. And in addition to this, seeking to differentiate oneself from others is precisely, as fashion shows, to become like everyone else, as the same means are used by everyone when they try not to resemble everyone else. To sing the song of the world in the chorus is to become oneself, irreplaceably. The voices that will succeed us when we have fallen silent here below will be able to succeed us only when they come in person, and not by taking our place. All these irreplaceable offerings draw their inspiration from the unique offering of the incarnate Word, and from the substitution, which he alone could bring about, in which he took our place in death, so that we might become free. It is in him and by him alone that the world is gathered and unified so as to be offered to the Father, and in the great variety of the hymns we sing, in their most intimate depths, there is always this hint of tremulousness, suspended, as it were, on the edge of silence, by which the *thank you* wounds a human voice, with a blessèd wound, and brings it about that it gives itself, the voice in which all is given.

NOTES

INTRODUCTION

1 Genesis 2:19–20. All Bible quotations are from *The New Jerusalem Bible* (London: Darton, Longman & Todd, 1990).

2 Genesis 2:20.

3 Jean Calvin, *A Commentary on Genesis*, tr. and ed. John King (London: The Banner of Truth Trust, 1965), p. 132.

4 Bossuet, *Élévations sur les mystères*, ed. M. Dreano (Paris: J. Vrin, 1962), p. 157. Albeit from another point of view, Hans Urs von Balthasar also sees in this scene the illustration of a power of speech that has been lost: see *Man in History: A Theological Study* (London: Sheed and Ward, 1968), pp. 234–5.

5 Genesis 6–8.

6 See Philo of Alexandria, *De mutatione nominum*, § 63, in *Works*, tr. F. H. Colson and G. H. Whitaker, 10 vols, with 2 supplementary vols (London and Cambridge, MA: William Heinemann and Harvard University Press, 1962), vol. V, 1968, p. 175.

7 St Thomas Aquinas, *Summa Theologiae*, Ia P., qu. 96, art. 1, ad 3um, tr. Father Lawrence Shapcote and the Fathers of the English Dominican Province, revised by Daniel J. Sullivan (London and New York: Blackfriars, in conjunction with Eyre and Spottiswoode, and McGraw Hill Book Company), vol. 13, *Man Made in God's Image*, ed. Edmund Hill, p. 127.

8 Philo, *Legum allegoriae*, II, 18, in *Works*, vol. I, 1962, p. 237.

9 See the chapter devoted to this theme in Henri de Lubac, *Pic de la Mirandole* (Paris, 1974), pp. 184–204.

10 Louis Bail, *Théologie affective, ou Saint Thomas en méditation* (Paris: J. Billaine, 1654), I, IV, 16 (p. 222).

11 Franz von Baader, *Bermerkungen über das zweite capital der Genesis*, in *Sämtliche Werke*, ed. Franz Hoffmann, vol. 7 (Leipzig: H. Bethmann, 1854), p. 227.

12 Franz von Baader, *Bemerkungen*, p. 228.

13 Hegel, *System of Ethical Life (1802/3) and First Philosophy of Spirit (Part III of the System of Speculative Philosophy 1803/4)*, ed. and tr. H. S. Harris and T. M. Knox (Albany, NY: State University of New York Press, 1979), pp. 221–2.

14 *Hegel and the Human Spirit. A Translation of the Jena Lectures on the Philosophy of Spirit (1805–6)*, with commentary by Leo Rauch (Detroit, IL: Wayne State University Press, 1983), pp. 89–90. Original in *Jenaer Realphilosophie*, ed. Hoffmeister (Hamburg, 1969), pp. 183–4.

15 Alexandre Kojève, *Introduction to the Reading of Hegel. Lectures on the 'Phenomenology of Spirit'*, assembled by Raymond Queneau, ed. Allan Bloom, tr. James H. Nichols, Jr (New York: Basic Books, 1969), p. 140.

16 Maurice Blanchot, *The Work of Fire*, tr. Charlotte Mandel (Stanford, CA: Stanford University Press, 1995), p. 323.

17 Blanchot, *Work*, p. 322.

18 Genesis 2:23.

19 Blanchot, *Work*, p. 322.

20 Blanchot, *Work*, pp. 322–3.

21 Jules Supervielle, *Oeuvres poétiques complètes*, ed. Michel Collot (Paris: Gallimard, 1996), p. 301.

22 Supervielle, *Oeuvres poétiques*, p. 300.

23 Martin Heidegger, *Vorträge und Aufsätze* (Pfullingen, 1978), p. 184.

2 WOUNDED SPEECH

1 This poem is collected in *La fable du monde* (Paris: Gallimard, 1950), p. 39, where Supervielle also evokes (p. 55) a 'very attenuated God'.

2 See respectively Luke 11:1 and Mark 9:24.

3 Novalis, *L'Encyclopédie*, tr. Maurice de Gandillac (Paris: Editions de Minuit, 1966), p. 398.

4 Ludwig Feuerbach, *The Essence of Christianity*, tr. George Eliot (New York: Harper and Brothers, 1957), p. 122. At the beginning of his important work on prayer, Friedrich Heiler calls it the 'central phenomenon of religion' and provides a great number of quotations to support his thesis. *Das Gebet: Eine religionsgeschichtliche und religionspsychologische Untersuchung* (Munich, 1923), p. 1.

5 St Teresa of Avila, *Way of Perfection*, ch. 23, tr. E. Allison Peers (London: Sheed and Ward, 1977), ch. 24–25, pp. 100–5; original text in *Obras completas*, ed. Efrén de la Madre de Dios (Madrid, 1972), pp. 264–5.

6 Feuerbach, *Essence*, p. 123.

7 St Augustine, *De diversis quaestionibus ad Simplicianum*, ed. A. Muztenbecher (Turnholti: Corpus Christianorum series Latina 44, 1970), book 2, qu. 4 (*Quo situ corporis orandum*).

8 Louis Jacobs, *Hasidic Prayer* (London: Routledge and Kegan Paul, 1972), ch. 5, 'Gestures and melody in prayer', pp. 54ff. I am grateful to Catherine Chalier for bringing this study to my attention.

9 Immanuel Kant, *Religion Within the Boundaries of Mere Reason and Other Writings*, tr. and ed. Allen Wood and George di Giovanni (Cambridge: Cambridge University Press, 1998), IV, 2, 'General remark', p. 186n. Original in Kant, *Werke* (Berlin: Königliche Preussische Akademie der Wissenschaften, 1902–67), vol. VI, pp. 195 and 197.

10 Feuerbach, *Essence*, p. 123.

11 Kant, *Religion*, p. 186n, original text p. 194. It is easy to see why these pages led Franz von Baader to say that 'Kant talks about prayer in the way a deaf man would talk about music' (*Sämtliche Werke*, vol. IV, p. 407) and that he did not so much treat of prayer as mistreat it (*behandelte oder vielmehr misshandelte*) (*Sämtliche Werke*, vol. I, p. 19).

12 Schopenhauer, *Parerga and Paralipomena. Short Philosophical Essays*, tr. E. F. J. Payne, 2 vols (Oxford: Oxford University Press, 1974): vol. 2, ch. XV, 'On religion', §178, 'On theism', pp. 377–8. The fact remains that the concept of idolatry is essentially religious and can be defined only with regard to faith in the true God – which makes Schopenhauer's phrase absurd.

13 Augustine, *De magistro*, I, 1 and 2; English translation in *The Greatness of the Soul, and The Teacher*, tr. Joseph M. Colleran (Westminster, MD, and London: The Newman Press and Longmans, Green and Co., 1950), p. 130.

14 St Thomas Aquinas, *Summa Theologiae*, vol. 39, *Religion and Worship*, ed. Kevin D. O'Rourke (1964), IIa IIae, qu. 83, art. 2, ad 1um, p. 53; cf. art. 9, ad 5um: 'Prayer is not offered to God in order to change his mind, but in order to excite confidence in us' (p. 75).

15 St. Bonaventure, *Breviloquium*, V, 10, tr. Erwin Esser Nemmers (St Louis, MO, and London: B. Herder Book Co., 1946), p. 170 (translation modified).

16 Aristotle, *De Interpretatione*, 17A 4–5, tr. J. L. Ackrill, in *The Complete Works of Aristotle*, The Revised Oxford Translation, ed. Jonathan Barnes, 2 vols (Princeton, NJ: Princeton University Press, 1984), p. 26.

17 Proclus, *Commentaire sur le "Timée"*, tr. A. J. Festugière, vol. II (J. Vrin, Paris, 1967), pp. 32–3.

18 Cf. F. Heiler, *Das Gebet*, p. 151, and D. Porte, *Les donneurs de sacré, Le prêtre à Rome* (Paris: Les Belles Lettres, 1989), pp. 35–6.

19 John Cassian, *The Conferences*, tr. and ed. Boniface Ramsey, (New York: Paulist Press, 1997), IX, 18, p. 341. Hence the *audemus dicere*, 'we are bold to say', which precedes the reciting of the *Pater* in the Catholic liturgy.

20 Cf. St Cyprian, *De dominica oratione*, 8; Eng. tr. *St Cyprian on the Lord's Prayer*, tr. T. Herbert Bindley (London: SPCK, 1904): 'Before all things the Teacher of Peace and Master of unity is unwilling for prayer to be made singly and individually, teaching that he who prays is not to pray for himself alone. For we do not say, *My Father Who art in heaven*. . . . Prayer with us is public and common' (pp. 32–3). This passage is quoted by Aquinas, *Summa Theologiae*, IIa IIae, qu. 83, art. 7, ad 1um (vol. 39, p. 65).

21 Aquinas, *Summa Theologiae*, IIa IIae, qu. 83, art. 9, resp. (vol. 39, p. 65).

22 Michel de Montaigne, *The Complete Essays*, tr. M. A. Screech (London: Penguin, 1991), I, 56, 'On prayer', p. 357. For the Roman incident, see Montaigne, *Journal de Voyage en Italie*, ed. Maurice Rat (Paris: Gallimard, 1962), pp. 1228–9.

23 Proclus, *Commentaire sur le "Timée"*, vol. II, pp. 33–4; cf. p. 29.

24 Louis-Claude de Saint-Martin, *L'homme de désir*, ed. Amadou (Paris, 1973), §28 (p. 59); cf. §42 (p. 77); §101 (p. 144). For a different interpretation, cf. §245 (p. 274).

25 Romans 8:26.

26 Proclus, *Commentaire sur le "Timée"*, vol. II, pp. 45–6.

27 Proclus, *Commentaire sur le "Timée"*, vol. II, p. 39. It is evident that the description of this circularity does not need the theology of grace, which is of course absent here.

28 This is one of Kierkegaard's *Four Upbuilding Discourses* of 1844, in *Eighteen Upbuilding Discourses*, ed. and tr. Howard V. Hong and Edna H. Hong (Princeton, NJ: Princeton University Press, 1990), pp. 377–401.

29 *Fifty Spiritual Homilies of St. Macarius the Egyptian*, tr. A. J. Mason (London: SPCK, 1921), 19, 3 (pp. 158–9).

30 Feuerbach, *Essence*, p. 256.

31 Karl Jaspers, *Philosophy*, tr. E. B. Ashton, 3 vols (Chicago and London: University of Chicago Press, 1969–71), vol. I, p. 546.

32 Synesius of Cyrene, *Oeuvres*, vol. I, *Hymnes*, ed. and tr. Christian Lacombrade (Paris: Les Belles Lettres, 1978), pp. 61–3.

33 St. Augustine, *De dono perseverentiae*, XXIII, 64, tr. Mary Alphonse Lesousky (Washington DC: Catholic University of America, 1956), p. 209.

34 William of St Thierry, *Méditations et prières*, tr. Robert Thomas (Paris: OEIL, 1985), Meditation IV, 13 (p. 76).

35 G. Van der Leeuw, *Religion in Essence and Manifestation*, tr. J. E. Turner, 2 vols (Gloucester, MA: Peter Smith, 1967), vol. 1, §81 (p. 538). On prayer, cf. §62 (pp. 422–9).

36 Cf. *Exposition of the Orthodox Faith*, III, 24, tr. S. D. F. Salmond (Oxford: J. Parker, 1899), pp. 70–1, in which he juxtaposes them.

37 Cf. St Bonaventure, *Breviloquium*, V, 10.

38 Sermon LXXX, 7, in *The Works of St. Augustine, Sermons III*, ed. John E. Rotelle, tr. Edmund Hill (Brooklyn, NY: New City Press, 1991), p. 355.

39 Von Baader, *Sämtliche Werke*, vol. II, pp. 514–15.

40 Jalal ad-Din ar-Rumi, *Masnavi*, Fr. tr., *Mathnawi, La quête de l'absolu*, tr. Evan de Vitray Meyerovitch and Djamchid Mortazavi (Paris: Ed. du Rocher, 1990), p. 542. This passage is quoted by Heiler, p. 225.

41 Paul Claudel, *La Rose et le rosaire* (Paris: Egloff, 1947), pp. 156–7.

42 Von Baader, *Sämtliche Werke*, vol. VIII, p. 29. Louis-Claude de Saint-Martin had already said: 'You cannot pray unless your God himself prays with you. What will be refused you, if he who grants is the same as he who asks?', *L'homme du désir*, §271 (p. 297).

43 Von Baader, *Sämtliche Werke*, vol. II, p. 515.

44 Von Baader, *Sämtliche Werke*, vol. II, p. 500.

45 St Augustine, *Enarrationes in Psalmos*, 85, 1.

46 Henri Michaux, *Ailleurs* (Paris: Gallimard, 1962), pp. 132–3.

47 Aeschylus, *The Libation Bearers,* lines 719–21, in *Oresteia*, tr. Richard Lattimore (Chicago: University of Chicago Press, 1953). Claudel translated these words as: 'Can we not by prayer/ Bring help to Orestes?'

48 Angelus Silesius, *Der Cherubinischer Wandersmann* (The Cherubic Wanderer), French translation *Pèlerin chérubinique*, I, 129, tr. Plard (Paris, 1946), p. 99. Cf. the following distich on the superiority of silence.

49 Montaigne, 'On prayer', p. 357.

50 Feuerbach, *Essence*, p. 123.

51 Cf. Christian Sudhaus, 'Lautes und leises Beten', *Archiv für Religionswissenschaften*, 9, 1906, pp. 185–200. I am grateful to François Guillaumont for having indicated this extremely useful article to me.

52 I Samuel 1:12–13. It is obvious that he is surprised that he cannot hear her.

53 *The Talmud of the Land of Israel*, ed. Jacob Neusner, vol. I *Berakhot*, tr. Tzvee Zahavy (Chicago: University of Chicago Press, 1989), p. 149. Somewhat unexpectedly, this is all discussed by H. A. Wolfson in his magisterial work on Philo of Alexandria, *Philo*, vol. II (Harvard, 1982), pp. 248ff.

54 Persius, *Satires*, V, 184.

55 Despite Calvin, who writes on this subject: 'For although on some occasions the best prayers are those which are not spoken, nonetheless it may happen that the heart's affection is so ardent that it impels the tongue and the lips without any hint of ambition. Hence it came about that Hannah, mother of Samuel, murmured between her lips, when she wished to pray. And the faithful daily make experience of the same when, in their prayers, they make loud utterances and sighs without having intended to' (*Institution de la religion chrétienne*, IX, ed. Pannier (Paris, Les Belles Lettres, 1961), vol. III, p. 167.

56 Jean Leclercq, in Leclercq, François Vandenbroucke and Louis Boyer, *A History of Christian Spirituality*, 3 vols, vol. II, *The Spirituality of the Middle Ages* (London: Burns and Oates, 1968), pp. 86–7.

57 Cf. Sudhaus, 'Lautes', p. 188, 190, and W. Eichrodt, *Theology of the Old Testament*, tr. J. Baker, vol. 1 (London: SCM Press, 1975), p. 175, 'The normal way of praying was to speak aloud'.

58 Aquinas, *Summa Theologiae*, IIa IIae, qu. 83, art. 12 (vol. 39, *Religion and Worship*, p. 83).

59 Claudel, *Emmaüs*, in *Oeuvres complètes*, vol. 23 (Paris: Gallimard, 1964), p. 82.

60 Cf. the curious passage in Horace, (Epistles, I, XVI), quoted by Montaigne, 'On prayer', p. 364. From the opposite point of view, John Cassian (*Conferences*, IX, p. 35) indicates as one of the motives of silent prayer, in which God alone hears our requests, the fear that the adversary powers might otherwise overhear them (p. 353).

61 *Ad Lucilium Epistulae Morales*, tr. Richard M. Gummere, 3 vols (London and Cambridge, MA: William Heinemann and Harvard University Press, 1967), I, 10, 5: vol. I, p. 59.

62 Montaigne, 'On prayer', pp. 364–5.

63 These quotations are taken from *Cahiers d'études juives*, Nouvelle série, 1, *La prière*, pp. 10 and 16.

64 Matthew 18:19–20.

65 Plotinus, *Enneads*, tr. A. H. Armstrong, 7 vols (London and Cambridge, MA: William Heinemann and Harvard University Press, 1966–88), V (1984), 1, 6 (p. 29). Cf. Heiler, *Das Gebet*, p. 229.

66 Proclus, *Commentaire sur le "Timée"*, vol. II, pp. 36 and 41.

67 Aquinas, *Summa Theologiae*, IIa IIae, qu. 83, art. 7, ad 2um.

68 Cf. Émile Mersch, *The Whole Christ. The Historical Development of the Doctrine of the Mystical Body in Scripture and Tradition*, tr. John R. Kelly (London: Dennis Dobson Ltd., 1938), p. 424.

69 John Cassian, *Conferences*, X, 11, p. 384.

70 Claudel, *L'Abbé Brémond et la prière*, August 1933.

71 *Tertullian's Treatise on the Prayer*, tr. Ernest Evans (London: SPCK, 1953), pp. 39–41.

72 Philo, *De plantatione*, §§130–1, in *Works*, vol. III (1962), p. 279.

3 THE HOSPITALITY OF SILENCE

1 This is true of Eugène Minkowski, in a passage that in other respects is not without its insights, on 'Silence and obscurity (differentiating the negative)', *Vers une cosmologie* (Paris: Aubier-Montaigne, 1967), pp. 173–8. In his fine reflections on silence, Louis Lavelle notes, from a different perspective: 'Silence is the atmosphere of our spirit. Light scatters the darkness, but sound crosses silence, which acts as its medium, without abolishing it' (*La Parole et l'écriture* (Paris: L'Artisan du livre, 1947), p. 129).

2 Cf. my study, 'Le silence dans la peinture' (*Corps à corps, A l'écoute de l'oeuvre d'art*) (Paris, 1997), which complements the present work.

3 Joseph Joubert, *Carnets*, ed. André Beaunier (Paris: Gallimard, 1955), vol. 2, p. 742.

4 On the silence of writing, cf. Louis Lavelle, *La parole et l'écriture*, p. 129 and p. 174. Jean Leclercq speaks of a 'literature of silence' in connection with certain monastic writings, in which one writes 'because one does not speak' and 'so as not to speak': J. Leclercq, *The Spirituality of the Middle Ages*, p. 158.

5 Roberto Juarroz, *Douzième poésie verticale*, no. 20, tr. into French by F. Versehen (Paris, 1993), pp. 58–9.

6 Aristotle, *De anima*, 430 A 1, Eng. tr. *On the Soul*, tr. J. A. Smith, in *Complete Works*, vol. 1, p. 683.

7 Alexander of Aphrodisias, *ad locum*, quoted and translated by G. Rodier, *Commentaire du traité de l'âme* (Paris, 1900), p. 457.

8 Max Picard, *Le monde du silence*, tr. J.-J. Anstett (Paris: Presses universitaires de France, 1953), p. 8 and *passim*.

9 Picard, *Le monde du silence*, p. 113.

10 Søren Kierkegaard, *Un compte rendu littéraire*, *Oeuvres complètes*, tr. Tisseau, vol. 8 (Paris: 1979), p. 216.

11 St Peter Damien, quoted by Jean Leclercq, *The Spirituality of the Middle Ages*, p. 158.

12 Samuel Beckett, *The Unnamable*, in *The Beckett Trilogy* (London: Picador, Pan Books, 1979), p. 282.

13 Beckett, *The Unnamable*, p. 274.

14 'While peaceful silence lay over all, and night had run the half of her swift course, down from the heavens, from the royal throne, leapt your all-powerful Word.'

15 Wisdom 18:14–15.

16 Herman Melville, *Pierre, or The Ambiguities*, XIV, 1 (New York: Literary Classics of the United States, Library of America, 1984), p. 240.

17 Friedrich Nietzsche, 'Of scholars', *Thus Spoke Zarathustra. A Book for Everyone and No One*, tr. R. J. Hollingdale (London: Penguin, 1961), p. 148; original in *Sämtliche Werke* ed. Colli and Montinari (Berlin), vol. 4 (1980), p. 162.

18 *Zarathustra*, 'Of redemption', p. 161.

19 *Zarathustra*, p. 163.

20 *Zarathustra*, 'Of great events', p. 153.

21 *Zarathustra*, pp. 154–5.

22 *Zarathustra*, pp. 167–8, as are the following quotations.

23 *Zarathustra*, p. 184.

24 *Zarathustra*, p. 130.

25 Beckett, *L'Innommable*, p. 37.

26 Cf. Louis Lavelle, *La parole et l'écriture*, pp. 139–40.

27 St Irenaeus of Lyons, *Against the Heresies*, tr. and annotated by Dominic J. Unger, revised by John D. Dillon (New York: Paulist Press, 1992), I, 1, 1.

28 Theocritus, *Idylls*, in *The Greek Bucolic Poets*, tr. J. M. Edmonds (London and Cambridge, MA, William Heinemann and Harvard University Press, 1912), p. 29.

29 *The Complete Poems of Emily Dickinson*, ed. T. H. Hohnson (London: Faber and Faber, 1975), no. 1004 (pp. 465–6).

30 Joubert, *Carnets*, vol. 1, p. 174.

31 Cardinal Giovanni Bona, *Principia vitae christianae*, II, 8, *Opuscula spiritualia* (Paris, 1667), p. 233.

32 P. Grou, *Manuel des âmes intérieures, Recueil d'opuscules inédits* (Paris, 1947), pp. 94–5.

33 Grou, *Recueil*, pp. 268–9.

34 St Augustine, *Enarrationes in Psalmos*, 86, 1.

35 Cf. Henri Maldiney, 'Événement et psychose', *Penser l'homme et la folie* (Grenoble, 1991), pp. 278ff.

36 Cf. my study, 'Perdre la parole', in the collective work *Kierkegaard ou le Don Juan chrétien* (Monaco, 1989, pp. 164–74).

37 Plato, *Phaedrus*, 230 D, tr. Alexander Nehamas and Paul Woodruff, in Plato, *Complete Works*, ed. John M. Cooper (Indianapolis, IN, 1997), p. 510.

38 Plato, *Symposium*, 174 D–175 B, tr. Nehamas and Woodruff, in *Complete Works*, pp. 460–1.

39 Plato, *Phaedo*, 84 B–C, 95 E, tr. G. M. A. Grube, in *Complete Works*, pp. 73 and 83.

40 Plato, *Parmenides*, 130 E, tr. Mary Louise Gill and Paul Ryan, in *Complete Works*, p. 364.

41 In Kierkegaard, *Christian Discourses and The Lilies of the Field and the Birds of the Air*, tr. Walter Lowry (Oxford: Oxford University Press, 1939), pp. 324–5.

42 Rainer Maria Rilke, *Sonnets to Orpheus*, II, 26.

43 Kierkegaard, *Lilies of the Field*, p. 325.

44 Plotinus, *Enneads*, III, 8, 4 (p. 369).

45 *The Imitation of Jesus Christ*, III, 2.

46 Alphonse de Lamartine, 'Ischia', *Nouvelles Méditations poétiques*, *Oeuvres poétiques*, ed. Guyard (Paris, 1973), p. 139.

47 Angelus Silesius, *Der Cherubinischer Wandersmann*, I, 299, tr. Plard (Paris, 1946), p. 109.

48 Johann Tauler, *Sermons*, tr. Hugueny *et al.* (Paris, 1991), pp. 13–14.

49 Tauler, *Sermons*, p. 17.

50 Tauler, *Sermons*, p. 20.

51 Nicolas Malebranche, *The Search After Truth*, tr. and ed. Thomas M. Lennon and Paul J. Olscamp (Cambridge: Cambridge University Press, 1997), V, IV (pp. 357–8).

52 Malebranche, *Conversations chrétiennes*, I, in *Oeuvres complètes* (Paris, 1959), vol. IV, p. 11.

53 Fénelon, 'De la parole intérieure', in *Lettres et opuscules spirituels*, X, *Oeuvres*, ed. Le Brun, vol. I (Paris, 1983), p. 590.

54 Fénelon, 'De la parole intérieure', p. 594.

55 Fénelon, 'De la parole intérieure', p. 594.

56 Fénelon, 'De la parole intérieure', p. 592.

57 Fénelon, 'De la parole intérieure', p. 592.

58 Fénelon, 'De la parole intérieure', pp. 597–8.

59 Psalm 76:9.

60 Isaiah 34:1.

61 Isaiah 41:1.

62 Zachariah 2:17.

63 Habbakuk 2:20.

64 Revelation 8:1.

65 Jean-Pierre Charlier, *Comprendre l'Apocalypse* (Paris, 1991), vol. I, pp. 194–5.

66 Euripides, *The Bacchae*, lines 1084–5, tr. William Arrowsmith (Chicago: University of Chicago Press, 1959), p. 203.

67 Attar, *Le Livre des secrets*, tr. Christiane Tortel (Paris: Les Deux Océans, 1985), p. 228.

68 Maurice Merleau-Ponty, *The Prose of the World*, ed. Claude Lefort, tr. John O'Neill (London: Heinemann, 1974), p. 146.

69 Merleau-Ponty, *Prose*, p. 64.

70 Merleau-Ponty, *Prose*, p. 30.

71 *Proclus' Commentary on Plato's 'Parmenides'*, tr. Glenn R. Morrow and John M. Dillon (Princeton, N J: Princeton University Press, 1987), p. 522.

72 Merleau-Ponty, *Prose*, p. 19.

73 Merleau-Ponty, *Prose*, p. 144.

74 Merleau-Ponty, *Prose*, p. 142.

75 Martin Heidegger, *Unterwegs zur Sprache* (Pfullingen, 1971), pp. 254–5.

76 Heidegger, *Unterwegs*, p. 252.

77 Blaise Pascal, *Pensées et opuscules*, ed. Brunschvicg (Paris, 1966), p. 132.

78 Merleau-Ponty, *Prose*, p. 46.

79 Cf. for example Oswald Ducrot, *Dire et ne pas dire. Principes de sémantique linguistique* (Paris: Hermann, 1972).

80 Karl Jaspers, *Philosophy*, vol. I, p. 206.

81 St François de Sales, *Traité de l'Amour de Dieu*, in *Oeuvres*, ed. Ravier (Paris, 1969), VI, I (p. 611). Further on, in the same work, VI, 11 (pp. 640–1), St François draws a very precise distinction between the situations in which we simply listen to God speaking 'by certain clarities and inner persuasions which take the place of words', situations in which we 'speak reciprocally' and situations in which we are dumbstruck.

82 Jean Rigoleuc, *Oeuvres spirituelles*, ed. Hamon (Paris, 1931), pp. 163–4.

83 Rigoleuc, *Oeuvres spirituelles*, pp. 164–6.

84 Pierre de Clorivière, *Considérations sur l'exercice de la prière et de l'oraison*, ed. Rayez (Paris, 1961), p. 138.

85 Plotinus, *Enneads*, VI, 7, 34 (tr. vol. VII, p. 193).

86 Jean-Pierre de Caussade, *Lettres spirituelles*, ed. Olphe-Galliard (Paris, 1964), vol. II, p. 111.

87 Caussade, *Lettres spirituelles*, vol. II, p. 29.

88 Caussade, *Lettres spirituelles*, pp. 29–30. On mystic death, cf. Alois Haas, 'Mors mystica', *Sermo mysticus, Studien zu Theologie und Sprache der deutschen Mystik* (Freiburg, 1979), pp. 392–480.

89 François Guilloré, *Les progrès de la vie spirituelle* (Paris, 1703), p. 625.

90 Guilloré, *Progrès*, p. 629.

91 Johann Tauler, *Sermons*, p. 244.

92 Elizabeth of the Trinity, *Ecrits spirituels*, ed. Philipon (Paris, 1958), p. 203.

93 Elizabeth of the Trinity, *Ecrits spirituels*, pp. 234–5.

94 Elizabeth of the Trinity, *Ecrits spirituels*, p. 223. Cf. the fine commentary by Hans Urs von Balthasar, *Elizabeth of Dijon. An Interpretation of her Spiritual Mission*, tr. and adapted A. V. Littledale (London: The Harvill Press, 1956), pp. 101–3.

95 Angelus Silesius, *Der cherubinischer Wandersmann*, III, 15 (Fr. tr. p. 155).

96 Cardinal de Bérulle, *Opuscules de piété*, ed. Gaston Rotureau (Paris, 1944), p. 234.

97 St Thomas Aquinas, *In librum beati Dionysii De divinis nominibus expositio* (Turin: Marietti, 1950), §44 (p. 16).

98 Angelus Silesius, *Der Cherubinischer Wandersmann*, IV, 11 (Fr. tr. p. 201). But two distichs before this, Angelus Silesius claimed that the inexpressible can be said, said in a single *Wort*, a single Word. The silence of *euphemia* is merely one moment in his thinking.

99 Proclus, *The Theology of Plato*, I, 3, tr. Thomas Taylor (Frome: Prometheus Trust, 1995), p. 57.

100 Proclus: *Alcibiades I. A translation and commentary*, by William O'Neill (The Hague: M. Nijhoff, 1965), p. 36.

101 Proclus, *Theology of Plato*, p. 165.

102 Proclus, Theology of Plato, II, 11 (pp. 166–7).

103 Werner Beierwaltes, *Proklos. Grundzüge seiner Metaphysik* (Frankfurt am Main: V. Kolstermann, 1965).

104 Proclus, *De providentia*, V, 31, in *Trois études sur la providence*, ed. Isaac (Paris, 1979), p. 54.

105 Plotinus, *Enneads*, VI, 7, 35 (tr. vol. 7, p. 199).

106 St John of Damascus, *Des premiers principes*, tr. Galperine (Paris, 1987), p. 158; cf. ed. Westerink and Combès (Paris, 1986), vol. I, p. 11.

107 St John of Damascus, *Des premiers principes*, p. 168/p. 22.

108 St John of Damascus, *Des premiers principes*, p. 168/p. 22.

109 St John of Damascus, *Des premiers principes*, p. 172/p. 27.

110 Leconte de Lisle, *Poèmes antiques*, ed. Lemerre (Paris, n. d.), pp. 313–14.

111 Leconte de Lisle, *Poèmes antiques*, p. 293.

112 Leconte de Lisle, *Poèmes antiques*, p. 55.

113 Jean-Paul Sartre, *The Family Idiot. Gustave Flaubert, 1821–1857*, tr. Carol Cosman, 5 vols (Chicago: University of Chicago Press, 1981–93), vol. 3, p. 409.

114 Karl Jaspers, *Philosophie*, p. 793.

115 Franz Rosenzweig, *The Star of Redemption*, tr. William W. Hallo (London: Routledge and Kegan Paul, 1971), pp. 37–8. This book also includes reflections on various aspects of silence.

116 Pseudo-Dionysius the Areopagite in *Patrologiae cursus completus*, ed. J. P. Migne (Migne: Paris, 1857), vol. 3, 997 A–B.

117 Maximus the Confessor, in *Patrologiae*, ed. Migne, vol. XCI, 229 A.

118 Jean Rousset, *Anthologie de la poésie baroque française* (Paris, 1988), pp. 236–7.

119 Hans Urs von Balthasar, 'Wort und Schweigen', in *Verbum Caro* (Freiburg, 1990), pp. 135–55; *La théologique*, vol. II, *Vérité de Dieu*, tr. Déchelotte and Dumont (Brussels, 1995), pp. 91–132. Cf. also the remarks in Alois Haas, *Sermo mysticus*, pp. 150–1.

120 St John of the Cross, *Spiritual Canticle*, XV, 4, *Obras* (Madrid, 1973), p. 745. On this passage, cf. the commentary by Max Huot de Longchamp, *Lecture de saint Jean de la Croix* (Paris, 1981), pp. 301–24.

121 Cf. my study 'La voix visible', *L'appel et la réponse* (Paris, 1992), pp. 45ff.

122 Max Huot de Longchamp, *Lecture*, pp. 307–8.

123 St John of the Cross, *The Dark Night of the Soul and The Living Flame of Love*, II, 24, tr. Benedict Zimmerman and David Lewis (London: HarperCollins, 1995), p. 156; *Obras*, p. 689.

124 Caussade, *Lettres spirituelles*, vol. I, p. 242.

125 St John of the Cross, *Living Flame of Love*, III, 3; *Obras* p. 961.

4 DOES BEAUTY SAY ADIEU?

1 Cf. my work, *L'appel et la réponse* (Paris, 1992), ch. 1.

2 In the ninth and seventh elegies respectively.

3 Isaiah 53:2.

4 Wisdom 13:3.

5 Wisdom 13:5.

6 Wisdom 13:6–7.

7 Plotinus, *Enneads*, V, 5, 3 (tr. vol. V, p. 165).

8 Aquinas, *In librum Beati Dionysii*, §343 (p. 114).

9 Denys Petau, *Dogmata theologica*, VI, 8, ed. Fournials (Paris: 1865), vol. 1, p. 547.

10 Petau, *Dogmata*, p. 548.

11 Louis Thomassin, *Dogmata theologica*, III, 19–21, ed. Écalle (Paris, 1864), pp. 251–69.

12 Aquinas, *Summa theologiae*, I a P., qu. 39, art. 8.

13 Thomassin, *Dogmata*, p. 259.

14 Karl Barth, *Church Dogmatics*, II, I, 2, ed. G. W. Bromiley and T. F. Torrance, tr. G. W. Bromiley, 2nd edn (Edinburgh: T. & T. Clark, 1975), vol. II:1, p. 651.

15 M. J. Scheeben, *Katholische Dogmatik, Gotteslehre*, ed. Schmaus (Freiburg, 1948), §85, pp. 134–40.

16 Scheeben, *Dogmatik*, p. 139.

17 Scheeben, *Dogmatik*, p. 139.

18 Barth, *Church Dogmatics*, II, I, 2, p. 650.

19 Barth, *Church Dogmatics*, II, I, 2, p. 653.

20 Barth, *Church Dogmatics*, II, I, 2, p. 653.

21 Barth, *Church Dogmatics*, II, I, 2, p. 657.

22 Barth, *Church Dogmatics*, II, I, 2, p. 661.
23 Barth, *Church Dogmatics*, II, I, 2, p. 665.
24 This is what Hans Urs von Balthasar did in his vast and brilliant work, *Herrlichkeit* (Eng. tr.: *The Glory of the Lord*).
25 Barth, *Church Dogmatics*, II, I, 2, p. 655.
26 Barth, *Church Dogmatics*, II, I, 2, p. 657.
27 St Anselm of Canterbury, *Cur Deus homo?*, I, 2 (London: Griffith, Farran, Okeden and Welsh, n.d.), p. 3.
28 Plotinus, *Enneads*, V, 8, 8 (vol. V, p. 263); cf. I, 6, 9.
29 Plotinus, *Enneads*, I, 8, 2 (vol. I, p. 281).
30 Plotinus, *Enneads*, VI, 7, 32 (vol. VII, p. 187); cf. VI, 7, 22, on 'grace', which gives this excess a phenomenal dimension.
31 Cf. my *L'appel et la réponse*, pp. 26–7.
32 Pseudo-Dionysius the Areopagite, *The Divine Names, and Mystical Theology*, IV, tr. John D. Johns (Milwaukee, WI: Marquette University Press, 1980), p. 140.
33 Pseudo-Dionysius the Areopagite, *The Divine Names*, 704 C, p. 140.
34 Gerard Manley Hopkins, 'Pied Beauty'.
35 St Augustine, *Confessions*, X, XXVII, 38, tr. Henry Chadwick (Oxford: Oxford University Press, 1991), p. 201.
36 St Hilary of Poitiers, *The Trinity*, I, 7, tr. Stephen McKenna (Washington, DC: Catholic Univeristy of America, 1954), p. 9.
37 St Hilary, *The Trinity*, I, 8, p. 9.
38 Rilke, *Sonnets to Orpheus*, I, 3.
39 I Kings 19:12.
40 Jacopone da Todi, *The Lauds*, tr. Serge and Elizabeth Hughes, Classics of Western Spirituality (London: SPCK, 1982).
41 Jacopone, *Lauds*, p. 238.
42 Song of Songs, 2:5.
43 Jacopone, *Lauds*, p. 227.
44 Jacopone, *Lauds*, p. 227.
45 Jacopone, *Lauds*, p. 241.
46 Jacopone, *Lauds*, p. 226.
47 Jacopone, *Lauds*, p. 231.
48 Jacopone, *Lauds*, p. 238. In the same poem, Jacopone takes up the words of St Augustine: 'Late have I loved you, beauty so old and so new.'
49 St François de Sales, *Traité de l'amour de Dieu*, II, 15, in *Oeuvres*, ed. Ravier (Paris, 1969), p. 454.
50 St François de Sales, *Traité*, III, 15, p. 523.
51 St François de Sales, *Traité*, III, 15, p. 524.
52 St Augustine, *De Trinitate*, VIII, IV, 7.
53 St Augustine, *De Trinitate*, VIII, IV, 7.
54 St Augustine, *Enarrationes in Psalmos*, 44, 4.
55 Bossuet, *Oeuvres choisies*, vol. 2, pp. 231–43 (Paris, 1866).
56 Bossuet, *Oeuvres*, vol. 2, p. 238.
57 Bossuet, *Oeuvres*, vol. 2, p. 238.
58 Jeremiah 20:7: 'You have seduced me, Yahweh, and I have let myself be seduced.'
59 Léon Bloy, *Oeuvres*, ed. Petit (Paris, 1983), vol. IX, p. 306.
60 Bloy, *Oeuvres*, p. 308.
61 Bloy, *Oeuvres*, p. 307.
62 Cf. Paul Michel, *Formosa deformitas. Bewältigungsformen des Hässlichen in mittelalterlicher Literatur* (Bonn, 1976).
63 Malebranche, *Oeuvres complètes*, ed. Robinet (Paris, 1976), vol. XII, pp. 21–2.

64 Cf. Jacques Le Brun, 'Esthétique et théologie au XVIIe siècle' (Coll.), *Penser la foi*, Mélanges offerts à J. Moingt (Paris, 1993), and Marc Fumaroli, *L'école du silence* (Paris, 1994), pp. 223–4.

65 Isaiah 53:2, quoted above.

66 *Tertullian's Treatise on the Incarnation*, IX, 5–6, ed. and tr. Ernest Evans (London: SPCK, 1956).

67 Justin Martyr, in *The Writings of Justin Martyr and Athenagoras*, tr. Marcus Dods, George Reith and B. P. Pratten (Edinburgh: T. & T. Clark, 1867), p. xxx. Cf. Clement of Alexandria, *The Tutor*, III, 1, 3, and Irenaeus of Lyons, *Against the Heresies*, II, 19, 2. This list is far from being exhaustive.

68 Origen, *Against Celsus*, VI, 75, tr. James Bellamy (London: B. Mills, 1660?).

69 Søren Kierkegaard, *Concluding Unscientific Postscript to 'Philosophical Fragments'*, vol. I (Text), ed. Howard V. Hong and Edna H. Hong (Princeton, NJ: Princeton University Press, 1992), p. 600.

70 Kierkegaard, *Training in Christianity*, p. 600.

71 Albrecht Dürer, *Lettres et écrits théoriques*, tr. Vaisse (Paris, 1964), p. 166.

72 Luis de León, *The Names of Christ*, Fr. tr. *Les noms du Christ*, tr. Ricard (Paris, 1978), p. 53.

73 Francisco Suárez, *Opera omnia*, ed. D. M. André, 28 vols (Paris: n.p., 1860), vol. XVIII, p. 173.

74 André Chastel, *Mythe et crise de la Renaissance* (Geneva, 1989), pp. 290 and 342.

75 The painting is in Bordeaux. The text is quoted in the catalogue *Le siècle de Rubens dans les collections publiques françaises* (Paris, 1977), p. 118. It dates from 1861, signed by one Marionneau.

76 St Bernard, *On the 'Song of Songs'*, II, tr. Kilian Walsh (London: A. R. Mowbray & Co., 1976), pp. 90–1; *Sancti Bernardi Opera*, ed. Leclercq (Rome, 1957), vol. I, p. 194.

77 St Bernard, *On the 'Song of Songs'*, p. 89; original in *Opera*, vol. I, p. 193.

78 St Bernard, *On the 'Song of Songs'*, II, p. 91; original in *Opera*, vol. I, pp. 194–5.

79 Munich, the Alte Pinakothek.

80 Erwin Panofsky, *The Life and Art of Albrecht Dürer*, 4th edn (Princeton, NJ: Princeton University Press, 1971). What he says about this work is disappointing.

81 Werner Beierwaltes, *Visio facialis – Sehen ins Angesicht. Zur Coincidenz des endlichen und unendlichen Blicks bei Cusanus* (Munich: Verlag der Bayerischen Akademie der Wissenschaften, 1988), pp. 51–6.

82 Nicolas of Cusa, *The Vision of God*, VI, tr. Emma Gurney Salter (London: J. M. Dent & Sons, 1928).

83 Nicolas of Cusa, *Vision*, VI.

84 Nicolas of Cusa, *Vision*, XV.

85 Cf. Robert Rosenblum, *Modern Painting and the Northern Romantic Tradition. Friedrich to Rothko* (London: Thames and Hudson, 1975), pp. 63–4.

86 In Oslo.

87 In Amsterdam and Los Angeles.

88 Iconoclasm is an age-old trend, and the controversy over images is not merely found in Byzantium. Kierkegaard's iconoclasm is especially violent. Cf. *Training in Christianity*: 'Would it be possible for me, that is to say, could I bring myself to the point, or could I be prompted, to dip my brush, to lift my chisel, in order to depict Christ in colour or to carve his figure? . . . And I answer, No, it would be for me an absolute impossibility. Indeed, even with this I do not express what I feel, for in such a degree would it be impossible for me that I cannot conceive how it has been possible for anyone. A person says, "I cannot conceive of the

calmness of the murderer who sits sharpening the knife with which he is about to kill another man." And to me, too, this is inconceivable' (p. 247). The painter is like a 'Judas', his act a 'sacrilege'. Cf. also the *Philosophical Fragments*, p. 58. – For Karl Barth, cf. *Church Dogmatics*, II, 1, 2: 'And this is the crux of every attempt to portray this face, the secret of the sorry story of the representation of Christ. It could not and cannot be anything but a sorry story. . . . If at this point we have one urgent request to all Christian artists, however well-intentioned, gifted or even possessed of genius, it is that they should give up this unlikely undertaking' (p. 666). These ideas are of a piece with the denial that the beauty of the world or that of art are able to say adieu. But if we are not allowed to paint Jesus, why accept that we can paint any other face? Is a semi-iconoclasm coherent? Christ countenances every countenance, and every countenance may countenance Christ.

89 Malebranche, *Dialogues on Metaphysics and Religion*, ed. Nicholas Jolley, tr. David Scott (Cambridge: Cambridge University Press, 1997), p. 155.

90 St John of the Cross, 'Spiritual Canticle', V, 5.

5 THE OFFERING OF THE WORLD

1 Seneca, 'Eum qui libenter accipit, beneficium redisse'. See *De beneficiis*, II, XXXI, 1, in *Moral Essays*, tr. John W. Basore, 3 vols (London and Cambridge, MA, William Heinemann and Harvard University Press, 1964), vol. 3, p. 113.

2 Stéphane Mallarmé, *Oeuvres complètes*, vol. I, ed. Carl Paul Barbier and Charles Gordon Millan (Paris: Flammarion, 1983), pp. 192–7. All subsequent quotations are taken from this edition.

3 Cf. Paul Bénichou, *Selon Mallarmé* (Paris: Gallimard, 1995), p. 125.

4 Arthur Rimbaud, 'Alchimie du verbe', *Une saison en enfer*.

5 Cf. my *L'Antiphonaire de la nuit* (Paris, 1989).

6 St Augustine, *De Genesi*, I, VIII, 14.

7 St Augustine, *De Genesi*, II, VI, 14.

8 Paul Celan, 'Speech on Occasion of Receiving the Literature Prize of the Free Hanseatic City of Bremen', in *Collected Prose*. tr. Rosemarie Waldrop (London: Carcanet, 1986), p. 33.

9 Plato, *Theaetetus*, 155 D, tr. J. M Levett, revised Miles Burnyeat, in *Complete Works*, p. 173; and Aristotle, *Metaphysics*, book A, 982 B 11–12, tr. W. D. Ross, in *Complete Works*, II, p. 1554.

10 Aristotle, *Rhetoric*, I, 1371 A 33, tr. Rhys Roberts, in *Complete Works*, II, p. 2183.

11 Aristotle, *Rhetoric*, 1371 B 28, p. 2183.

12 Aquinas, *In libros Metaphysicorum Aristotelis expositio* (Turin: Marietti, 1964), §55 (p. 18).

13 Aristotle, *Parts of Animals*, I, 5, 645 A 16–17 and 645 A 7–10, in *Complete Works*, vol. I, p. 1004.

14 Descartes, *On the Passions*, II, 76, in *The Philosophical Writings of Descartes*, vol, I, tr. John Cottingham, Robert Stoothoff and Dugald Murdoch (Cambridge: Cambridge University Press, 1985), p. 355.

15 St François de Sales, *Traité de l'amour de Dieu*, VII, 4, pp. 677–8.

16 Kant, *The Critique of Judgment*, tr. James Creed Meredith (Oxford: The Clarendon Press, 1952), part 1, p. 124; Akademie-Ausgabe, vol. V, p. 272.

17 Kant, *Critique of Judgment*, part 1, p. 125.

18 Kant, *Critique of Judgement*, part 2, p. 11; original, p. 365.

19 Kant, *Critique of Judgement*, part 2, p. 9; original, p. 363.

20 Kant, *Anthropology*, §68; Akademie-Ausgabe, vol. VII, p. 243.
21 Franz von Baader, *Sämtliche Werke*, vol. I, p. 31.
22 Franz von Baader, *Sämtliche Werke*, vol. VIII, p. 23.
23 Franz von Baader, *Sämtliche Werke*, vol. X, p. 264.
24 Franz von Baader, *Sämtliche Werke*, vol. I, p. 42. To this can be added the remarks of Schelling, *Werke*, ed. Manfred Schröter (Munich: Beck, 1956), pp. 500–1, in which philosophy as astonishment passionately seeks 'das letzte absolut-Erstaunenswerthe zu finden', and the comment by Kierkegaard in *The Concept of Anxiety*, ed. Reidar Thomte in collaboration with Albert B. Andersen (Princeton, NJ: Princeton University Press, 1980), p. 146.
25 Plato, *Symposium*, 198 C–199 B, in *Complete Works*, pp. 481–2.
26 Pierre Teilhard de Chardin, *Oeuvres*, vol. XII (Paris, 1976), *Ecrits du temps de la guerre*, pp. 19–20.
27 Philo, *De plantatione*, §§126–31, in *Works*, vol. III, p. 277. Subsequent quotations are from this edition.
28 Cf. Richard Rolle, 'The Song of Love', 45.
29 Philo, *De plantatione*, §131, p. 279.
30 Philo, *De specialibus legibus*, I, 96, in *Works*, vol. VII, p. 155.
31 Philo, *De vita Mosis*, II, 133 and 135, in *Works*, vol. VI, pp. 513–15.
32 Philo, *Quis rerum divinarum heres sit*, § 200, in *Works*, vol. IV, p. 383. On all these questions, cf. the work by Jean Laporte, *Théologie liturgique de Philon d'Alexandrie et d'Origène* (Paris, 1995), ch. 1, 2, and 7.
33 Philo, *De somniis*, I, 215, in *Works*, vol. V, p. 413.
34 Cf. Henri de Lubac, 'Petit monde et grand monde', *Pic de la Mirandole* (Paris, 1974), pp. 160–9.
35 Pico della Mirandola, *Oeuvres philosophiques*, tr. Boulnois and Tagnon (Paris, 1993), pp. 4–5.
36 Pico della Mirandola, *Oeuvres*, p. 153.
37 Pico della Mirandola, *Oeuvres*, p. 5.
38 Bérulle, *Opuscules de piété*, XIII, ed. Rotureau (Paris, 1944), pp. 118–19. Subsequent quotations are from this edition.
39 Jean-Jacques Olier, *Oeuvres complètes. Explication des cérémonies de la grand'messe de paroisse selon l'usage romain*, c. 4, col. 388–89 (Paris, 1856).
40 Martin Heidegger, *Sein und Zeit*, §4.
41 St Augustine, *Concerning the City of God against the Pagans*, XI, 29, tr. Henry Bettenson (Harmondsworth: Penguin, 1984), pp. 464–5. Of course, Augustine is referring to the angels and their knowledge of the evening. But this possibility is just as much a human one, and can be expressed in the same terms.
42 Cf. A.-M. Dubarle, *La manifestation naturelle de Dieu d'après l'Écriture* (Paris, 1976), pp. 21–2.
43 Psalm 19:1.
44 Psalm 145:10.
45 G. von Rad, *Old Testament Theology*, tr. D. M. G. Stalker, 2 vols (London: SCM Press, 1962), pp. 361–2.
46 G. von Rad, *Wisdom in Israel* tr. J. Martin (London: SCM Press, 1975), p. 162.
47 Psalm 98:7–9.
48 Psalm 96:11–12.
49 Cf. my *L'appel et la réponse* (Paris, 1992), ch. II.
50 St Augustine, *Confessions*, X, VI, 9 (p. 183). The quotation is from Job 12:7–8. Cf. G. von Rad, *Wisdom in Israel*, pp. 163–4.
51 Charles Baudelaire, 'Spleen et Idéal', IV, *Les Fleurs du Mal*.
52 It is worth recalling that this theological term refers to universal reconciliation and the total dissolution of evil. 'Evil will die,' says Victor Hugo.

53 Victor Hugo, *Oeuvres complètes*, Poésie II, ed. Gaudon (Paris: Laffont, 1985), p. 535.
54 Hugo, *Oeuvres complètes*, Poésie II, p. 535.
55 Hugo, *Oeuvres complètes*, Poésie II, p. 550.
56 Hugo, *Oeuvres complètes*, Poésie II, p. 551.
57 Romans 8:22.
58 Hugo, *Oeuvres complètes*, Poésie II, p. 552.
59 Francis Ponge, 'Les façons du regard', *Tome Premier* (Paris, 1965), p. 137. Cf. Henri Maldiney, *Le legs des choses dans l'oeuvre de Francis Ponge* (Lausanne, 1974).
60 Guillevic, *Le chant* (Paris: Gallimard, 1990), p. 87.
61 Guillevic, *Le chant*, p. 162.
62 Paul Claudel, *Oeuvre poétique*, ed. Jacques Petit (Paris: Gallimard, 1967), p. 284.
63 Claudel, *Oeuvre poétique*, p. 262.
64 Claudel, *Oeuvre poétique*, p. 527.
65 Claudel, *Oeuvre poétique*, p. 267.
66 Claudel, *Oeuvre poétique*, p. 274.
67 Claudel, *Oeuvre poétique*, p. 261.
68 Claudel, *Oeuvre poétique*, p. 281.
69 Claudel, 'Du sens figuré de l'Écriture', *Introduction au livre de Ruth* (Paris: Desclée de Brouwer, 1938), p. 102.
70 Claudel, 'Du sens figuré', p. 76.
71 Claudel, 'Du sens figuré', p. 61.
72 Claudel, 'Du sens figuré', p. 61.
73 Hans Urs von Balthasar, *Liturgie cosmique*, tr. Lhoumet and Prestout (Paris, 1947), p. 123.
74 von Balthasar, *Liturgie*, p. 122. Similar remarks are found in Alain Riou, *L'Eglise et le monde selon Maxime le Confesseur* (Paris, 1973), p. 150.
75 *Patrologie grecque*, ed. Migne, 91, 685.
76 Alain Riou, *L'Eglise et le monde*, p. 158.
77 *Patrologie grecque*, 91, 685 C, tr. Riou in *L'Eglise et le monde*, p. 159.
78 von Balthasar, *Liturgie*, p. 126.
79 *Patrologie grecque*, 91, 669 D, tr. Riou in *L'Eglise et le monde*, p. 150.
80 Cleanthes, in Von Arnim, *Stoicorum Veterum Fragmenta*, vol. I, §537 (Stuttgart, 1958).
81 Cleanthes, §537.
82 Epictetus, *Works*, III, 26, 29–30, tr. W. A. Oldfather, 2 vols (London and Cambridge, MA: William Heinemann and Harvard University Press, 1928), vol. II, p. 237.
83 Epictetus, *Works*, I, 16, 16, vol. I, p. 113.
84 Epictetus, *Works*, I, 16, 19–21, vol. I, p. 113. Cf the commentary by M. Pohlenz, *Die Stoa* (Göttingen, 1984), vol. I, pp. 340–1.
85 Cf. M. Spanneut, 'L'Hymne au monde', *Le stoïcisme des Pères de l'Église* (Paris, 1957), pp. 362–77.
86 St Augustine, *Enarrationes in Psalmos*, 148, 17.
87 J. Moltmann, *God in Creation. An Ecological Doctrine of Creation*, tr. Margaret Kohl (London: SCM Press, 1985), p. 71. This finds confirmation in the Psalms. Only the dead man does not praise God, and he who does not praise God is dead. Cf. G. von Rad, *Old Testament Theology*, vol. I, pp. 369–70: 'Praise is man's most characteristic mode of existence: praising and not praising stand over against one another like life and death.'
88 St Augustine, *Enarrationes in Psalmos*, 49, 21.

89 F. Suárez, *Opera omnia* (Paris, 1861), vol. 21, p. 602; cf. p. 618 – a transferred epithet.
90 St Augustine, *City of God*, X, VI, pp. 379–80.
91 St Augustine, *City of God*, X, V, pp. 377–8. Cf. Aquinas, *Summa Theologiae*, III a P., qu. 22, art. 2.
92 St Augustine, *Enarrationes in Psalmos*, 148, 3.
93 St Augustine, *Enarrationes in Psalmos*, 148, 3.
94 St Augustine, *Enarrationes in Psalmos*, 148, 15.
95 Cassiodorus, *Expositio Psalmorum LXXI-CL*, *Opera*, Pars II, 2, ed. Adrian (Tournai, 1958), p. 1314. Cf. Roberto Bellarmine, on Ps. 148, *Opera omnia*, ed. Fèvre (Paris, 1874), vol. 11, p. 470.
96 St Jerome, *Tractatus in Psalmos*, *Opera homiletica*, Pars II, ed. Morin (Tournai, 1958), pp. 344–8.
97 This 'voice' of the living creature was already a theme in Plotinus, *Enneads*, III, 3, 5.
98 Desbonnets and Vorreux, *Saint François d'Assise, Documents, écrits et premières biographies* (Paris, 1968), p. 196.
99 St Bonaventure, *Legenda minor*, 3, 6, in Desbonnets and Vorreux, *Saint François d'Assise*, p. 738.
100 St Bonaventure, *Legenda major*, 9, 1, in Desbonnets and Vorreux, *Saint François d'Assise*, pp. 663–4.
101 Mark 3:35.
102 St Bonaventure, *Quaestiones disputatae de mysterio Trinitatis*, IV, 2, 8.
103 St Bonaventure, *Collationes in Hexaëmeron*, III, 8, tr. Marc Ozilou, *Les six jours de la création* (Paris: Desclée/Cerf, 1991), pp. 154–5.
104 St Bonaventure, *Breviloquium*, II, 11, 2, p. 73.
105 St Bonaventure, *Collationes*, XIII, 12, tr. Ozilou, pp. 307–8.
106 St Bonaventure, *The Soul's Journey Into God*, I, 9, tr. Ewert Cousins (London: SPCK, 1978), p. 63.
107 A. Gerken, *La théologie du Verbe. La relation entre l'incarnation et la création selon Saint Bonaventure*, tr. Greel (Paris, 1970), p. 79. In fact, the One of Plotinus is intimately linked to all things, but the fact remains that it is in no way the same as the Word.
108 Gerken, *Théologie*, pp. 108–9.
109 Ephesians 1:10.
110 von Balthasar, *Man in History*, p. 233.
111 von Balthasar, *The Glory of the Lord. A Theological Aesthetics*, vol. 2: *Studies in Theological Style: Clerical Styles*, ed. John Riches, tr. Andrew Louth, Francis McDonagh and Brian McNeil (Edinburgh: T. & T. Clark, 1984), p. 324.
112 St Bonaventure, *Quaestiones disputatae de scientia Christi*, qu. 6, resp., tr. Weber (Paris, 1985), pp. 156–7.
113 St Augustine, *De Genesi ad litteram*, VIII, 8, 15.
114 St Augustine, *De Genesi ad litteram*, VIII, 9, 17.
115 St Augustine, *De Genesi ad litteram*, VIII, 8, 16.
116 Colossians I:19–20.
117 'Nur im Raum der Rühmung darf die Klage/gehen': Rilke, *Sonnets to Orpheus*, I, 8.
118 Ephesians 1:10.
119 St Augustine, *Enarrationes in Psalmos*, 149, 2; cf. 149, 7, on the choir.
120 St Augustine, *Enarrationes in Psalmos*, 95, 2.
121 Cf. my study, 'Le corps mystique dans la théologie catholique', in *Le corps*, ed. J.-C. Goddard and M. Labrune (Paris, 1992), pp. 91–106.
122 Ephesians 1:4.

INDEX